A JUDICAL TERROR IN TEXAS

CROSSING THE NATION..A FIFTEEN YEAR NIGHTMARE OF BEING FALSELY ACCUSED

by

D. LAINE

This book is a work of non-fiction. Names of people and places have been changed to protect their privacy.

First published by AuthorHouse 07/02/04

ISBN: 1-4184-5592-X (e-book)
ISBN: 1-4184-2836-1 (Paperback)

This book is printed on acid free paper.

This book is dedicated to my loving,
supportive family, for all they have endured,
never considering defeat! And my precious husband,
for such support and the patience of Job
and for the loving support, in keeping the fire burning.
Sharing my passion for such an injustice,
with the capacity to endure the last five years.

But, especially to our unselfish,
innocent brother, my hero!
Choosing prison over his own life,
refusing to provide doubt for
another innocent victim, his son.

In loving memory of dad,
January, 2004
And to our mother,
who will never see this.

ACKNOWLEDGMENTS

I gratefully acknowledge Attorney Gerald.
A fine, honest, rare breed, with his hands tied behind his back,
going into battle anyway! Always there for me. Al White of <u>THE FACTS</u>, who knocked himself out to help me, still calling to check on me, after five years. He continues to fight the good fight in California!
Go Al!

To my friends Darryl, and Shirley, for all your support,
encouragement and assistance!

Thanks to the many Prayer Warriors, who have contacted me with hope,
prayers of encouragement, with the inspiration, to keep on keeping on.

With special thanks to Donna and Sheila, with
<u>"Truth In Justice."</u>
Who's caring and support are beyond measure.

Last, but not least, my Lord, for sustaining me all these years!
Who placed the fire within me,to fight the good fight for justice.
Not for one, but for all!

INTRODUCTION

This book is not for cowards, nor for those minds, much like concrete, are thoroughly mixed up and permanently set! Having prayed about it for over five years, I found, not only is it the thing to do but, the timing is excellent. My goals are not to hurt or offend any. An impossible mission. Without a doubt,

I will offend many, through no intention. I am amazed at the journey this project has taken. I found myself writing the introduction, following the completion of the book. Not as I had planned. I love that old joke, how do you make God laugh? Tell Him your plans. The book is a horror story of a false accusation, a corrupt lawyer, inept Departments of the Government, the Courts and the State Bar of Texas. Our entire system!

I have been led to include Politics, Religion and other controversial subjects that my husband felt should be in another book. I listened and value his opinion, but in this case, I cannot comply with his suggestion. Why? Because, I cannot separate my brother's life from politics, corruption or any of the subjects I have taken on. In essence, they are all neatly entwined, therefore, I cannot eliminate any of the topics included. Each horror comes in one package, thus, they must be addressed in whole. It's a road map to a judicial terror. This is a story of the most horrific crime any father can endure. A false accusation of sexual assault of a child, only requires an angry, unstable, unhappy wife to speak for a four year old child. It's a text book scenario, becoming a national epidemic. Encouraged by our Government, in their haste to protect the children, (I too, want them protected) have created a monster, run amuck! A system out of control! The issue is finally getting some media attention, but falls way short, with little results. You will find it to be the most popular accusation for close to two decades, with the highest sentencing rate.

I watched C-SPAN covering the hearing on Capitol Hill, with that poor man having spent thirty-three years in prison, while the FBI and Police knew of his innocence, but protected a criminal drug informant! Don't tell me the prisons aren't full of innocent men and women. As for Prosecutors, they couldn't care less if one is innocent or guilty, a win is all that counts. I would be any Prosecutor's nightmare, were I on a Jury. I know that most evidence is never allowed in a Court of law. Therefore, with my experiences, my first thought is the defendant is most likely innocent! A Jury of our peers holds no hope, as for the limited evidence allowed, combined with the desensitized public. Sorry, I no longer believe any receives a fair trial! Most lawyers prefer the easy way out, with a Plea. We have become a toxic society. In as much as our hearts, minds and souls being desensitized to violence, corruption and even death.

The fire began in my heart as a mission, soon becoming what is known in Washington, as a litmus test. I questioned every thought, every word, with my goals rapidly becoming a chore. I lost focus and more importantly, the fire within had grown cold. Thus my work slowed to a crawl, finally, to a halt. I'm a God fearing, loving, practicing Christian. I know full well that Christians are very unwelcome in Washington and much of the nation. I question why one that fears the wrath of the Lord, strives to be a good, honest, responsible person, is to be feared? As a Christian, forgiveness is not an option. I can finally say I have forgiven them all, but I cannot forget the facts.

I watched the Filibuster on Capitol Hill! I soon learned there is nothing like a room full of Politicians to get one fired up! A travesty of legislation, time and the taxpayer dollars! Elected men and women acting like children, actually, spoiled brats. I pray I am not alone in being ashamed. I could see the direction in which this country is going! Mix in the ruling of Alabama's Chief Justice Roy Moore, being crucified over the Ten Commandments Monument. This man is far more educated in the Constitution than the Supreme Court. He campaigned on Christian values and won overwhelmingly. He upheld his oath. We need so many more just like him! I now have what it takes to speak up! The fire is back and burning hot. The system will not silence me nor take my faith or hope. As long as I have a voice I will have something to say. I will find a way to be heard. This opens the door to what may be viewed as revenge. A charge I do not wish to be guilty of. I will risk it, refusing to detour this mission of corruption and injustice!

I am not an angry, vengeful woman. Allow me to interject. I am angry, but I see it as a righteous anger. Weary of the vast ignorance I see daily. I chose the term ignorance opposed to stupid because I feel any-one truly ignorant, is one that is innocent of the facts. Stupid is stupid and this makes me angry. I fear the stupid because they generally have some facts, but too programmed to care, with the attitude of, "Self," being the only thing worthy of concern. Few are willing to see an injustice and speak up. Fewer yet, are willing to do anything about it. The same problems we have in Texas, crosses state lines. I intended to concentrate on my state and the nightmare our family has endured, for fifteen years, compliments of a broken, corrupt system, with many Governmental departments involved, whom I shall name. The good, bad and the ugly. I have undoubtedly, exercised my freedom of speech, absent of any Political Correctness. This is not intended to make friends. My desire is to stir your soul, wake you up and encourage you to at least think for yourself!

Recall the old Hee Haw show? That hilarious lawyer skit, "Are you unhappy with your spouse, boss or neighbor?" "Then do something about it, Call BR-549, we'll sue anybody?" It's no longer funny is it? It has become a harsh reality. Terms of accountability and responsibility no longer exist, except for we, the Christians, who must be both daily. Lawyers on the battlefields and in Washington. TV commercials encouraging you to sue your Doctor for the prescription you generally asked for. Yes, I am angry with politicians and the bulging pockets of lawyers that are in office and writing legislation for our nation! Our so called Judicial System does not work! Nor, does the Supreme Court! This is an election year! We must open our eyes and become radically aware of the downward spiral our nation has taken, for much too long. It will not improve or heal us, if we don't arise to the occasion, we might as well give up. I cannot stress the perilous times we are living in.

Read the Declaration of Independence and the Constitution! Separation of Church and State do not exist, outside of the cultural mind. Fifty-two of the fifty-five signatures on the Declaration were practicing Christians and active members of their Church. Don't tell me this nation was not founded on the Word of God, including the Ten Commandments. When we lose our way we open ourselves to disaster. Let's stop being victims! God is angry with us! Why? Because we have turned our backs on Him. Pat Robertson asks, "Why have the "Ten Commandments" become the "Ten Offenses?" It is more important to come out of the closet than to clean it! I'm not here to convert you but, I sure pray you will be enlightened. Now, the far left wants the middle and suddenly, it's okay to have faith. Let's deal with TRUTH and issues that are truly life threatening. And, let's have a point, a valid point. It is not the economy, stock market, jobs, etc., it's our lifestyles, values and a busted system. We spent a fortune on building prisons, then forced to fill them. Even California is running over and releasing fifteen thousand in the next few years.

I love my country. I am a true Patriot. I care to the point of pain and anger. I want America to stand for what it once stood for. I prayed daily in school and said the Pledge of Allegiance, with pride. I was raised in the Midwest as a champion of the status die-hard Democrat. After the assassination of Bobby Kennedy, I felt forced to register as an Independent. My first introduction to the vast power and bias of the media, compliments of Life magazine. I saw how badly Kennedy was treated in my state, leaving me ashamed and appalled! Then I read the Life issue, which contained a huge article printing the exact opposite!

Decades later, I find I have the opportunity to make a difference. I have arrived at the point of having absolutely no concern for self, but I must insure the safety of my brother, at all costs! Therefore, I have no choice but to fictionalize the names. Unfortunately, not using the real names is somewhat like setting the criminals free. This angers me deeply. I so desire to name the corrupt attorney, the questionable Judge as well as those at Human Services, the State Bar of Texas and the accuser. However, I also wish to protect the innocent, as there are many. I have no option in this, as the charges against my brother could place him in real danger. You know what happened to the Priest convicted of molesting children! Prisoners don't consider an inmate being falsely accused. This story must be told, but his safety is top priority! I also resent not being able to use my real name. One day I will come forth, boldly. I long for the day I can stand up and say, "Here I am, take your best shot." I have chosen to use all the of names of the Politicians and many Governmental departments I have tried to enlist in my personal campaign. I will include the actual names of those in office, though a couple have retired since then.

I will expose the complete failure of the local Police, the FBI, CIA, Departments of Human Services, CPS, Planned Parenthood etc. I truly believe the latter departments were designed to tear families apart. Our father, (deceased long ago) told me something at the time I didn't understand. He said it was simple, "Power is in numbers, break up the unity of a family and the numbers are gone. Without unity, Politicians gain all the power!" In retrospect, I am a witness to this transpiring. I'm convinced, our father was indeed a very wise man!

We have huge problems when an unstable woman, with a history of false accusations, (unfortunately a victim too) well versed in the system, can destroy an innocent man and his family. Not alone, but with the assistance of Human Services and the Courts, simply by pointing a crooked finger. Should the truth be allowed to come forth, nothing can come back on her or them. Not that I wish to, finding it just another injustice, we as a nation are forced to deal with. In other words, she can lie, force the taxpayers to pay for her divorce, receive a $150,000.00 grant, schooling, food stamps etc., and not be held accountable for any wrong doing! All of this, compliments of our Government, paid for by we, the taxpayers.

I am against any form of abuse! Sexual, verbal, physical, even emotional, it is still abuse! The very thought of any child or adult being abused makes me ill. I would never condone such behavior. If one is that sick, brother or not, I would expect them to pay the price and get help. I am so blessed in knowing the truth in this matter. I was there. I know the truth. I know her and I know my brother. I must give her some grace here, in that I truly believe for the first time in her life, things got out of her control. I do not believe she thought it would go this far. But, having an innocent brother sentenced to prison for twenty years for sending his son a birthday card, is impossible to live with.

I will take you down a path that should frighten everyone to the core, not just in Texas, but across the nation. This is a real issue. Horrible, ugly, unjust and full of corruption, from the lowest level to the very top. Our battle has raged for years with no relief in sight. Truth is, it continues to worsen. I have fought non-stop for over five years. Our family has spent well in excess of $60,000.00 on two lawyers and I still owe $8,500.00.

I will share the ugly and frightening facts with two goals and a prayer; (A) A warning that this could happen to anyone of you! No one is exempt! The information provided may help spare another family from our life in the abyss. (B) With the hope of getting the case reopened, exposing the broken Judicial System in Texas and the inept, Criminal Attorney, that truly is, the real criminal. I demand my brother receive his God giveth, man taketh, Constitutional Rights! (C) I realize I have another motive. An attempt to wake America up and to get the complacent, silent Christians and true patriotic Americans, to finally stand up and let their voices be heard!

Where? At the Polls! We, as a nation, have yielded to a dangerous state, with the inability to act independently in allowing our Government to take care of us. What have they done to gain our trust? Do we really want more Government in our lives? Do any truly believe they care enough to look out for us? God help those that do! (My prayer, is that I am not giving any reader the idea of doing the same horrible thing, falsely accusing another.)

In closing, I have a very important and valid question which should scare any parent to death. Why would any Judge allow a potential child molester to receive a ten year Deferred Adjudication Probation, that he said he _thought_ guilty, to walk out of a Courtroom, climb into an eighteen wheeler, then driving the lower forty-eight and into Canada for the next seven years? Brother or not, I would not want him on the streets! Would you? But, this is Texas. The same County that sent that little child back to her parents to be locked in a trailer closet, sexually abused and almost starved to death. Again, our judicial system is beyond repair. Something must be done and the quicker the better. I've heard for years that one person cannot change this country, but I have since come to realize it has to begin with one. The complete failure of our Courts, especially the Supreme Court, over filled-prisons, corruption running rampant, is a problem that will not just go away. It is time to take a stand. After all, our elected Politicians work for us! We pay their salaries. A fact few are aware of. In short, wake up America, before it's too late!

I cannot ignore something I received in my e-mail, regarding the former Chief Justice Roy Moore. I enlarged it, printed it and have it on my wall.

GOD BLESS JUDGE ROY MOORE

The Ten Commandments display was removed Wednesday from the Alabama Supreme Court building. There was a good reason for the move. You cannot post "Thou Shalt Not Steal," in a building full of lawyers and Politicians without creating a hostile work environment!

I can add nothing to what Truth in Justice says, **"There is no crueler tyranny than that which is exercised under cover of the law and with the colors of justice."** (US v Jannotti, 673 F .2d 578 (3d Cir. 1982)

Now, I will take you to a reality not many will believe and few will accept. The location is in "Anywhere City and County," in Texas and beyond! I simply cannot afford to be too informative in order to protect the innocent.

CHAPTER 1
OH HAPPY DAY?

On Rick's drive to work, one beautiful summer morning, he was actually smiling. Realizing the smile wasn't as big as yesterday or the day before, but he still had one. It was one the happiest days of Rick's life. Sue had finally agreed to seek help and above all, she had dropped the divorce just three days ago. Now, he wondered when he could return home to his family. There had been enough turmoil the past year to last him a lifetime, especially the last six months. He reflected on all the years they had been together, even though they had only married the previous December, after the last son was born. According to Sue, the hospital refused to release his son until they were married.

Yes, a strange situation indeed. Sue, still a patient, would leave the hospital, having made all the arrangements. Directing Rick to a Funeral Home, just down the street to sign a piece of paper, stating they were married, then back to the hospital to sign her release and retrieve the baby. But, Sue is Sue and certainly all his years being single, he had nothing to compare her to. In fact, after all those years, the only thing definite about Sue he had learned, was nothing was definite! Oh well, maybe today he would hear from her or better yet, see her. Yes, perhaps today would be the day, after all, she had promised!

But, why had he not heard from her the last five days? Nor, had he seen her since she left his shop, having announced the wonderful news. BB was there and heard her tell Rick, that after much thought, she finally agreed Rick was right, she needed help and was seeking it, and "Don't bother going to Court, I dropped the divorce too!" BB was quite upset with Rick, begging him not to believe her, vowing she could not be trusted. BB never liked Sue, Rick reminded himself. Sure, BB had been his best friend for over thirty years, but Sue was his wife and he thought he understood her, unlike so many others. Actually, more like accepting, than understanding her.

Rick was also aware his side of the family didn't like or trust Sue either. Actually, very few people liked Sue, but he felt he had invested far too many years in the relationship to just give up! There had to be a way to make it

1

work and now, obviously, Sue agreed also. She was his wife and mother of his two sons, and three other children, whom he dearly loved and felt they needed him. Rick had spent the last eight months trying to open Sue's eyes to the fact the family had some real problems, but he was not the problem. He had even stopped drinking for over two and a half years to be a better father, husband and person. Surely Sue wouldn't have lied to him. No, she was serious and he would just have to be patient.

Patience? Hadn't he cornered the market on that the last five months? Yes, there was still a bit of anger at Sue's wild accusations of his cheating on her and being gay? These, he considered to be a part of her mental state of mind, due to recent childbirth, and that, he could live with. But, the anger and pain, still very present at her accusation of him molesting his son, was a giant hurdle to overcome. Not only absurd, by the fact of the child sleeping between them, but he would die for his son. Never would he do something so despicable as she claimed. The final straw, so to say, was the fact she was in desperate need of professional help, an assignment he wasn't capable of. Sue definitely needed professional help. He had done all in his power to help, without any positive results. He practically lived at the Human Service Dept. begging for any tests to prove himself innocent. He was painfully aware of the many problems in that house. He welcomed as much help as he could get, but first, he wanted to clear himself.

After all this time, had anyone heard him? He urged CPS and Human Services to drop by the house, unannounced, to get a better picture of what really transpired inside, but no, they couldn't do that. So, what brought about this new Sue, a seemingly rational woman at the time, to change her mind about everything? He chose not to over analyze the situation and just be grateful that Sue had come around to reality.

Dare he believe the storm had passed? That dark cloud his sister had warned him about for well over a year now? He certainly would not want to relive the last year again, but it might be worth it now, if Sue kept her word. That thought was so pleasing, he chose to believe the worst was over! Everything would improve now. A warm, comforting thought he accepted as a possibility, now.

Arriving at the shop, he noticed a couple of cars had been left on the lot. With the ones inside the shop, his day had been predetermined. It would certainly be a busy day. Well good, that would help pass the time until he heard from Sue.

He didn't have a clue of the impending doom. He never considered he wouldn't have time to finish half his work before the Police swarmed the place with a Warrant for his arrest! Nor was he aware that no officer from his county was present, not that it matters now, but another glimpse of how the law, or lack of it, works in Texas.

He was arrested and charged with a felony crime, "Aggravated Sexual Assault of A Child."

His own child. His oldest four year old, the apple of his eye! Booked with bail set at one million dollars and the DA asking for ninety-nine years in prison! For what? He committed no crime!

Detectives all over him, yelling how he was guilty and they were going to get him to confess! Twenty-four days, but they never got a confession of any kind!

He was released on $20,000.00 bond, not the million. This was not the beginning, this was six months later. This was the beginning of our experience with the Texas system of law. Notice, I intentionally omitted the term, "Judicial," for that implies justice. There was never, nor is there yet to this day, any justice in this nightmare.

It would take well over a decade to put the pieces of the puzzle together. We still do not have all the pieces and never will. The Courts confess to having no transcript from either of two Court appearances in the same month, same year, and we are expected to just accept this! We have enough to expose corruption from day one. Forged legal documents from the lawyer, the Courts and that's merely the beginning.

There are attorneys and then there are lawyers! Since Max was not Court appointed, perhaps it would have turned out differently, but too much of a risk. I have witnessed how tight the entire county is. To be perfectly honest, we would have been better off with a first year law student, than the lawyer we retained, based on his false credentials, and that's simply the prelude.

I shall now relate this horrible nightmare. I am Rick's sister. I have POA, (power of attorney) one reason I have been able to accomplish anything, little as it may be, it's something. I was at his side all along. We are very close. I call him brother and he calls me sis. I know Sue better than any, yet with all my knowledge I can honestly state, not even I know her.

In knowing one well, you can most always predict what they will do, say or think. In regards to Sue, you cannot assume anything, other than the worst. This always occurs when one is unstable.

3

I think prior to Rick's dilemma, the only fear I ever knew was from an unstable person. You simply cannot know or predict what an unstable person is capable of.

Without any malice I must say this, Sue would be the perfect experiment for the most highly accredited Doctors in the field of mental illness. I think they will find a histrionic personality to be possibly, her finest trait. Believe it or not, I do have compassion for this woman.

I've been warned not to write this book until Rick gets out. Being told that THEY will figure out who he is and that Rick will be punished, possibly, with his life! God have mercy on any that touches him, if you think I am angry now? It is a righteous, perfect anger, like David speaks of in the Book of Psalms. By faith, I will trust God to keep His hand over Rick, keeping him safe in order for me to come forward, exposing this gross injustice, corruption and scam, to help others.

Along with the inept, pompous, know-it-all, ignorant, misguided and more importantly, protected employees, by and of our Governmental Departments, devoid of any accountability. All above reproach, which no one, and I do mean no one, should be entitled to!

If the Courts and the lawyer are so intent on concealing the facts, then I can only wonder why.

Why have they taken the extreme steps to get rid of him, if they have nothing to hide? Apparently, they are fearful of the truth. We have no fear of the truth, nor have we ever agreed to play their game. In the hands of a DA who wants a conviction, at any cost, whether you are guilty or not.

Know this now. Rick chose prison over confessing to a crime he didn't commit. He didn't have to go to prison, but he made the only choice he could live with. Anything else would be selling his soul to protect his own life. He felt it would give his son a reason to believe what his mother told him may be true. An innocent, loving child of four years of age, so devoted to his daddy. Being told by his mother, that if he said what she told him to say, daddy could come home!

I will now relate the horror we have been forced to live with. I have no need to lie. I will not embellish, (no need to) I don't even have to exaggerate. I will merely share the facts as I know them to be. The facts will stand on their own. I'm not seeking revenge or writing this with malice, wanting no one else in prison, except perhaps the lawyer, who is the real criminal. But, only then, if that would allow the truth to come forth. Truth coming forth and real justice are my requests, my goal and prayer!

This has been our prayer all along, "Stop suppressing the truth!" Isn't obstruction illegal? Prior to the Clinton era, I know it was a crime. The "truth shall surely set one free," perhaps, even in Texas. Unfortunately, again, we must follow the money trail. It always comes down to the dollar. Beginning with the meager amount a court appointed attorney gets, (which we did not have) to the huge bucks for the Counselors, Victim/Witness program and up. In short, just another huge enterprise! As well as the State's income per inmate, with the money being mishandled!

CHAPTER 2
A LARGE SIMPLE FAMILY IN THE MIDWEST

Life seemed so simple back then. Not that we were problem free, but we had the staples in which to live life. Three girls and two boys, in that order. Rick is the youngest, naturally, always mother's baby and our baby brother. We were raised to be honest, to always tell the truth. That the truth, indeed, would set you free. We were taught not to steal, lie and above all else, we were held accountable and responsible for what we said and did. Again, that was decades ago and many realities ago. We grew up, went to school, married and gave birth to most of our children there, in the Midwest. Our folks moved to Texas in the late sixties. Eventually, we would all end up in Texas by 1973. Still, all are here, except for one brother. Texas is huge and apparently thinks they are America or a sovereign country, regarding law.

Texas no longer hangs the bad guys. In fact, Texas suffers intensely in discerning just who the bad guys really are. Now, as with most of this country, you are guilty until proven innocent! Once Texas gets you into the system, there is no getting out. And trust me, when you go on probation in Texas, the system will see that you never get off, you will end up in prison, no matter what! Having to fill the once empty prisons we were forced to build. Otherwise, the state threatened to release the bad criminals! "Shucks folks, here in Texas, if y'all are accused of anything, you got no rights, the accuser has 'em all." If you are not wealthy, you don't stand a chance. Sorry for the bad grammar, but what little sense of humor I have salvaged, helps me on this endless journey.

In Texas, you can kill a man, cut him up in pieces, drop the body parts in Galveston Bay, and walk out of the Courthouse a free man (even violating bail). But if you are accused, falsely or otherwise, by a woman with a history of false accusations of molesting a child, forget it. You're as good as done for. Some might kill another and get less than fifteen years. Take an accused man that the Judge says ___*he*___ thinks is guilty but, gives him ten years Deferred Adjudicated Probation, then allow the accused to serve over two thirds of his probation, then send him to prison for twenty years for sending a Birthday card, and in arrears of $188.00 final probation fees! Is this a great state or what? You do not want me to answer that.

The story you are about to read will emerge more like a movie or a fairy tale. I wish! I have the facts, documents, stacks of endless, error filled legal papers. If we were to embody such blatant conduct in our own lives, we would surely be held responsible, most likely serving time. Your chances are better with the IRS than in the Texas Courts. Is the state of Texas, or any state, above the law? Not even Stephen King could top this. It is not a novel, it is life, a nightmare we have known for over fourteen years. The alarm ringing here is the fact that this could happen to you, without warning. You could live the same nightmare. I shutter to think how many other innocent people have been or will be railroaded in Texas!

I would like to stipulate right here, I will use negative terms as secretive, darkness, evil and others, but please do not think I hate Sue. Absolutely not! I know for a fact that one can change. My prayers, years prior to this book, is that she would come forward, confessing she lied and correct the record. Since she has yet to do that, I am forced by love, belief and the gross injustice for my brother, and for so many others facing the same thing or worse, to write this book. I will not use names, cities or counties, including real names for a reason. Rick could pay a heavy price and I desire to protect him and the innocent. My goal is not to ruin her life in order to save Rick! I am not attempting to make her look bad, with the hope of making my brother out to be a Saint.

On the other hand, Sue's reputation precedes her. I have little need in attacking her. Had either one of the two Investigators, I paid for, been allowed to do their job, the situation would never have come down to this. Rick would most likely, never have gone before a Judge in his defense. But, that blame belongs to the so-called lawyer, Max, and I cannot blame Sue for that.

When I speak with references to darkness and such, I am not being sanctimonious. I am being real, in a dark world. I know the enemy and how he works. I know full well, what Sue got into with her so called religion. This statement will be dealt with, in good time, in another book. For now, I stand by what I say. I am attempting to achieve a better understanding, as to how any Christian can speak the words I am applying in defining Sue. I hear voices yelling out against me, but I can't afford to care if I offended you. I am simply exercising the same rights as you, my right to freedom of faith and speech! Actually, **Judeo-Christians** have fewer rights than any other faith in America. I warned you, I am not concerned about being "Politically Correct!" In fact, I said I refuse to be.

As for Rick, he is a fine, honest, loving, very pensive man, having done nothing to be sentenced to twenty years in prison. Unless being naive, gullible, trusting the system and the wrong people, (especially his attorney) is punishable by law, then Rick does not belong behind bars! I would place his reputation against Sue's, anytime.

As for the accuser, Sue, I have forgiven her and to my surprise, I have learned to love her and have great compassion for her. This book is something you must decide for yourselves. I will simply relate the facts and truths, as I know them to be. (Along with the documents, letters and such I have in my possession, which has taken years to obtain, and I still don't have them all.)

It never ceases to amaze me how no one cares. How so much evidence is considered too old.

I wasn't aware that in America, one's Constitutional Rights could expire. Not to mention, how any lawyer can forge legal documents, lie, cheat, extort and embezzle money. Never doing one simple step of only two, required by law in Texas. (Investigate the case and interview witnesses.) Max was allowed to walk without any repercussions, all because we were too late in finding the evidence! Evidence withheld from us for years! The sole purpose of Max withholding Rick's files. I assure you, Max could ill afford anyone to have access to those files or the lack of! Of course, an attorney by law, must release the files, but no one would tell me how to force him to do so. Max had to sit on them until the four year statue of limitations expired. Which is exactly what he did.

I wish I could find solace in Max not being eligible to practice law in Texas at this time. I know him and trust me, he will be back to terrorize another victim and their family. He has got to be stopped. Max has already been on probation, once. He will be back, but not if I can help it!

I highly suspect Texas is not alone in this. I fear this disease in our judicial system respects no state line. A national epidemic, keeping the lawyer's pockets bulging, the Courts running over, tearing families apart, with a trail of destruction. Laughing at us on their way to the bank. Does this not infuriate you? If you said no, then you are a lawyer or perhaps a

Politician or both. I am convinced the "Plea," was offered twice because the DA had no case and the DA knew Max was inept and not capable of fighting the case. Max knew his only way out in protecting his own butt and the corruption, was to coerce Rick into a plea.

CHAPTER 3
RICK'S FIRST WIFE

Rick and Rhea married very young. Rhea was soon to be a mother to a beautiful baby girl, Sarah. A couple of years later they had a daughter together, DeDe. She was just as beautiful as Sarah. The marriage did not work out. Perhaps they were too young. Actually, Rhea was more mature then Rick. Rick was never perfect, but kind and more generous than most. Rick always loved children, especially Sarah. Rhea was more stable and I think a year older than Rick. Rhea was an excellent mother then and now! She was always very attractive, warm, loving and very intelligent. They divorced, but remain friends, to this day. Love wasn't the reason for the divorce.

Prior to their marriage and the birth of Sarah, Rick and Rhea were the only baby-sitters my children ever knew, except for their grandparents. I seldom left my children, but when I did I would not hire a "baby-sitter." I would only allow family to be with them. Of course we paid them to watch our children, knowing they would have done it for nothing. They were so young and just getting started. After Sarah was born they would bring her along. I never questioned or had a doubt regarding the safety of my children in leaving them with Rick and Rhea. Actually, Rick watched my children before he met Rhea. Rhea was always very loving to my children, as Rick was. I trusted her completely.

Rick and Rhea moved to Texas also, prior to their divorce. After the divorce, Rhea and the girls returned to the Midwest. Rick did not spend the time he should have with the girls. The distance was an issue, but not good enough. A part of me resented Rick for not being more of a father and a part of the girl's lives. Rick soon felt a failure as a father and a husband. Honestly, I have often wondered if Rick felt he was deserving of Rhea and the girls. I think he relied too heavily on the fact of Rhea's strength, and being the great mother that she was. I have so much respect and admiration for Rhea. This single mother spent years in school, working full time and raising her girls. Rhea would put herself through college, with a 4.0 GPA! I always took great pride in being a good mother, but I must bow to what

Rhea has done. I cannot over-emphasize all of Rhea's accomplishments! I'm so grateful we are still conversing after thirty years. Rhea remarried a wonderful man, (she so deserves). They all reside several states away.

Many years later, Rhea accepted a fantastic job in south Texas, therefore she and the girls were back. (about thirteen years later) Sue was never pleased at Rick having other children! Sue was openly defiant and determined to keep the girls and Rick apart. When DeDe would call Sue's house asking for her daddy, Sue would tell DeDe that Rick no longer lived there! Rick was not aware of this in the beginning, but when it did come to his attention, he should have stood up to Sue more!

I know life was very difficult for DeDe and I still hurt for her. However, I am so proud of her! DeDe had enough of her mothers strength and influence to make it through a lot of very tough times. As for Sarah, I felt somewhat guilty in feeling closer to her, but I knew her longer, and better, as DeDe was younger. I am so proud of Sarah also!

I have gone into depth on Rhea for a purpose. Sue would soon suck Rhea and DeDe into her hellish scheme against Rick. Sue knows no limits and will resort to any level in using anyone for her personal benefit. "Open season" for Sue. No one was safe in order to win her games, leaving a trail of innocent, hurting victims to live with the pain that Sue eagerly spread around!

CHAPTER 4
RICK'S LIFE BEFORE SUE

Soon after the divorce, Rick moved to St. Louis and became involved with a woman, Paula. She had a son, Scott. Paula would transfer to Texas right after Rick moved back. Of course Rick loved Scott, but was very concerned that he needed a male role model. Rick felt that Paula was far too nurturing. Scott was an only child and very pampered. Rick was convinced Scott needed some outside hobbies. He felt the child needed to be around other boys more. So, with absolutely no experience, Rick coached a basketball team at the YMCA just for Scott.

That year the team won a trophy, for what I don't recall, but I have it here, somewhere. I was very surprised, but more astonished, as Rick's only knowledge of sports was NASCAR and drag racing. I was the sports nut, most all of them, yet here he was coaching a basketball team. I was, and still am so proud of him. I saw it as sheer dedication and a loving concern for that little boy. Another note here, as this would be used years later, in such a painful manner. Not through the courts, but it still continues to sting Rick and infuriate our family. It wasn't enough that Sue had falsely accused him of such a revolting crime, but would continue to destroy his life. As well as his business, friends and his very future, not to mention selling all nine vehicles, tens of thousands of dollars, but it didn't end there either.

Another example of Sue on the loose, using any form of weapon at her disposal.

Sue would proclaim to any that would listen, how Rick molested the entire YMCA team, his own nephews and it wouldn't stop there. Sue would even lie to her attorney, stating that Rhea would not allow Rick to see the girls for the same reason! Using our tax dollars, Sue would make a trip to visit Rhea, in order to recruit Rhea to go along with the lies Sue had told her lawyer.

As many times as Sue lied to DeDe, after as she accused Rick of that horrible crime, she then invited Rick's girls to spend that very summer with her! It looked good on the surface, but they would see Sue first-hand, as the abusive mother she was.

I heard horror stories of Sue's physically abusing the children. I do believe it, for numerous reasons, given her history, which I shall elaborate on later. For now suffice it to say, I knew her temperament. I've had a front row seat many times, witnessing too many of her despicable performances and unhealthy reactions to what I deemed insignificant matters. I noticed some days were somewhat mild, others were completely unexplainable, an absolute contradiction to the previous day.

A pattern of total inconsistency in every matter. I was forced to merely expect the unexpected.

I could never attempt to predict a single thing Sue might say or do regarding the most diminutive situations. Each and every day was an experience. As for Rick's girls, to my knowledge, they never returned. Why would Sue be so nice and accepting of Rick's girls so suddenly? Remember, Sue didn't do a thing without a motive. Yes, she had one. A huge one. Sue needed Rhea to back up the lies she told her lawyer!

Sue would lie to Rhea and hurt DeDe unnecessarily, while violating another law. A law called, "CONSPIRACY." Nothing more than a misdemeanor to Sue.

CHAPTER 5
WHEN RICK MET SUE

Rick had worked for a small company in ST. Louis. A computer tech when his company merged with a huge corporation in a large city in Texas. Rick was quickly promoted to an Executive Field Engineer. Rick and Paula didn't last long. Rick traveled extensively and moved into a house with his oldest friend, BB. Rick wore three piece suits and drove a Corvette. Rick was very handsome with a personality to match. Yes, women loved him, but he was a gentleman also. He was raised to respect women. We sisters were older, but Rick would never let us forget that we were ladies!

Rick met Sue in a small bar near an Airport. She was working as a barmaid. Rick told me she had a college education in Real Estate. Why was she working in a bar, I asked. He said she had come through a bad divorce. I met Sue, as I did all of Rick's girlfriends. My first impression of Sue was one of extreme disappointment. I knew he was a sucker for long hair, but I was amazed at her features. I saw her as dark. With questionable morals, values and ethics. On the surface Sue was attractive. I was quite disturbed to learn of her three small children, living with her mother, in a town about forty-five miles south and seldom seeing them, due to her schedule and commuting time.

Being a mother, I had real problems with this. Rick felt sympathetic towards her. I felt uneasy! How does any mother see her children only once or twice a month? I went through a divorce too, with many problems, but I couldn't wait to see my children every night, no matter what time I got off work. If I just watched them sleep, at least I saw them and knew they were safe. I would later learn Sue's mother was a Nurse, working with in-home patients, evenings. Wait, if Sue worked nights too, just who was watching the children? I had too many questions regarding Sue and the situation. Try as I might, she was so secretive, so dark and mysterious, I could seldom, if ever, get a straight answer from her. Rick was mesmerized. I was curious with fear of the unknown.

Within weeks, Sue moved into the house Rick shared with BB. As Rick's job required him to travel extensively, therein I found hope, sensing her opposition to him being gone. I felt Sue was out to get him with whatever it took. I couldn't blame any woman in wanting Rick, but in this case, I didn't want her to have him. I simply failed to see the connection between such opposites. Rick was outgoing and passive. Sue was quiet and withdrawn. Her eyes bothered me. Too dark, void of light. Eyes are important to me, as they are the mirror of the soul. I detected her resentment for me and a passiveness for Rick. Sue was so darned dark and secretive, with an inexplicable evilness that I sensed could detonate, without warning!

Rick and I were so close, it actually caused problems in our personal lives, regarding relationships with the opposite sex. We vowed to marry spouses that could accept one another. My jealous boyfriends, his girlfriends, were all intimidated by the closeness of our family. We didn't know life any other way, being taught God first, family then Country.

Rick drank beer, even more after moving to ST. Louis without family there. He never drank on the job, only after work and weekends. Sue didn't like his drinking, yet she would never go near him without alcohol. Sue and I often had words over this. I asked why she took Wild Turkey home every night from the bar. Wild Turkey 101 is very strong alcohol! Why did she drink with him? Why work in a bar, if she had such an education and being a Realtor? Simple, if that's what it took, then so be it. BB cared no more for her than I did, and soon moved out. This told me something. BB was even more passive than Rick. I deemed this as a warning signal, rightfully so.

Of course, they are still very good friends. BB never warmed up to Sue. Actually, his dislike for her intensified.

Within weeks of BB moving out, Ellie, Sue's mother, demanded that Sue be more responsible. Ellie had to work and wanted Sue to spend more time with the children. Soon after, Sue brought the children to Rick's. This lasted a couple of years. Rick quit his job and moved into Sue and her mother's house, south of the city. Sue didn't want Rick traveling and eventually, he would have to leave his job to please her. Rick was not only living with Sue, her mother and three children, but Sue had a brother living there too, Bill Sr. He didn't just reside there, he hid there AWOL and behind in his child support. There were Warrants out for him on both issues. Sue and Ellie had a small room off the pantry for him to hide in, whenever anyone would come looking for him. This bothered Rick and our family. Bill Sr. had a dark side too. He was very handsome and polite, but we found him disturbing and somewhat alarming, without knowing why, at the time.

Rick told me about a huge rift existing between Sue and Bill, and when it would flare up, it was ugly! He could never figure out what it was, but recalls hearing remarks (possibly being made about a cousin.) Rick thought he heard, "It doesn't matter, no one will find her anyway." Very disturbing, but Rick said, "When they drink, God only knows what they will say." Rick always told me, "Don't even try to figure her out sis, just try to get along with her." He naturally felt that her brother should not be AWOL. Rick received an honorable discharge right after the loss of our father, years prior to meeting Sue. Rick was uneasy and didn't trust Bill Sr., saying, "He is Sue's brother and I'll just have to make the best of it." Rick hated strife and turmoil. Rick was passive, <u>loved children</u>, living for peace and harmony. This was the main reason Rick didn't ask questions and would allow things he didn't approve of, to continue.

It bothered him that she would hide her brother from paying child support, while she would wait for a year or so, then take her second husband to court for a large, lump sum. She told me her first husband, was a drug addict, living in Washington or Oregon, with the state providing his needles etc. She collected a substantial, monthly check for his son, (Bill Jr.) from the state, until he turned sixteen. We found it troubling that Sue better get her child support, but her brother wasn't expected to pay his. Quite a double standard, with the exception being when it came to Sue's children! Rick tried to give her children the love and attention they seemed to be starved for. Sue was verbally abusive to them and this, Rick simply would not tolerate. Very seldom would he put his foot down, but in this area he did. That worked fine, as long as he was around. Little was he aware of her physical abuse, for years to come. He would eventually learn of many events having occurred in his absence

Again, now as then, all my memories consist of terms of darkness, evilness and secrets. That <u>house</u> did indeed have a very real darkness about it! More like a dungeon than a house, never was it a home. Big difference. Rick began confiding in me of the many concerns and questions he had. He said their father had built the house. As soon as it was completed, he walked out of their lives and never returned again! Sue had other siblings, that would come one time a year, at Christmas, for an hour or two, then leave.

The oldest child, Bill Jr., was by her first husband. Bill Sr. was Sue's brother. A brother and son with the same name. Confusing? Yes, but it will become even more so. A younger boy Jeff, (named after his father) and daughter (Wendy) were by Sue's second husband. Sue was pregnant with Wendy, before and after the divorce. Bill Jr., was several years older than Jeff and Wendy. I think the youngest ones were around three to five when we first met them, and so cute. Wendy's voice was so unorthodox. I can only describe it as extremely masculine, very deep, and a rather harsh voice for such a small child, with an extreme speech impediment. So deep, and raspy, frankly we felt she was possessed. Many do not believe such as this, but had you the experiences I have had, you would well know the possibility. When you consider how conducive the environment was, it would be so easy.

It explains the fear of the strange woman, with long dark hair, always at the end of the hallway, all through the night. It frightened the poor children so badly, they chose to wet the bed and be punished, rather than going to the bathroom in order to avoid her. All three children witnessed this numerous times and shared this with our sister, Lori, our mother and myself. I am aware that Wendy's symptoms could also indicate a sign of severe sexual, physical abuse. Under the circumstances, I feel anything is possible. In reality, Jeff and Bill Jr., exhibited the same signs, but not as severely, to my knowledge. Some might see them as signs of classic abuse and trauma.

Sue's brother, Bill Sr., was very strange indeed. Lori, and I always suspected he was gay, but treated him well just the same. He was always nice to us, and we tried to bestow the same in return. Much later, we learned he had been married and obviously had a child. However, the child didn't look a thing like him. In fact, the child had a color of hair very unusual for their family, but matched his wife's live-in lover perfectly. Bill Sr., actually seemed to want us to believe he had a son, very few, if any believed this though. I am not judging, simply attempting to discern the weird situation and how often things are not as they may appear. If Bill Sr. was so proud to be a father, why would he not pay child support? All the years we knew him, none of us, including Rick, ever saw him with a woman or knew him ever have a date. This could be construed as being symptomatic of an abuser. The more I learn about dysfunctional people, the more I see Sue and her brother, including their mother too, as formerly abused children themselves. This is sorrowful, but I must remain focused on Rick. I confess, the more I study Sue and her family, the easier it has become to understand true dysfunction. Mix this knowledge with faith and prayer, and you might better relate to the fact of how I have been able to forgive her.

I soon recognized that cold rift between Bill and Sue. One day they were best friends, then not speak for days on end. Having real arguments, with remarks no one could understand. At times they would yell and scream at each other. This was most always while they were drinking, so Rick took the off-the-wall remarks as alcohol. I tended to lose patience with Rick and his aloof attitude at their so called off -the-wall remarks, urging him to pay more attention to them. I was convinced they were more serious than Rick considered. Again, you have to know Rick and how he lived for peace. Myself, I tend to check the eyes and smiles, searching for that which one doesn't want me to see. I wont settle for the mere surface, I want to go deeper, much deeper.

Bill Jr., about twelve years old, appeared to hate his mother. I say this, because he told me often enough. I would stand outside the corner of the house and hold him while he cried, proclaiming his hatred for her. With his declaration of how he wished her dead, always frightened me. I would console him, saying I knew she tended to expect too much out of him, but that she loved him the best way she knew how. Sue pretty much expected him to raise the younger two, a very difficult position for a child. I prayed for years that he would not kill her. I honestly feared he would. In fact, I spent years expecting it to happen. He was a child not the ordained, "caregiver." Sue would place to many burdens on Bill's young shoulders. That in it's self is a form of abuse!

Sue's mother, Ellie, a nurse and very quiet, strange and seemly afraid of Sue. In her own home? The house was owned by Ellie, but Sue ran everything. Ellie took care of in-home patients mostly at night or late evenings. Apparently, Ellie would bring medicine home to Sue. I have always wondered how many patients were missing their medicine, or not taking them, where else would they come from?

I was there one night when Ellie came home with nothing. It was not a pretty sight! I know, I was there. I saw Valium a couple of times. I hesitate to accuse her. I'm expressing a well founded concern. Now, after all this time, I learned that Sue is in the same profession, which I'm sure the taxpayers paid for. I find this an aggravating thought! How can I not suspect the worst, when this was considered so mainstream? Sue called all the shots, having full control over everyone in the house.

I know from cards and letters Sue wrote Rick while he was still traveling, that she smoked pot, did some drugs and such, while he was out of town. This surprised me, as I never new Rick to do any drugs, actually he was very opposed to it. He always said his alcohol was a bad enough vice, he didn't need another. But, if she would wait until the children were in bed, he could better live with the problem. Compromise can be very hazardous, as he would learn, too late. Much of it she proclaimed was medicine. Right, but it bothered me how she came about that also, aside from her mother's assistance. Was this the classic abused becoming the abuser?

Many things bothered me about Sue, especially her constant boasting of how much smarter she was than others and how she would always get her way. Often Sue would proudly proclaim, "God have mercy on anyone that gets in my way." I knew that was one of her ways of threatening me too. I have never been one easily intimated and Sue was aware of this. However, Sue would never lose an opportunity at taking a shot at me. She especially enjoyed laughing and flaunting her superior ability over the Government and their stupidity. I'll back off of that one for now, I shall be more detailed later, but suffice it to say, she was right!

And how she proudly stated she was an animal in bed! I decided, I had heard enough this time. Sue was at the kitchen sink and repeated it with vigor, "And Clar, I do mean I am an animal!" I finally told her straight out, "Sue, I don't want to know what transpires in your bedroom with my brother, it's none of my business, so please, in the future spare me the details!" Sue was insulted and angry at my attitude! I was bewildered and confused at hers. I didn't discuss my love life with my family. Perhaps you don't have a problem with this, but I do. I would understand better, years later, upon hearing of Rick's disgust at picking up the X rated movies for her. I warned you we were old fashioned, not goody, goody, but we girls were ladies and our brothers were gentlemen. Rick wouldn't even allow me to light my own cigarettes, to his last day of freedom!

Rick reiterated again, how her mother feared Sue, but never knew exactly why. He confessed she did rule and controlled everything in the house and tried to do the same with his job. That is why he would eventually quit working at home and get his own shop, a few miles a way. Rick wanted Sue to stay home with the children. This did not set well with her, not at all. I thought I was competitive, but I couldn't hold a candle to her, nor did I want to. Fact is, Sue unknowingly helped me to become a better person because of seeing her in action exposed some of my faults.

As bad as I hate to say it, she certainly has proven her point. I hate the fact that she used the system to the hilt, but more so that our tax dollars paid for it all. Yes, I am convinced she was right, in that our Government is so ridiculously stupid. Completely stupid or severely unaware of such insidious behavior. This should have easily been detected with any professional investigation. I confess she is good, but for God's sake, where were all the experienced, intelligent employees?

She was good enough to con Lee Iacocca and Chrysler, out of three months car payments, based on a lie! Perhaps I expect too much of the Government. It's more acceptable in understanding how easily Rick was taken for such a fool. I began to think that perhaps he was more conscious of Sue's behavioral pattern than I thought, as he still had not married her, after all this time. I found comfort in that fact, against my belief in marriage.

Rick told me he overheard Sue and Bill Sr., laughing and talking one night about the time their mother had become involved with a man. Sue and Bill didn't like him. He told me it bothered him that they took such pleasure in running him off. He never got any details of how, but they were very proud of themselves and thought it quite funny. This concerned Rick greatly, he liked Ellie and just couldn't comprehend them not wanting her to be happy and having a relationship with someone. She was elderly and alone. As for her children, where was their duty in the best interest of their mother? Such selfishness on their part.

Our whole family had to work very hard to like Sue, as she gave us very little reason. The way she drank, abused her children, smoked, not just cigarettes, took drugs and treated Rick. We could never get a question answered. So secretive about everything. Very demanding and yes, Rick was right, she wanted control over everything. Our family is not like that, in fact, don't even attempt to control us. Rick was more passive and always quick to forgive and even make excuses for anyone, especially those he didn't know well. He simply enjoyed peace and harmony. That made it all the more difficult for any of us to understand such a relationship. Sue seemed to prefer strife and turmoil. Rick was an extrovert. Sue? An Ex-introvert. I think he did it for the children.

Rick worked from that house for about a year, but with Sue's maddening drive to control all, he knew he had to get a shop away from the house. Rick actually thought it would improve the situation. Sure it would. Just as well as pigs can fly. If only life would be that simple.

When I say Sue was unpredictable, I mean it. You never knew what she would say or do! One day, out of the blue, she turned to me in the kitchen with a remarkable statement, "You know, your brother is the only man I know that I don't have to worry about my children being around." Of course, I took it as a compliment, but had to wonder where that came from and why.

Sue's mind always brings back memories of those old cartoons, where you would sing along. Cartoons with music and the lyrics to the song would be on the screen, and we would sing along with the bouncing ball. Sue was that bouncing ball.

Twice I went grocery shopping with her and learned she had no problem with shoplifting! Sue truly feels the world owes her a living. Even at a fast food place, Sue would attempt to beat them out of something. Needless to say, I no longer shopped with her. I was embarrassed, too many times, so I brought my trips, anywhere and everywhere with Sue, to a halt!

For years, I wondered if Rick was aware of this. I was sure he wasn't. We just weren't raised that way! I remember when Rick took little Rick back inside a store, upon finding some bubble gum that wasn't paid for. His son had to tell the lady at the register, he stole the gum. Just like mother did to me over pink nail polish in Oklahoma City, when I was five. No, I knew Rick would never go along with stealing! Just another syndrome of Sue's, she had kept from him.

This may be the appropriate time to inform you, I do not believe in luck! I believe in curses and blessings. Good and bad. Deceit and truth. Black and white. Right and wrong.

CHAPTER 6
WE ARE CHRISTIANS, NOT SAINTS!

Sue was very abusive. Mostly verbal abuse. Although, mother and I had each witnessed Sue throwing her little girl Wendy, all the way through the kitchen, dinning room and into the back door! We were appalled! I blew up asking, how she could do such a thing? All the child asked for was a drink of water!

I picked Wendy up and took her outside, calmed her down, getting her to play with Jeff, then went back inside the house to confront Sue, on how I felt about what I had seen. She refused to back off of her feelings or actions. No matter how angry I got, she would top it with her own fury. I demanded to know how she could mistreat an innocent child? She was now screaming as loudly as ever, and with such profanity! "I hate every little G-d child in the world, I wish I had never had one little M-F, and I wish they were all dead." She often spoke only four letter words and I don't mean simple ones, like conversing with a child. Little Wendy didn't actually walk. It was far more like creeping around the house in boys, cowboy boots, that were too big. Wendy seemed as though she was constantly fearful of her mother.

With Sue's state of mind, knowing the children could hear her every word, was inconceivable to me. (I had to gain my composure before asking) "Then why did you have so many? "There are ways to prevent getting pregnant Sue." Her response was cold and callous, with a wicked smile and a much calmer tone, she replied, "Well, they do have their advantages." Sue and I argued numerous times, over the way she treated and spoke to the children. In my departure, I told her one day she would need them, and they wouldn't be there for her, and she should think about that. This is the absolute truth. I was there, I saw, I heard. Our mother witnessed the same thing on another occasion, without my presence, because Wendy said she was hungry. I would gladly take a polygraph, if necessary, anytime!

I asked Sue if Rick was aware of her treatment of the children. She let me know exactly who they belonged to, suggesting I mind my own business. She implied that he did know, but also, he could do nothing about it! I should have gone directly to him, but she certainly led me to believe he had no say about it. I kept quiet, for a while.

So, I was to assume Rick knew about the situation, the abusiveness. That sure didn't sound like Rick. I had no desire to cause turmoil, so I continued to remain quiet for the time. I would learn years later he didn't know a thing. Yet, neither did I!

Again, so secretive. As much as I hate saying it, I have never known one more cruel, evil, or devious, then perhaps the next day, a rather decent person. The only thing definite was, nothing was definite, other than never knowing what to expect from Sue.

However, I must confess, we did manage to have some beautiful and wonderful times. The memories of the good times were rare indeed, but Sue did have some good days. When she was good, she was good, even with a sense of humor at times. There were times I felt hopeful, but as always, they were short lived. We did have two incredible Christmas days with them. I so wanted Rick to be right, proving me wrong about her.

I honestly did give Sue a lot of breaks, trying desperately to like her, for Rick at least. I had to respect his choice. A task Sue didn't make inviting nor with any encouragement on her part.

CHAPTER 7
HE HAD A SON

Rick was a natural born mechanic, with a knack for repairing just about anything. He always loved working on cars, for a year or so he worked from home on vehicles. A few years later Sue became pregnant and Rick was thrilled. September, he had a son, named after him. Rick and his son were so close. Sue was obviously, openly jealous. Little Rick wouldn't get more than six inches from his daddy. I can still see him holding tools and helping daddy. What frightened Rick was something Sue told him in the hospital, after the birth, **"Rick, if anything ever happens to us, you will never see your son again."** He told me he believed her too, according to what he had observed over the years with her former husbands. It disturbed him greatly. They were still not married, but his son had Rick's last name. Keep this in mind, as it holds a great mystery, yet unsolved.

Rick soon moved his business into a shop. He wanted Sue home with the children! As stated, Sue still had to control everything and this included Rick's business. Rick's patience finally came to a halt. He was aggravated and concerned at her writing checks for parts and wrecked cars he would purchase and rebuild. He knew checks for $900.00 or more would not clear. Sue assured him of her ability to handle the situation. He learned she was using her mother's checking account to do so. Inadvertently, it came to his attention that she was running most of the checks through a nearby gas station. Rick's biggest concern was that the station owner had a daughter, the biggest drug dealer in the county and a lesbian. Not that Rick cared, but he had heard rumors that Sue, at one time, dabbled in that and he knew Sue had a knew friend. The possibilities alarmed Rick.

Rick's shop was only a few miles away. He worked endless hours, but never forgot the children. Busy as he was, he got Bill Jr. a motorbike, against Sue's wishes. Rick felt Bill deserved it and was old enough. He taught Bill how to be respectful of the dangers, laying down the rules. Little Wendy wanted to join Brownies. Sue threw a fit saying she wasn't going to run a bunch of brats back and forth etc. Rick got so angry he told Sue that if she would let Wendy join, he would take her and pick her up. I don't know how he could have pulled it off, with him working fourteen to eighteen hours a day, often seven days a week. But, I knew he would find a way. When I say Rick loved children, I mean he had a huge heart for them.

I could never get him to spank or punish my children. When I say spank, I mean a swat on the bottom to get their attention. He has eighteen nieces and nephews, two of his own and with Sue's three, not including the baby, he and Rhea's children, he has yet to ever lay a hand on any child!

When they were all younger, Uncle Rick and Aunt Clar were favored. Not that we were more loved, but we were much like children ourselves. I know I wanted to grow up with my children.

My years as a mother are filled with good times. I was Chairman of both their classrooms, Vice President of the PTA., Cub Scout Den mother, Blue Birds, coached baseball and softball. What ever they were into, I was there. Let's face it. They know how to have fun, and Rick and I really enjoyed that. Children are so innocent. Young lives longing for themselves. We were keenly aware of the impact adults can make in their lives. Both Rick and I have often stood in line at stores, with many little ones being ignored in order to serve us, the adults. This always infuriated us. We would stand back and announce, "they were here first!" So many suffer with an attitude, "They are just children." As though they have no value until they become an adult? Too often, the damage has been done and they end up feeling like a second class citizen. This is wrong, very wrong, and Rick and I refused to participate in such.

CHAPTER 8
TRYING TO HELP SUE, HELP SUE

Rick virtually had no say in much of anything that went on. He just tried to make the best of whatever he had to deal with. He was working such long days to provide to the best of his ability.

He did see signs of things that bothered him greatly. I think he agreed to accept her as a very different type of person than most. Notwithstanding, she was the mother of his son, therefore he tended to make excuses for what he couldn't understand. He asked me, often to try and get along with her. I did try. It became more like a mission, but after having spent one night in that house was enough for me. I was helping Rick to put an industrial engine in a truck and stayed over to be there early, plus it was a long drive home. But, what a night! Like the children, I wouldn't go to the bathroom or walk that hallway.

We were aware that Sue was a Mormon, which is her right, but you can't know Jesus and not talk about Him or void of the desire to share what you know. Again, I have nothing against the Mormons, in fact I have several Mormon friends and neighbors that I respect and love dearly! It's just that Sue abused her faith, just as she tended to abused everything else in her life.

Lori and I took tapes, books and a Holy Bible to Sue. At first she was very reluctant, but she gave it a chance. We got them into Carman, a Contemporary Christian singer/author/actor. They would call us at any hour, regarding some of the lyrics. Laughing and asking if Carman really said what they thought they heard. Rick said they thought Carman was incredibly talented and admired the gift he had in relating Bible stories in songs. Rick said he never realized how much fun it could be in listening to Christian music. Lori and I got so tickled over their amusement of the tapes we had made them. Even Sue appeared to thoroughly enjoy them. For a while, Sue was actually fun to be around. A more calm, serene Sue than we had ever seen. There were a few good times.

This went on for several months, to our delight. Then I paid Sue an announced visit. Upon my arrival, I found her in a frenzy. She didn't appear to be the Sue of late, more like a wild woman, with glazed eyes. I found her tearing through her closets, throwing things across the room. The house was in total disarray. Tapes strewn all over the place, especially the materials we had given her. I hold no degree in psychiatry or sociology, but I know how to look into eyes. The mirror of the soul. What I saw chilled me to the bone. Sue asked if Lori and I wanted any of the items we had given her, otherwise she would throw them in the trash!

I prayed for peace and strength, as well as knowledge, before attempting to speak with her. I asked Sue what was happening. She stopped, as if frozen and out of nowhere she asked me, "You want to see me move a lamp with my mind?" No, I did not. I then noticed the books on the table where my Bible lay. I was completely caught off guard! Books on Witchcraft, the Power of the Mind, Occults and even movies, with covers I wouldn't touch! On the floor, couch and all about.

I picked up my Bible, trying to tell her I was leaving. I couldn't get a word in for her jabbering on and on about how she had learned to control minds. Anyone she chose, and was so eager to show me, begging me to stay. Again, with more emphasis, she assured me how good she had become in controlling lives and their very thoughts. Proclaiming, "I can make anybody believe what ever I want them to." The smirk on her face defied anything I had seen. I replied, "Then Sue, make me believe what I am seeing, with a healthy rationalization." She didn't appreciate that. Noticing her expression of anger, which was very visible. I wanted out. Now! Finally, I was able to speak, and be heard, telling her in no way would I stay and my Bible wasn't going to lay along side such books from hell, that I was indeed leaving. I walked out. Actually, I felt as though I was running for my life. I could not get out of there quickly enough.

On my way home I recalled Rick's remark, "Sis, Sue's getting into some really weird things." Sue had Rick picking up rental movies for her that she would call and order. Movies that Rick strongly disapproved of and books he found very disturbing. Rick knew very little about Sue's "newest thing." Upon his arrival home, Sue would immediately place the questionable items under the couch cushions or anything close by. He said she always jumped into one thing after another, how he just gave up trying to understand. Bless his heart, he tried to relate to her, but said he had to give up, as each time he would get just close enough to get a handle on it, she would be off into something else entirely different. He'd laugh and say how she would make him dizzy, trying to keep up with her.

As for her newest craze, if Rick would ask anything about them, Sue would throw a fit and scream that it was none of his business. Other times she might just laugh and say it was no big deal. Regardless, Rick could never get a satisfactory or comforting answer.

He often mentioned Wendy and Jeff had a lot of bad dreams. Nightmares of monsters and such. He jumped Sue numerous times, saying he wished she would be more selective about what she allowed the children to watch on TV. Now, little Rick had begun having nightmares too. Waking up all through the night, in fear of them, and they seemed to be increasing. Rick confessed to me, "Sis, there are some real problems in that house, but I don't know what to do about it, or if I can do anything." He added, he didn't even know where to start. I asked, "Is it that bad brother?" Rick answered, "Yes, maybe that bad sis, I only wish I knew." So, did I!

I knew why little Rick was having nightmares. I was convinced he really did see those monsters. I wasn't sure Rick could handle it, possibly not believing me. It simply wasn't time yet. I thought of that strange woman with the long, dark hair in the hallway and I recalled the night I had spent in that house. Without sleeping, all night, just from the dark, ugly feelings I felt surrounding me. I vowed I would never stay another night there again, and I never did.

I also recall Lori and I praying for them and the children one night. We asked the Lord to fill that house with His ministering angels and He wouldn't allow it. We asked for His warring angels and again the answer was no. The best we could do was to place them on the boundary lines of the land. This He allowed. That really threw us a bit, but also the realization of just how bad and dark the house truly was. Lori and I were aware of the words in the Bible, regarding how there was no darkness in Jesus. The house was so dark, void of any light, and therefore we were not allowed to place His angels of light into the enemy's camp of darkness. It was years later before I shared this with Rick, knowing he wouldn't be capable of accepting the facts, at that time.

I began to experience a growing fear of doom for Rick. A fear so real I wanted to drag Rick out of that house, kicking and screaming, I didn't care! Every time I prayed for Rick, I saw a dark cloud hanging over his head. I attempted to reason with myself, that it was simply an "after-effect" in knowing what Sue was into. It didn't work. The cloud continued to increase in size and the gloom only deepened. I began dropping hints to Rick about getting out of that house! All of my warnings fell on deaf ears. Rick couldn't understand. I didn't quite understand. Rick was always aware of my ability to somehow know the unseen, but this was too much for us. Again, I knew that I knew of that impending doom!

CHAPTER 9
RICK WAS DELIVERED FROM ALCOHOL

Lori and I were living together, in a duplex, with her youngest daughter. A month later we moved into a larger two story townhouse, just before Thanksgiving. Naturally, we prayed over the new place before moving in. I was told in my bedroom, that due to my prayers, miracles would spring forth. Many did, but the best was the deliverance of Rick's drinking!

Lori and I went to the folks for Thanksgiving. Rick was there, drinking and alone. Sue and the family stayed behind, due to colds. He returned home the next day and Rick and Sue had a huge argument about his drinking. No one could blame Sue for not wanting to live with a drunk!

Less than a week later, Sue called us to announce the news! Rick wanted to wait and surprise us, but Sue couldn't wait to share the news. Sue said, when he finally went to bed, he woke up without any desire to drink. She didn't believe him at first and I couldn't blame her. Days passed and he was still sober. She encouraged him to join AA, but no, Rick said he didn't need to. He simply had no desire for alcohol. She became a believer and called us with the incredible story.

A few days later, Rick came by our place to help us decorate for Christmas. He didn't look the same or act the same. He wasn't the same. He spent the entire day with us. We shopped for lights and went out for lunch. I tried to tell him why he didn't desire alcohol, that he had been delivered. He didn't agree, but did confess, he just "woke up" that way. I let up, knowing full well it was an answer to our prayers, but didn't wish to force him. By the time we finished decorating both floors, outside and inside, it was well past dark. What a wonderful day that was! I shall forever remember it. Lori and I were blessed in seeing this new man! Even Sue had calmed down again, being once again receptive to the Lord. It was the best Christmas we ever had!

Often over the two and a half years of Rick not drinking, when seeing one under the influence of alcohol, he would ask me, "Sis, is that what I looked like?" I'd smile and nod my head. He'd appear embarrassed and ashamed. I laughed, assuring him he needn't worry about that anymore. That part of his life no longer existed. What a wonderful time we had during those years. So, why did I still sense such impending doom? Every night in prayer, I would feel such a darkness in the atmosphere, that I couldn't explain. I truly wanted to think the enemy was so perturbed at Rick's unbelievable growth, that he was fighting me tooth and nail. I chose to just enjoy!

Rick had become so strong, in such a short period of time. I knew only the Lord could do such an amazing, life changing miracle. In the beginning, I was concerned that his old drinking buddies would come by the shop. I knew they would be drinking and I feared Rick might be tempted. Praise God, he never wavered or weakened. BB told me, everyone would offer him a drink, but Rick always refused with a "thank you, but no thanks." BB said Rick would drink that phony beer on occasion, adding, that it was obvious Rick honestly didn't want to drink. BB was astonished.

We girls often got on BB's nerves, regarding our faith, but he loved us in spite of it. BB and I were closer than the other two sisters. BB is not perfect, but he has always been a perfect friend to me and Rick.

My problem was that I still had not convinced Rick it was the Lord that had delivered him from alcohol. Rick didn't just wake up without a desire to drink. We do not live in the land of IF. We reside in a land of IS. Rick has always had three loving, believing and praying sisters. At least we knew why he was no longer drinking! I backed off and decided to allow God to be God, not me.

CHAPTER 10
WENDY'S MOLESTATION!

Sue went to our mother, with a problem. Apparently, Wendy had been molested by Bill! Which Bill? Son or brother, we do not know, but strongly feel it was the son. We had been concerned, in regards to the sleeping arrangements in the <u>house</u>. The mother, Ellie, had her own room at the far left end. Across from her was a back bedroom, for the two boys. (generally the oldest son Bill Jr. slept with the grandmother) Wendy slept in the front bedroom with Sue's brother, Bill Sr. Bunk beds or not, no one was pleased with this. Rick and Sue slept in the living room, on a couch that made into a bed. After little Rick was born, he slept between Rick and Sue. Details later.

Mother and I were very upset as to what Wendy must be going through. Sue said she wasn't sure how to handle it. Two weeks passed. I had to go out there to check on Wendy, and learn what Sue had decided to do. I wasn't there long at all. Having asked what she had done, I got a very distinctive, "Go to hell," look, with two sentences; "Hell no, I haven't done anything, and I don't plan to. My brother and I were molested by our grandfather and we turned out all right!"

I stood in horror, replying, "Oh, you really think so, do you?" After regaining my composure, I asked if Rick was aware of the awful event. With the same expression, Sue stated Rick knew, but he had been informed that she would handle it. I left in a state of disbelief, shock, confusion and anger! My heart broke for Wendy.

Okay, if Rick knew of this, no matter what Sue said, he would never <u>just</u> <u>let it go</u>. I found consolation in knowing Rick would do something about it. Regardless of Sue's sick attitude, victim or not, I was sure Rick would step in.

I cried all the way home, wondering how I would handle <u>my</u> daughter being molested. The thoughts that ran through my mind horrified me. My God, how could any mother take on such a "No big deal attitude?" I shivered all over, thinking of what I might be capable of doing, were it my baby girl! I was unable to stop the awful thoughts running rampant through my mind. So many questions of what I might be capable of doing, ushered in a fear unfamiliar to me. I felt a force of unknown and unrealized fear, rising to a peak of horror. A fear of the probability that I could actually take a life! Never, had I ever risen to the brink of hate or a desire to physically harm another life. Dear God, I came to the reality of the potential, stirring deep within. It was horrifying and suddenly, I felt such compassion for those that have retaliated when the Courts failed. You never know until you walk in those shoes, just what your capabilities are! What if the offender is a relative, friend or another child, or even your own child? I can be this angry and it's not my child? None of my business?

I was always under the impression, that her mother had known about her father molesting Sue and Bill. But, never doing anything about it. I found this shocking yet, perhaps it was not true. I seldom knew anymore than Rick, whether to believe a word Sue said, or not. Again, how could a mother, any mother, tolerate such a ghastly incident? Oh Lord, she must be right. It really does run in the family. Well, it didn't run in ours and I was persuaded that in no way would Rick stand for such as this!

It would be years before I would learn that Rick never knew about Wendy! The real truth is, Sue was right, again. She made me believe a lie! No, that's giving her too much power. I allowed myself to accept her lie about Rick's knowledge, regarding Wendy's real molestation. I should have known better!

CHAPTER 11
THAT WARNING OF DOOM

I had known for over a year of that dark cloud. I felt something awful was about to happen to Rick. But, even I had no concept of how truly nefarious things would become. As the weeks passed by, that black cloud became more ominous than I could conceive. Then months passed and the warnings evolved to more of an <u>apocalyptic symbol of the coming doom</u>! I could feel it closing in. Now, it was as though a heavy cloak was falling down all over Rick. Each time I saw Rick I could actually see that black cloud above his head. It would enlarge steadily, becoming even more darkening.

I was going through a divorce, which was finalized in May. It was very difficult, in that I saw it as a personal failure. I spent much time helping Rick out at his shop. This caused a problem with Sue, as she was jealous of the closeness of our family, especially Rick and I. I stopped going out there, but didn't tell Rick why. By early August I had become so depressed that I quit my job and hid in my townhouse, alone. What could I do to help Rick? Was I missing something? Was my depression a part of it? Was I being overly protective? God, are You not talking to me? No answers, just that cloud, growing larger, darker and more threatening.

My husband and I had separated two years earlier. I told Lee he would have to file if he wanted his freedom, as I had no intentions of doing so. I spent months trying to recover, in a two story, three bedroom townhouse, alone. By the end of August, I had pretty much given up on life and prepared to walk out, leaving everything I owned. My folks showed up unannounced, put my things in storage and took me home with them, to the country.

Twenty-five acres of land, with nineteen natural springs. A country girl at heart. I spent over seven months there, working the land from sunrise to sunset, six days a week. In doing so, the Lord used the time to heal my broken heart and restore me. Daily, I would spend the first hour or two reading my Bible. I had my radio for my music and worked hard, very hard. I would almost have to crawl the huge hill in order to get back. I got so much closer to Him, spending hours on end in prayer. I was much stronger and felt I needed to rejoin the world again. I was filled with concern for Rick and the desire to be there for him, as **IT** was much closer now. No, it was not me, my depression nor my imagination. **IT** was as real as the sun that rose that day!

I had gone back for a visit in late winter. Lori was having car trouble and Rick came to her place late one night to work on it. It was very cold, but I stayed by his side the entire time. I sat on the curb and began questioning him about what was going on in his life. We could always talk about anything. But that night's conversation was strained, to say the least. I had to warn him of my fears and attempted to share what knowledge I had. It was more difficult than I was prepared for.

I began questioning him about little Rick's nightmares. Was he still having them? Yes. Again he expressed his concern about what she allowed the children to watch on TV. I asked him to explain the details of what the little guy would say or do when he had them. Rick said he would hold him and ask him to show daddy where they were. The little guy would point to numerous places in the room. Rick would tell him they were not there and at times he said he would wave them off, and tell him they were gone and it was just a bad dream. My heart was pounding, I had to speak up. I stood up, asking him to hear what I had to say, whether he liked it or not. Even if he didn't believe me, I had to tell him what I knew. I realize now, at the time, I knew very little.

But, when you know that you know, you know! It is settled, a done deal, so make the best of it. I told Rick, "You are dead wrong about your son!" When he points to a location saying he sees a monster, it's because he really does see them. They are all over that house!" I began to weep, begging him, once again to get out, to run for his life before it was too late. I couldn't make him understand. He kept saying he couldn't leave, not just because of his son, but the other children needed him also. Could I be more specific? Yes, "Your world will blow up in your face, it will happen so quickly and horribly, you won't know what hit you, and life will never be the same for you again!" I confessed I was not saying it well, but I couldn't stress how imperative it was that he get out as soon as possible! The condensed Readers Digest version, "Run for your life brother, get out of that house!" Run, Rick, run!

After a long period of silence, Rick back working on the car, asking me if that was why the family had stopped coming to the house? I confessed it was a part of it, as well as all the darkness Sue had gotten into, plus we couldn't stand to hear the awful way she spoke and screamed at the children. Sue had a mouth like a Sailor and her words cut like a knife. I asked him if he was aware that she would beat the children with a vacuum cleaner cord. His body language told it all. No, in fact I learned that night just how little of anything my brother was aware of. He said Sue was the most secretive woman he had ever known, (where have I heard that?) and when she drank or did drugs he was amazed at the things he heard come from her mouth.

He mentioned one day, the previous year, one of the children had come home from school with a letter. Rick said Sue went ballistic and pulled the children out of school. Sue announced that she was going to home-school them. Rick said he never saw the letter, but got the impression that the child had said something about their home life that angered Sue terribly. The Mayor had somehow become involved, and threatened to have Sue arrested if the children were not back in school. They did go back to school. "That's it brother, that's all you know about it?"

He added, Sue had allowed the two younger ones to spend a weekend with their father. Sue told Rick, the father had sexually abused Wendy. Sue called Human Services and they said not to press charges, because of the child's speech impediment. Sue was told they could not win in a Court of Law! He said for weeks Sue would take the children and be gone all afternoon. I asked why? According to Sue, upon Rick questioning her, they were all going for counseling. Rick said that was the most he could get out of Sue. Rick never got any details but, he always thought their father a pretty all right guy. I think so too!

Oh my Lord! I realized exactly what Sue had done! Sue set their father up for the fall. She had to find some sort of cover for whichever Bill, had molested Wendy! Sue is shrewd, cunning and unpredictable. Obviously her secret had been exposed, most likely through the school. I was now burning hot, in spite of the bone chilling cold, just seconds previously. How could this woman live with herself? Sue always found a way out or a scapegoat! Never accountable for anything. I do believe the accused father is a decent man. I can only imagine his hell, but he got a "free pass," from the Dept. of Human Services, "Because they couldn't win, due to Wendy's speech?" Damn!

I knew without a doubt, Rick never knew about Wendy's horrible ordeal. Did I dare tell him? Was it time? Yes, perhaps it was. Before I could tell him, he said he couldn't leave Sue. He was too afraid he would never be able to see his son or the other children again. He appreciated what

I told him, but he couldn't do it. I hugged him, told him I loved him and I had to return to the folks, but that he knew where to find me if he needed me. I lovingly urged him again, to pay as much attention as he possibly could, to everything that was going on in that house. He stood back and said he knew I was convinced of what I told him, but he just couldn't understand, adding, that I was scaring him. All I could say, was that he had every reason to be scared. "Be afraid my brother, be very afraid! And above all, watch your back!"

I no sooner returned to the country, when I felt a strong urge to go back to the city. The folks were doing pretty well. I wanted to be closer to Rick and I felt ready to go back to work, but in a new profession. I stayed with my sister Lori, and her daughter. I was able to see Rick much more and how I loved that! I went into retail, a very refreshing break. Anything other than management.

Soon, the folks weren't doing so well. Again, I had to return to the country. I was the only one available to go. Our other brother lives thousands of miles away. Both sisters still had children at home. I was the only one available to watch over the folks. A labor of love, but difficult to do. By now I was overwhelmed and consumed with concern for Rick and that dark cloud!

I spent every minute I could with Rick, before leaving. I still hadn't told him the truth about Wendy, and to a degree, I'm glad I didn't. His plate was running over. He didn't need anymore problems. We talked about Sue a lot and he shared many more, disturbing facts he had become aware of. I continued to encourage him to leave. I was relentless for two years, because I loved him so much and saw the storm coming.

Sue was still trying to run his business. Still writing checks that made him crazy, but also, there seemed to be a potential problem at the parts store. What did he mean? The payment of them or the guy that worked there? Rick wasn't sure, but quite alarmed. We couldn't figure that one out and wouldn't, for a couple of years yet. I left town with a heavy load. My burden of the forth-coming doom was increasing for Rick, to the point of mother sensing it. I had to pacify her as best I could. I have never been able to fool my mother about something that I knew to be and she would do her best to get me to open up. Not this time. I told her as little as possible. Rick is her baby and she spent most of her life concerned about him. As a child, his health was not good. He was always undersized and underweight. Finally accepting, he was just smaller, healthy, but small.

With mother suffering from hypertension and an enlarged heart and with dad's health, I just had to be as nonchalant as I could. I offered no more details than absolutely necessary. Mother never cared much for Sue either, but like all of us, if she was Rick's choice, she would make the best of it. She had noticed that Sue had become extremely more distant. Sue had literally stopped calling mother and it bothered her greatly. She was afraid it indicated there may be problems between her and Rick. I laughed and asked her if she really wanted to chat with Sue? Well no, she didn't, but she sure did miss talking with the children. Mother worried for years about how Sue was treating them. We honestly loved all the children. It means nothing when a child has another type of blood. They are all lives, longing for themselves. Children are innocent, needing love and acceptance. I still refused to reveal to mother what I knew in my heart. My younger sister Lori, was the only one I confided in, though she saw no visible signs, she took to heart what I shared. In just a few months, she too picked up on something very disheartening with Rick's life. Now I had a prayer warrior! A witness for me, of not being crazy.

Within weeks of my return to the folks, I would hear from Rick, with the worst news possible! The last thing I wanted to hear was the worst thing that could happen to Rick. I hate to confess my lack of enthusiasm, but I must be honest. Rick was happy. I was miserable, angry, shocked and utterly bewildered at the news. How could he possibly be happy? Why not just sign the remnants of what life he still retained, and surrender to her? Another form of death. Another child is on the way. Sue is pregnant!

CHAPTER 12
A NEW FRIEND AND ANOTHER CHILD COMING!

Yes, Sue was pregnant again! My heart was torn between Rick's happiness and what I saw on the horizon! I felt ill. I mean very ill. I seldom spoke with Sue, once the announcement was made. Funny, I couldn't see or detect any happiness on her part. Fact is, she became a recluse. I didn't even speak much with Rick. I knew my warning of doom had to be difficult for him. I knew without a doubt, this was the worst possible scenario. No way would Rick leave now! He told me about Sue's new best friend. A lesbian drug dealer. Rick was right. The new friend was the daughter of the man that owned the business Sue used to cash all those checks! That dark cloud just got darker! Rick said he forbade Sue to have her friend around the house and the children. Sue didn't like that! All I could do was pray about it. Nobody tells Sue what to do!

I knew in my heart something was very wrong with this. In spite of all my prayers, I became even more concerned. I knew **IT** was close. That dark, ominous cloud was about to burst forth with a vengeance! I felt so helpless. What could I possibly do? It was Rick's life. Had I stepped over the line in revealing what I knew? Had all I accomplished served only to drive a wedge between Rick and I? I couldn't recant. I wouldn't if I could. I honestly tried to warn him, to spare him of that which was to come.

I became angry at God several times. I wanted to know why He showed me such doom, yet failed to give me any instructions as to what to do with that knowledge. I got over that pretty quickly, when I realized I sure wouldn't want Him mad at me! It was over and done. I warned Rick. What was left to do? Have faith, with Lori's, mixed with heavy duty prayers.

Apparently the pregnancy was far more difficult than any Sue had experienced previously. The baby came early. He was born days before Christmas. We found out by chance when we called them Christmas day! When little Rick was born, Sue called us from the hospital. Why had she not bothered to notify anyone of the arrival of this one?

39

Mother was shocked and angry. Mother said Sue wasn't even friendly when she called to wish them a Merry Christmas. The announcement of the baby was, more or less, as though Sue had gone shopping and made a purchase. Not to mention the name! We had no idea where that name came from. An unusual first name, but the middle name was more foreign. The reason for that would soon come out, in due time. We would find out, without any data from Sue, save for a slip of the lip. An off-the-wall remark we put together. The parts store! The guy at the parts store?

I began hearing from Rick in January. He was so concerned about Sue's state of mind! It seems she was notably depressed. I had suffered terribly with the "baby blues" with both my children. Rick wanted as much information as he could get, in order to help. I remarked, " For Pete's sake Rick, her mother is a Nurse, why don't you talk to her?" Well, that seemed a problem too. He felt Ellie was completely unconcerned! "Unconcerned?" What did this say? I dismissed it and told him as much as I recalled, ending with I would pray for them all. Rick thanked me for any prayers!

February, and he is still calling. Sue is actually worse. I suggested he get her to a Doctor. Sue refused to go, telling Rick she was already taking medication. I asked, "what medications." Rick had no idea. Sue wouldn't tell him. Whoa! This is not good and I told him so. I then asked for symptoms. Rick said she would sit and stare at the ceiling most of the time. The baby wasn't well. Sue was not talking and half the time she didn't seem aware of him being home.

Rick said Sue was once again, reading questionable books and concealing them. He said he had come home early, one day, to check on her and found her watching a movie. Rick didn't like it at all, telling Sue how he wished she would watch something more uplifting instead of something so morbid. She exclaimed, with a smile, "But, it's a true story." Rick said he didn't care, that he didn't like the story line. The fact of it actually being true, Rick found even more disturbing.

It was a movie about a woman wanting a divorce, so she falsely accused her new husband of molesting her daughter and enlisted her best friend to go along with the lie. The man was went to prison. However, the friend that went along with the conspiracy, was diagnosed with terminal cancer. While on her deathbed, she refused to die before confessing the truth. She confessed she had lied about the innocent man, who was still in prison. Rick was appalled at Sue enjoying the movie. In fact, she hit rewind to watch it again, so Rick went back to work. All I could say was, that he had some real problems. I asked the title of the movie, but Rick didn't know. What? Didn't you have to pick it up Rick? He said no, that he assumed her "new friend" brought it to her. "The one you won't allow to be there?" He said yes, he was pretty sure of it.

Sue was taking long, extended baths, with candles and wine or other alcoholic beverages. He said, "Sis, I mean hours at a time." I withheld my true feelings and said, "Hey, women love such as that, leave her alone brother." I did caution him that she shouldn't be mixing alcohol with her medications, if she was still on them. Yes, she was. He saw two more prescription bottles. I asked what they were, but again, Sue wouldn't let him close enough to read them or tell him what they were. I told him I was more concerned for him than I was for Sue. I suggested he bring the family for a visit to get Sue out of the house. He felt that would be too much for her, so I suggested that just the two of them come and bring the baby. Rick said he would let me know.

He called a couple of days later. Sue refused to come! He had no idea why she reacted like she did, quite cold. I shouldn't have said what I did, but it came out, "Well, sure sounds like she has something to hide." Rick was stunned at my remark, asking why I would say such a thing. I did apologize. I hated what I said, but that was my thought and without thinking, I just spouted off. He said that wasn't like me. What else could I say? I hated hurting Rick's feelings, but I detected something else in his reaction. Rick knew me well enough to know it wasn't a slip. He was right. It wasn't like me to say hateful things without a reason. Yes, I usually did say what I thought, (with discretion) but, I did get his attention! I knew Rick's confrontation with Sue about her new friend, forbidding her to be at the house, there would be hell to pay. Nobody told Sue what to do.

A week later he called, convinced she was suffering with, "After baby blues." He said he had no idea who this woman was. I'll never forget his remark, "Sis, Sue has always been weird, but I've never seen anything like this, Sue is too weird, even for Sue." He said she was making off- the- wall remarks again that really scared him. Like what I asked. He said the night before, as they were about to go to bed, Sue was standing in the kitchen, looking at the walls. He came up behind her and put his arms around her. Before Rick could say a word, Sue spoke, "Rick, I'm sorry, but I've done something and either you or mom, (her mother) will have to take the fall."

"Rick, what on earth is she talking about?" He said he had no idea. I asked him rather loudly, "What do you mean? Didn't you ask her what she meant?" Yes, he asked her, but she clamed up and refused to discuss it. Rick said it was as though she went into a twilight zone and he could get nothing else from her and how she took a long bath.

In March, I heard from him once. He was mentally exhausted and more concerned than ever.

CHAPTER 13
THE DARK CLOUD BURSTS WITH A WRATH

A knock at the door, Rick and sis were there, at the folk's place. The visit was unannounced. I saw a problem all over their faces. I knew that cloud had burst open, to what extent I had no idea. Mother, bless her heart, was so thrilled to see them and completely unaware. I went to my room to pray, giving them some time with mother. How they held up so long, I'll never know. I braced myself and finally joined them. I hugged Rick and whispered in his ear, asking if he wanted to talk alone or visit with mother. Mother finally caught on to the fact, something was very wrong. Rick started trembling all over and Lori spoke up, saying they had something they had to tell us.

He broke our hearts with his shaky voice. Fighting tears, he attempted to explain what all had happened. It took over six hours to finish the nightmare and for us to absorb what we had just heard. It sounded more like a horror movie than real life. He couldn't go home or CPS would remove all the children! Had sis not been there with him, it might have taken days for Rick to get it all out.

Mother spoke up saying Sue had called her in January. The only time she had called in months. Her call disturbed mother greatly. Sue asked her about a refrigerator mother had bought from Rick years ago, when Sue and Rick moved south, into her mother's house. Sue claimed that mother bought it on a contingency basis, that they could buy it back and apparently it was needed. Mother became angry telling her that no such deal had ever been made. Sue stressed to her that the sale was set up just as she declared. Mother let her know she purchased it from Rick, that Sue never had a thing to do with it. This was typical Sue, attempting to manipulate and control minds, but it didn't work. Mother said she knew she angered Sue, but really didn't care, then asked Rick if he was aware of it. Rick was quite perplexed, as he knew nothing about the call or the purpose of it. Scratching his head, Rick said he had no knowledge of their needing another refrigerator. I gathered she had been planning in advance, all along. This Sue I knew.

We begged Rick to share every detail he could. He began with the staggering story. It was like a horror novel. I told him I knew all he had been sharing with me about his concerns with her state of mind, but to proceed with the latest details. He described his last three days at home.

In mid March Rick had gotten home very late. Sue met him at the door yelling he was cheating on her, that she knew he had a girlfriend. You have to know my brother. He simply told her it was late, he was exhausted, and wanted a shower and to go to bed. Asking, just when would he have time for an affair? Nothing more was said. A shower and on to bed in silence.

The next night, the same thing, but with a twist. Now he was gay and having an affair with BB.

Rick told her she has some serious problems, but that he was too tired to discuss such a ridiculous charge. He declared he was taking a shower and going to bed. Nothing more was said. Rick truly felt it was her depression and perhaps medication or the combination of the two. He said it was too wacky for him to even consider Sue believed those wild accusations.

The third night, the same thing. But, now she accused him of molesting his own son! This time my mild mannered, passive, easy going brother was none of these. He confessed in tears, how upon hearing the sick allegation, he lost it. He confessed he became so enraged, he grabbed her around the neck, pushing her up against the wall, telling her in no uncertain terms, she was sick and come hell or high water, he was going to get her some professional help!

He was still torn up over his loss of control, with him physically touching her in anger. The allegations of having an affair and even being gay, he thought, were directly related to her state of mind, but to accuse him of such a despicable act? He wept, saying, he could not deal with this. The accusation had no rational explanation. This was far more serious than he imagined!

Rick didn't work at all that weekend. He felt he needed to stay home with the family, talking to Sue, telling her the entire family was screwed up and they had to have some help. He told us he was amazed at how calm she was the whole weekend. Rick said, "Actually, the old Sue surfaced but, even better." And, that she finally agreed to counseling. Rick held himself largely to blame, in working such long hours. He felt he could have been more helpful to Sue. He said the weekend went very well, quiet and even tranquil, but determined not to relent on their getting professional help.

Monday morning, at the door on his way to work, he asked Sue, "Honey, what are you going to do today?" She replied she would find a Counselor and make an appointment. He was happier than he could recall that morning. It was a very short morning. His happiness became pointless before he would get out of the driveway. He just didn't know it yet.

Within an hour of Rick's arrival at the shop, Sue's brother appeared with three large, black plastic trash bags, containing Rick's personal effects and a message. "Rick, Sue said if you return home, the Department of Human Services, and CPS, will take the children out of the house!" Have you figured it out yet? It took three days to find the right button to push, his son! Now she could go forward with her plan. He literally gave her the weapon she needed. She found the right button to push! His son was his life, his weakest point, her winning weapon of choice. Let the games begin!

Rick went to Lori's place and called Sue for an explanation. He called her numerous times to at least check on the children. At first she was nice, but wouldn't answer any questions about what happened. She said he couldn't come around or they would lose the children, but met him at various places for visits. He couldn't figure out which side she was on. She loved him, but things got out of control. A walking, talking enigma, armed and dangerous!

We spoke for hours. I knew Rick was still in shock. I decided I would return with them if only to support him in this nightmare. He told me he thought I was the only one that could truly see through Sue. And oh, how he wished he had listened to me. Did I know? Yes. Did I want to be right? No! Oh Lord, I would've done just about anything to be wrong! Oh how I would have loved being wrong. So often I prayed to be proven wrong. In matters like these, who would want to be right? I'm talking about five innocent children, a father, (my brother) and his chosen love, with a scared mother/grandmother, plus Rick's entire family about to be devastated.

Most of my knowledge involved impending doom. Oh, I would know great and positive things too, but not enough of them. I have never taken any joy in being right, especially in hurtful or dangerous situations. My goals and prayers are always for the ability to be able to spare them.

I never questioned Rick's intentions. I knew what kind of man he was. Leaving Sue, and the children, would break his heart, were he capable of doing so. I was well aware of his love for all the children and the feeling he had of being needed by them. They did need him! I felt he was more dedicated to the children than Sue, not that he didn't love her, but he never asked her to marry him either. Another enigma or a possible blessing?

I returned with Rick and Lori, to do whatever I could do for Rick. We stayed together at Lori's place. I worked every day with Rick. I badgered him to death with my questions. I wanted every detail. I wanted to know everything!

Often times, I would realize the more I knew, the less I knew! I would soon realize I merely received a glimpse of the entire realm. The ugly fact that Rick was surrounded by such darkness was only a hint of what was to come. There were no words to define the coming storm, but God knows I tried. Oh, how I tried.

Rick begged me to share all I knew about that <u>dark cloud</u>. How did I know? What could he do to mend this horrible situation? Surely this was just Sue's state of mind, again from having the last child. I wished that could be true, but I knew better. This had been a plan for sometime. I had no clue as to what Rick could do, but felt in my heart, it was too late. At least for this segment of his life. I strongly felt the new baby was instrumental, or a very important element, regarding the course of action Sue had taken. Why? I wasn't sure.

How does one say, "Forget it, there is nothing you can do, it will not get better, in fact, it will only get worse!" Her state of mind? I was convinced, it had nothing to do with the "baby blues." Sue had a plan. Rick had served the role she had need of, for the time. Now, it had become an evil battlefield and Rick was in no way prepared for it. I wanted to scream for him to spare me of all the excuses he was making for Sue, yet admiring such devotion.

I abhor, "I told you so." I candidly told him only time would tell. I felt he would have to be prepared for what he was about to learn, regarding Sue and her family. He wouldn't like it and the problem was not about to just go away! I warned him not to be so vulnerable, but to be hopeful. (very hard to say, but without hope I feel life is not worth living) I suggested he not trust Sue in any way. "Hope for the best brother, but without Sue."

I made it clear, that I knew he had many things to share with me. I knew it had been several years but, he didn't for fear of my attitude towards her becoming even more negative. I added, "Brother, no matter what you tell me, I will not be surprised, in fact, I expect the worst and I don't think anything you share with me could increase my negativism towards her." I was right, yet, I was wrong! Several events did surprise me, but more often I would become so enraged, and even angry at Rick for placing himself in such a hazardous position.

I would eventually, come to learn that Rick actually feared Sue. He finally shared an event that occurred while they were dating. He had gone to a friend's house, after work, to fix an engine on a boat. Rick had the same group of friends for years, some went back over three decades. Sue wanted him to have nothing more to do with them. It was Sue or nothing, not just with friends, but family too.

Rick had told Sue where he was going, but apparently she didn't like it or didn't believe him. So, Sue went looking for him. He saw her car westbound, as he was returning home. She made a illegal U-turn on the freeway, speeding to catch up with him. He wondered why she would be upset. The sun was still out and he hadn't stayed as long as he first thought.

He pulled off on to the shoulder, waiting for her to approach his car. In the rear view mirror he could see the angry expression on her face, knowing Sue was furious. What he didn't see was the 38 she placed to his head, asking where the F-- he had been. A mental image of this is staggering! Remember the gun, as I will expound upon it again, with her testimony on the stand, years later.

I knew it was hard for any man to confess he was afraid of a woman, but he certainly did have reason to fear Sue. I was furious at the mental vision in my head. My brother with a gun to his temple! "Brother, if you saw this dysfunctional, blatant side of her, why didn't you run for your life, right then and there?" Rick had become too attached to the children. This I knew.

He replied, he felt Sue had been abused by many men and he wanted her to be able to trust one, him. Rick had also fallen in love with her children and he didn't really think she would have pulled the trigger. "Really brother? It happens every time you pick up a paper or watch the news, and most always, they didn't think they would do it either!" I wanted to shake him and hug him simultaneously. Shake some sense into him, hug him for his honorable intentions.

But Rick, she did this on a freeway, in broad daylight and you think that wasn't a pretty strong indication of her not having a full measure of sanity?

His reaction was one of retreat. I know it was also an embarrassment, so I yielded for the time being.

Can anyone imagine your brother having a gun to his head? Am I alone in being completely repulsed, angry and frightened of such a woman, professing her love for him? Is this any form of sanity? The same person accusing a good man of such a crime, he wasn't capable of committing?

I begged and encouraged Rick to think, think hard and recall everything he could, no matter how trivial it may have seemed at the time. I was convinced everything Sue did had a motive of some sort. I had to find a way to reach him and assure him, there was no innocence in her! Sue resented Rick and I being so close and did her best to keep us apart. Rick would suffer with migraines at times. I was the only one that could relieve them. It was merely massaging his head and feet, mixed with prayers. Sue was determined she could do the same. She couldn't and it was nothing for me to get a phone call anywhere from midnight to two AM. I would make a twenty minute drive to relieve his headache. He told me Sue did it too hard, hurting him. Sue hated this.

He continued to recall many unexplainable events. Like him bringing in the mail one day, about a week or so before the **explosion**. Generally, he wasn't allowed to check the mail, but with bad weather and Sue's condition, he did, to help her. He recalled seeing a large brown envelope from Human Services. Sue became quite stressed and defensive upon Rick's inquiry. Could that be a part of it? There were so many possibilities and candidates. Where do we begin? What to do?

As hard as I tried to walk in Sue's shoes, and to think like her, I found it short of an impossible task. I simply couldn't think like her, so I checked with several friends, Doctors and a couple of private investigators I knew. Eventually, I was able to think in ways I never knew I could. I had to learn to become a devious, shrewd, conniving, evil woman. One hell bent on destroying a life in order to gain a clue, as to why Sue would do this. Obviously to cover up a deep, dark secret, she had wanted kept concealed. I finally became rather good at it, resenting her for such a downward spiral in which I felt I must venture. Without a doubt, I knew she was in deep and out to save herself, and too willing to take Rick down for it. Uncomfortable? Oh yes, but it was for Rick. It had to be something enormous to go to such unlimited lengths. A "fall" was necessary for someone. Rick, was the chosen one! But, why Rick? What was she concealing that was so awful that she would, without hesitation, destroy her husband's life?

Rick was fearful for his son and very protective. His worst fear was the fact that his son may well have been molested. It was impossible to know by whom, but we were fully aware of the horrible possibility of it actually happening.

CHAPTER 14
BROTHER RECALLS EVENTS!

As time passed, he would recall even more, and question many things. Up to now, no one in the family had ever seen the baby yet! In late April, Rick became even more depressed and terribly worried about the children. I questioned him constantly, insisting there had to be more signs of this coming. Had he ever heeded my warnings and encouragement in paying closer attention to events and her nonsensical remarks? Things slowly began to come to him, like how the oldest son had gotten into trouble.

It seems they had a new neighbor. A very dark, secretive man, just like Sue. Bill Jr. and some friends broke into the man's house, stealing a gun and some electronics. When Rick found out he was furious. Rick gathered up all the items he could find and returned them to the man's house, demanding the man call the police. It was difficult to tell the man's age. He seemed older but, Rick couldn't be sure how old. He had a long beard and was very shabbily dressed, in a dark, cabin like house. Rick found the man's attitude troubling. The guy wouldn't look Rick in the eye.

The man had two young children there when Rick arrived. Rick asked about the children, (feeling that something was very wrong with what he saw. Especially when the man explained they were just relatives and flatly refused to call the police, seemingly very nervous.)

Rick told Sue, he never wanted his son, or any of the other children, over there again and Sue better pay heed to it! No matter what Sue said, Rick had been in that filthy place and had no use for the guy. Rick, had a bad feeling and was convinced the guy was hiding something! Sue was very angry at Rick, stating the man was nice and all the children hung out there. Rick told me, "Sis, there was something very wrong about that whole thing, but Sue refused to listen to me." Years later, we learned about a serial sexual child molester, arrested in LA. The accused had been in that very area, at that very time! Leaving a trail of molested children in other states!

Compound the situation of the neighbor and her new, drug dealing, lesbian friend. With Rick's refusal of allowing her in the house, and forbidding the children to go to that cabin and you have one furious woman! I think Sue felt she was being somewhat controlled. Control was like a gift to Sue. A right of passage she would never relinquish, willingly. What a thorn in her side that must have been! Rick laying down rules for her! A combination for disaster, for sure. He worried that she would resist his demands, so Rick began working less hours. He would come home at unexpected hours, to her displeasure. He found her friend there many times, quickly departing upon his arrival.

He was trying to spend more time at home to help her. One evening, he was home early enough that his son was still up. Little Rick wanted daddy to give him his bath. Rick found a red, swollen spot on his little penis. He asked how it happened. Getting nothing of value from his son, Rick stormed into the kitchen, asking Sue about it. To Rick's dismay, she expressed no concern. Much like, "big deal!" Rick told Sue he wanted little Rick at the Doctor's office, the next day! Sue was quite upset with his attitude! Rick said, "You will take him, because I want some answers!"

The next afternoon, Sue called Rick saying, it was nothing more than a spider bite. Was it? Did she really take him? She whined about spending money for nothing. It was like she told him the previous night, it was nothing. Did she take him to the Doctor? Was it a spider bite? Rick felt unsettled. Now, he feels stupid for listening to Sue and wonders what else he might have missed.

He recalled it happened a couple of months prior to his shattered world! He really bore down on every detail, thoughts, questioning her irrational remarks. He remembered something else he had heard about Sue getting stopped on I-45. He said she was pregnant with one of the children. He heard Sue proceeded to kick the police car door in. Sue claimed the officer then took her out for coffee. "Sis, I never know what to believe when she says something." He agreed it sounded pretty wild and most likely never happened. I wasn't so sure at all. I would never put anything past that woman and the way she controlled so many.

I had a real problem comprehending how he could sexually molest his son, especially when his son slept in the same bed, between the two of them. Sue's explanation was inconceivable! At first, she claimed Rick thought she was sleeping! This angered Rick so greatly that she soon altered it to, her being sure he wasn't aware of it. Now, Sue was now trying to convince Rick how she was positive that Rick wasn't cognizant of doing it, perhaps he was doing it in his sleep! Mind control!

Well, Rick isn't that gullible, so he went right out and purchased a Polaroid camera. He placed it above the bed and said, "Next time, get a picture." This was on a Sunday, his last full day at home. I wonder, had he not purchased that camera, if things would have been different. It did place the burden of proof on her, but perhaps it forced her hand too. I must confess, it appears that her plans were already in motion. In reality, she was racing the clock. It took her three days to find the right button to push in order to learn which accusation struck the reaction she seemed to be in need of, to implement the ability to pull her scam off. I can think of nothing that would have upset Rick more, than accusing him of abusing his son, or any of the children for that matter.

He also recalled, maybe in February, of Sue making the remark that her mother wanted them out of the house. The more he thought about it, the more suspicious he became. It was always perceived, Sue ruled over everyone and everything. No one ever heard, or saw, her mother or brother, defy or oppose Sue. In her mother's own home!

That triggered something else in Rick. He relived that night of the accusation, of him molesting his son. He said he got rather loud, remembering how he became so consumed in anger, and that he had his hand around her neck, against the wall, but no one came out of their rooms to check on what was transpiring between the two of them! Strange indeed.

He confessed it mysterious. Why did no one come to see what was going on? Unless, they already knew, being advised by Sue not to intervene. I think he got it. It was a setup and not long after that, we were positive of it. Obviously, they were aware of her plans, being told to stay out of it! The day he went to pick Sue and the baby up from the hospital. Having been left in limbo with her mother leaving Rick stranded for hours, to run an errand. She had actually gone to the hospital. Why? It has to be one of two reasons. Did Sue's mother go to the hospital to talk Sue out of her scam, or possibly, her mother actually made all the "wedding" arrangements? It makes a lot of sense. A four hour journey, at night for an elderly woman, has to have an explanation and a motive.

After all the hours we spent conversing, again, I came to accept the fact, that the more I knew about her, the less I knew her. I doubt that there is a living person, anywhere on this earth that truly knows Sue and probably never will! I had promised Rick, years earlier, I would do all I could to like, accept and understand Sue. I labored exceedingly in doing so, failing, miserably. Knowing full well, now, why I couldn't complete the impossible mission!

CHAPTER 15
YOU'VE GOT TO BE KIDDING

Rick and I were together 24/7. I went to work with him everyday. We talked nonstop trying to come up with some sort of an answer. I asked him about the IRS. He had no idea, as Sue always handled that too. Do what? Rick never saw any forms, never signed any either. I couldn't believe anyone could or should be that trusting, especially with one with a history such as Sue's. "Rick, you really know nothing about your taxes? What about her writing all those checks you got so upset about?" <u>No</u>. I asked if he had any idea of the amount the checks may have totaled. All the cars he bought and sold, not to mention parts? Well, he felt it might be around $90,000.00. Oh no! My alarm at such news made him feel distraught. I backed off. He had enough to deal with. I would wait for another day.

I was saturated with questions. I had to find a way to sustain them in order to function and support him, opposed to attacking him. He was down on himself, bad enough, I had to be more vigilant to his state of mind. Never had I seen him so thoroughly devoid of any self-esteem.

He went to the offices of Human Services/CPS, sometimes daily, demanding answers. He begged for tests, a polygraph, anything to prove his innocence, to no avail, for months to come. Rick told Mr. J., he was well aware of problems in <u>that</u> house, but Rick was not the problem. He asked them if they couldn't just pop in for a visit. Oh no, they could never do that! He learned that <u>Wendy was now in Brownies</u>. Of course, why not? Would not that make her look like the excellent mother? All the more reason he wanted them to make an unscheduled visit, catching her unaware and unprepared, but again, they couldn't do that! Thus, Sue could be quite prepared.

When Sue found out Rick was going to the CPS/Human Services offices, she was furious. I left early one day. I wish I hadn't, but I did. That very night, Rick was working late when he saw them drive up. He saw Sue, Bill Sr. and her drug dealing friend drive up. Rick immediately knew what was to come. He was working on an engine, and had a huge screwdriver in his hand. Rick instantly threw it across the shop, fearing he would use it on one of them in self defense. Rick was right. They physically attacked and beat Rick badly. His ribs were badly bruised, making breathing very painful and difficult. Rick finally made it to Lori's. He would not allow to call the Police. He feared involving the police would only anger Sue and she would take it out on the children. Rick spent about a week on Lori's couch, with us tending to him. Did Rick fight back? No, he merely defended himself as long as he could. He couldn't remember everything, but knew that Sue used a fan belt on him. Lori and I were furious! I so wanted to call the Police, but Rick begged me not to.

When Rick was finally able to get up and around, he went out to Human Services, CPS again. Sue beat him to it, telling them he came to the house late that night and they defended themselves! If this was fact, why didn't she contact the Police? She could have had him arrested, why didn't she? Because she lied. Rick was never there and her neighbors, not liking her, would never be any type of witness for her! I told you she was good!

On this trip to Human Services, Rick demanded some answers! He asked MR. J, "If I am such a sick SOB, why wouldn't I do that to one of her children, opposed to my own." J. leaned back in his chair and replied, "Well Rick, we wondered the same thing, but in truth all the children speak very highly of you." Well, go figure. Why wouldn't they? They knew Rick loved them and would never hurt them in any way. How can these people be so blind and stupid? Are they all idiots?

Suddenly, little Rick came up with an arm broken in more than one place. It happened at the drug dealer's ranch, about 1:00 AM. What's a four year old doing out at that time? But of course, we couldn't get any kind of explanation. Rick had no rights! We could not go to the schools to check on the children, to learn more about that note from the school. We couldn't get medical records on his son! Our hands were tied. All we could do was speculate, because Sue was protected by the Government. Rick had no rights. Sue had them all, because she was the accuser.

My question is, if a person accused of such a crime, to the point that he was not allowed to return to his home or even see the children, then why was he not arrested? Not that I wanted him in jail! But, should any potential molester be allowed to roam the streets, for years? No! I knew without a doubt he was innocent, but where is the law to protect the potential victims, were he guilty? Does this not frighten you? Well, I hope it does, as it certainly should! How ironic, the accused, is in truth, the victim! A perfect example of a real victim!

I shall state again, our system is a bust, nothing short of a joke, lacking humor. And yet, no one in our family had seen the new baby. Not even Rick. Sue would take Wendy, little Rick and Jeff, (her middle son) to the shop often, but not Bill Jr. nor his new son, why? A very interesting question, with a more interesting answer to come later. An enigma fails miserably in defining this woman. She could be the Poster Child for the Mob! Pretty strong, I know, yet true.

Before you come down on me, remember, I have forgiven her. I love her and I pray for her, but my priority and focus must be on my brother and the corruption we have endured. To call it a gross injustice sounds far too inadequate.

We had not hired an attorney yet. Rick still hoped there might be a chance for them. Rick didn't see the need of an attorney and felt that too, would intimidate Sue even more. Sue had begun to drop in at Rick's shop, if I wasn't there. Sweet, kind, loving and then at times angry. One day Sue would claim Rick was right. Sue would confess her need for professional help, vowing she would get it. The next day, everything would be all Rick's fault. Again, the only thing definite, is nothing is definite with Sue.

As long as I worked with Rick, she stayed away, but an unexpected automobile accident transpired, involving me. I would be unavailable to help Rick at the shop. Sue took great advantage of the situation. In my absence, as I feared, she went there many times, with far too many stories, plots and plans. This gave her complete access to Rick and his weaknesses, which were his son and her children. I don't mean to imply Rick is brainless, I just knew Sue was very aware of his weaknesses and would use any, and all, to get to him.

How do you out-think a crazy woman and how do you stop one? I was getting pretty weary of waking up every day, compelled to "be every where, at all times," in order to protect Rick. Daily, I would ask myself, when was this going to come to a head? I constantly wondered exactly what her plans were. The dark cloud did burst open, but now the sky was black! I knew that Sue hadn't even gotten warmed up yet.

I stated Rick's faith wasn't as deep as his three sisters. We were all praying night and day. Rick had no problem with this, but we knew he wasn't expecting an answer from God almighty, but more so with the

Judicial System. We too, took some hope in that, for a while. We would learn as time passed, just how dismal the likelihood of that appeared. Eventually, we could see that Sue was not the only opponent, but Governmental Departments as well. This was a real scare upon meeting a few of them!

No matter what, we tried to stay upbeat and positive for Rick. It was difficult to convince Rick that God didn't do this dirty deed. We jumped on any opportunity to reveal the power of God, in any way possible.

I began pulling things on Rick. For instance, we had a car we had built a transmission on three times. Every time we tried to put it in, it wouldn't line up. Three times, three separate problems on three consecutive days. The last time Rick attempted to tackle it, I was on the other side of the shop putting a water pump on another car. I could hear Rick's frustration and foul words under his breath. Finally, I had enough. I left my job, walked across the shop, up to the rear of the car that Rick was under. I laid hands on it, asking God to line it up and click! I heard it go right into place. Rick rolled out from under the car, eyes big as half dollars, lit up with amazement asking me, "Sis, did you just pray?" I smiled, answering, "Yes, do you mind?" I then returned to my job smiling all the way back to the car. We girls did things like this all of the time and it never ceased to amaze Rick.

Again, not that Rick didn't believe in God. He did. He just didn't get into faith as we did. He, like many others, tended to limit God. Much like keeping God in a box until he needed Him. As I said, Rick was and is a wonderful man, but had his own snakes to kill. Funny, he did fear snakes but, spiders even more. He feared rodents as well. Rick never owned a gun or shot anything. I don't think he ever killed anything other than spiders and flies. On the other hand I did hunt, with a rifle. I never killed anything I didn't eat, except a couple of rattlesnakes, in order to protect the folks.

Rick's shop was surrounded by open fields and very tall weeds. Rick would set poison out, but no traps, otherwise, he would have to deal with those caught. I recall a huge rat that would enter all through the day. Rick called him the "Killer Rat." That rat really bugged Rick, but he said he had made a deal with it. It could do whatever it wanted, if the rat wouldn't bother him, Rick wouldn't bother the rat! I told him I was not going to put up with that evil looking, creepy, ugly, filthy rodent!

It aggravated me at how brazen the rodent was. It would enter in broad daylight, then choose which car he wanted to go under. This would often predetermine which car Rick would work on! I really teased Rick about this. Rick's response was, "Sis, that thing is bigger than a dog, I'm not taking him on and I don't see you doing it either!" I replied, "Well, if you're willing to allow a rodent to choose your job, that's your choice, but I will not tolerate that evil rodent's presence to dictate anything to me. God gave me dominion over the earth and it's creatures!" I finally told Rick if he didn't get rid of it, I would. Rick laughed and said, "Okay sis, you take him out then." He thought that so humorous. It did eventually come down to exactly that!

That killer rat, (was huge) made me crazy! The way it would enter and select a car, then just sit there under it and watch us with those beady, evil eyes. I caught myself talking to it and issuing threats. Rick would crack up with laughter, telling me how he didn't converse with it, since their deal.

One afternoon, (the rat having been there for at least an hour). Rick announced he had to run for some parts. I ragged on him about being scared of the rat. I swore he was using it for an excuse to escape the rat, as I was the one that did the all the "parts runs." Rick left. I was there alone with the "enemy, killer rat." I still can't believe how long I talked to it, warning it to back off or I would kill it, as it moved closer to me. Okay, that was it. I had enough of the rat business!

It moved to the car right next to me! I can still see those evil eyes, daring me. I jumped up and found a huge whisk broom across the shop. I grabbed the whisk broom, attacking it as a wild animal. That had to be a sight. I was beating and pushing it out of the shop, onto the gravel drive and into the field. Yelling at the rat that I had warned him. Now it was war! I think it took it's last breath as Rick returned.

He jumped out of the car yelling and asking me what I was doing out in the field. I answered, "I just killed your buddy." With a big grin and baby steps into the tall weeds, he finally located me and the rat. It was under the broom. He jumped and ran back onto the gravel drive. Then Rick began laughing. He laughed so hard, for so long I became agitated and asked what he thought so funny. He could hardly speak for laughing.

I was finally able to picture the scene he was trying to describe. He had seen me from the road. His five foot-three sister, in a field with weeds as tall as she was. A huge whisk broom beating the hell out of something. I must have looked like a wild woman beating that rat to death! When I got the mental image of this, I too burst into sheer, uncontrollable laughter too. We laughed until we cried. He still wouldn't go near the rat, but told me, "Man sis, I hope I never make you that mad, I can't believe you killed that killer rat!" I got cocky and asked, "Okay, who's the man now?"

That was an inside joke between the two of us. I would be having a problem getting a certain part off of a vehicle and fuss about it. I would finally complain loudly, vowing that it would not come off. After a while, Rick would always say the same thing, "Sis, if a man put it on, a man can take it off." I would then proceed to throw my tool at Rick and say, "Fine, you're the man, you take it off!" And, he would.

Oh, what wonderful, beautiful memories I have, and I demand more! Dear Lord, I miss him so much. I resent not having my brother around, because of an unstable, demented woman, in an effort to conceal something to save her own bottom! My heart breaks for all he has endured due to a false allegation! I wonder how Sue sleeps at night. How does she face another day? The most unsettling thought is, with her mind control, has she been able to convince little Rick in believing his father is guilty? The child was only four years old at the time, and I can still hear Sue's words, "I can make anybody believe anything I want," that still frightens me.

I am sure Sue has convinced little Rick of the lie. Think about it. Wouldn't she have to? But, we have prayed for years that he would know, deep within his heart, that it never happened. To allow an innocent child to grow up with such thoughts, is beyond my comprehension. I have often wondered, with this train of thought, without the memory, is little Rick aware of only what Sue has told him? Could the lack of memory cancel out her words? I know Sue dealt with this issue, as a child, and I am sorry for that, but that will not condone such perverse actions or any excuse to force a child to suffer just because she did. If Sue wanted a divorce, then why not just seek one? At least be honest about it, but Sue couldn't afford to be honest. Sue had something to hide.

Had we been able to afford a Loftus, Wakefield, Underwager and others, I know we would not be in this situation.

Drs. Wakefield, Underwager, Ross, Bush and Campbell are but a few that have investigated and studied over 2500 cases, to learn that the vast majority are false, manufactured and malicious. In 1991, according to Wakefield and Underwager, 80% of the allegations of child sexual abuse made during divorce, custody and visitations disputes are blatantly false! It's textbook. A mother speaks for a four year old child. These doctors can go right to the source, knowing a scam when they see it.

I look back and recall Sue's dark eyes, so threatening and often, almost void of life. I always go straight for the eyes when conversing with a person. The only part of the anatomy that cannot lie. I found myself avoiding Sue's eyes, to lesson any attempt to interrogate her mind and her dark thoughts. Sue must have picked up on that as she began to avoid looking at me. Sue is much like a chameleon, instead of her changing color, her eyes would. I know it sounds absurd, but true.

After a while, I would enter the room Sue was in, checking her eyes to know if I should stay or go. Eyes are the mirror of the soul and incapable of deceiving. Smiles can mislead you, but eventually, that too, will line up with the eyes. I know this believe this and I practice it. In all my years on this earth, I recall being wrong but one time. I honestly feel this was due to my prejudice, regarding the influence a certain DJ had on my son. I have twice seen death in eyes and once stared into eyes with no soul. That one I will never forget. Eyes cannot lie. I encourage you to try this for yourself.

I saw Sue in the lobby at the Courthouse during the Grand Jury meeting. I saw her bringing the children for visitation or picking them up afterwards. As angry as I was with her, I felt as though I was looking at an empty shell of a person. I had thoughts of what all Sue would have to stand accountable for one day. I would say a quick prayer, then snap back into the reality Sue forced upon us. The reality of her apparent desire for Rick's complete destruction. I had to be prepared for her next move. I never had to spend much time on the possibility of her doing anything good or productive.

Sue always left me merely wondering, how many more people she could fool and for how much longer? I prayed she would stop with Rick, but I seriously doubted that. Where was Sue now with her "mind control?" I had an unexplained perception of her being involved with another man. If so, I already felt empathy for him.

When I would finally see the baby for the first time, much of this would be explained, without a doubt. OOPS, getting ahead of myself here.

CHAPTER 16
WHEN YOU THINK IT CAN'T GET WORSE

After weeks on end, I had to have a day off, thus Rick worked alone and came home drinking. I was devastated, but had to remain mindful of the fact, I couldn't walk in his shoes. Sue had gone to his shop that day in May, to inform him she had filed for divorce! Actually, she filed less than two weeks after Rick was cast out. Rick was very upset about the divorce. I knew he loved her, but I still felt he loved the children more. Married three months, if you call that piece of paper at the Funeral Home a <u>wedding</u>.

We had been staying with Lori, in a one bedroom apartment. Lori worked full time. I often wonder how we all got through it. I know it was not just family, but God's loving grace and mercy. With Lori and I still badgering Rick to recall anything and everything he could. Begging him to think, to reflect on the most seemingly, meaningless things, events, remarks, whatever!

Even while drinking, he never came home without Butterfinger candy bars, the mega ones at that. Night after night, we would sit and talk, grasping for anything that might help us understand what was happening. Again, I suggested an attorney. Rick wouldn't consider it, still in hopes of resolving the problems. With Sue dropping by the shop often, hinting of getting help, opening doors to give him just enough hope to carry on. I knew they were "Sue" mind games, but I was not successful in convincing Rick to accept the facts, regarding Sue!

Suddenly, out of nowhere, Rick recalled another remark Sue made, about how her brother had to come down on the guy at the parts store, to leave her alone! Rick had no clue of the implication, but I did, immediately. I wanted details. He was not American, but Rick didn't know where he was from. Could this be a clue as to the foreign name of the baby? It's a thought! We were talking about Sue, where anything and everything is possible.

Another day, he recalled another off-the-wall remark Sue had made. Apparently Sue ran over a woman while in college, and her dad got her off.

Her best girlfriend's father was a wealthy Realtor and Sue ended up moving in with them. She received a new car and, obviously, a very comfortable life, until she woke up in bed with the father, in Las Vegas. She was immediately thrown out of the house. I now feel Sue never finished college. Rick said it took about two years to get that much information from her. Apparently, Bill Sr. knew the whole story. That was all the data Rick was able to get. Not much, mostly bits and pieces of a puzzle. I was convinced those bits and pieces would eventually form a picture. We took what we could get, little as it was. I knew Sue would go to great lengths in order to cover herself, but is anyone that good? There had to be gaps somewhere, and I wanted to find them.

Rick and I were at the shop, working, when I brought up Wendy's ordeal again. Did Rick ever learn the truth yet? Was I going to have to be the one to tell him? I received my answer the very minute I asked him to go over it once more. Dear Lord, do I have to tell him the absolute truth?

Truth, as I saw it, with the knowledge I had. Knowing I still wasn't certain which Bill did it. Was it the brother or the son? I have to be very careful here, or I might falsely accuse the wrong one! Believe me, I know how painful and devastating it can be, to be falsely accused!

I was stunned hearing the same explanation! Rick knew nothing more than since we last spoke of it. I guess it was time for me to inform Rick of the horrible truth! I hated giving him the sordid details. Especially, with my lacking the knowledge of "which Bill" molested Wendy? I finally decided, at this point, it really didn't matter, Rick had to have the cold, hard facts, as I knew them to be.

I told him the truth. I told Rick how months prior to Sue's false accusation, she had confided in mother and I, what had happened to Wendy. I told him the brutal truth, breaking his heart. He went from one emotion to another with confusion turning to fury. Rick asked me why I had not told him sooner. I went over that awful day again, including my confrontation with Sue. How Sue had assured me that Rick did indeed know, emphasizing the fact that <u>Rick knew who was in control</u>. Sue clearly stated that I needed to mind my own business. I finished with, "<u>Rick, don't you see, Wendy's father never touched her! In other words, she set him up just like she has done to you!</u>"

I watched Rick's body go limp, as he slumped into the front seat of a vehicle in the shop. The pieces fit perfectly. The picture was quite clear.

Rick was so crushed, scattered and not really able to accomplish anything, so I suggested we go home early that day. Rick never spoke a word all the way to Lori's.

We did talk that night, all night. Rick was feeling guilty and very naive, with such a burden for little Wendy. He said he never felt more stupid in his life, asking me how he could have missed the signs? I reminded him who we were discussing, Sue. I told him he was dealing with a career pathological liar. I stressed the endless hours Rick spent away from the house, working, in order to support the family.

I don't think either one of us slept more than two hours that night. Rick was quiet during most of the drive that morning. He finally broke the silence, asking me if there were other things he needed to know about. What else did I know?

I told him I didn't think I could be much help, at the time, that I too was having to rethink a lot of things. It was a Friday and I told him that I would help him again the next day, then take a day off to go to Church. I really needed that and he understood. I told him I would not tie up the car, that I would call Randy, a dear friend and member of my Church. I knew he would come and get me and I was sure we would return for the night service.

Rick really startled me by what he said as I was leaving. He turned right to me and said, "Sis, please be very careful." I didn't know where that came from, but I assured him I would. I sensed the seriousness, but then again, I was his best friend. I was his confidant and supporter and more available for him. I thought he was just very dependent on me and I could easily understand that, dismissing the rest.

However, this time he would be right!

CHAPTER 17
I DIDN'T HEED THE VOICE!

I needed to visit my old home Church. I loved my sister's Church, but I needed to take in a service at mine. My dear friend, Randy, picked me up. A beautiful day and night, in May. It was Memorial weekend. We chose to have dinner before the night service. Randy stopped and bought me a fountain coke and a bouquet of mixed flowers. I thought he was taking me home, but made a left turn. I asked where we were going. He said it was just too nice out and wanted to continue to ride, with the windows down. It was perfect weather for Texas. I felt a tinge of fear, with no logical reason. The next turn was a right turn and suddenly, I felt very ill at ease. I wanted to go home. That was when I heard a voice telling me to slow down. I looked up, seeing next to no traffic, on all six lanes. At a distance, I noticed the light was green. I could see nothing to indicate any hazard, so I ignored the voice and looked down at my flowers. Again the voice, louder and more firm saying, "Slow down now!" I heard myself yelling, "Randy, slow down, now!"

Randy never said a word, but immediately hit the brakes, when I saw the car. Out of nowhere, it came over a hill at a high rate of speed, running the red light. I saw several cars going in all directions to avoid what was to come. Cars that had stopped on roads opposite to us in other directions, throwing their cars in reverse to clear a path. I don't know how many times we spun around. Upon finally coming to a stop, I had to raise up to see out the window. I saw nothing, but the hood smashed against the shattered window. I was twisted like a pretzel, seat belts on both of us, but I was on the floorboard. I fought to get back into my seat. People were running in all directions checking on us. The fire trucks, ambulances and Police cars everywhere.

A precious paramedic was on his knees asking me if I was all right. Yes, I thought I was, asking him to get me out. He couldn't. I had to be cut out and that took time, but he never left me. He asked me repeatedly if I hurt anywhere. I told him no, I just wanted out. I was having a bit of trouble breathing, but I was quite shaken too. Randy had hit his head on the door post, but claimed he too was all right. Finally, about thirty minutes later, I was freed.

In my exit of the vehicle, I felt a tinge in my ribs as I moved and noticed my foot hurt a little. As I attempted to get out and stand up, I saw the pavement coming right at me, with the paramedic catching me. I couldn't stand. I could barely breath, having no choice but to go to the hospital. I was hurt far worse than I imagined. I spent the next two years in therapy, five times a week at two Clinics. Eventually, the therapy would become twice a week for another year. I was told to file for disability or early retirement. I qualified for both, but refused it. It was like throwing in the towel and accepting "disability." Not me. I have too much faith, and after all these years, I have defied five out of six Doctors. The sixth one is a Christian and has stood by me for over twenty years, now. Healed? No, but deliriously pleased at my capabilities. Randy would have surgery on his neck, but I was told surgery would not give me the results I wanted. No problem, I'll get by.

But, this wasn't going to help Rick. I blamed myself. I knew better than to ignore that voice! I was able to contact my daughter about midnight to come get me. Randy's car was totaled. I was sure Rick and Lori would be worried, but I wasn't going to call them that late. Genie had called them and Rick was at my daughter's house by 1:30 that morning. He had known since 10:00 PM something bad had happened to me. The accident occurred at 10:15. He told sis that he wasn't going to bed until he heard from me. I allowed it to happen and I was furious at myself. I knew better and I would pay a price for it.

CHAPTER 18
GIVE US A BREAK!

Now, I wouldn't be able to help Rick at the shop. I had to stay at my daughter's for weeks. Worse yet, Sue had been calling Rick at Lori's place for weeks, non-stop. Sue wouldn't come to the shop as long as I was there. Now, I knew she would. I was right! Sue was going there constantly. She began a new project of attack. She sold little Bill's motorbike, that Rick had bought him, in order to turn Bill Jr. against Rick. She told Bill Jr., Rick took it back and sold it.

Sue took Wendy to the shop demanding Rick beat her for hitting little Rick in the head with a bat. Rick had never whipped a child and was furious with Sue for expecting him to. Sue was in a rage with Rick, but he told her to leave his office, that he would talk with Wendy, which he did. Sue left so angry, she threw gravel and rocks everywhere on her departure. I told Rick what she was up to. All the children not only loved him, but told Human Services so. Sue was forced to do whatever she deemed necessary, to turn the children against Rick. The children, apparently were making it difficult in assisting Sue on her mission of making Rick the bad guy.

This is a form of abuse in my eyes. I had both of my children by my husband. Divorce or not, we went out of our way to see they were not directly involved, affected or suffered any guilt, because we, the parents, could no longer live together. We shared joint custody. We argued for months over child support, because I felt he was willing to pay too much. I had no desire to take advantage of him. We made our own conditions, to the attorney's dismay. I fired my first attorney because of the dollar signs I saw in his eyes, regarding all he was going to get for me!

I didn't even go to Court that day, but we had lunch prior to the hearing and dinner, later going to my house to spend time with the children, together. Wanting them to see we were all in this as a family, both of us loving them. The worst times were when they would move in with their dad, usually for about six months at a time. They would generally spend a year or so with me. Their father and I always lived close to one another, for the children's sake, wanting their happiness, and frankly, he and I actually liked each other. We shared many meals together, as a family!

I am not this wonderful person. I am just a mother that had never planned to not be married to their father for the rest of my life. I risked my life to have my daughter. I wanted and prayed for each of my children. I loved being a mother, a wife, and homemaker. It was my world, but it didn't work out. Through no fault of the children, would we want them to pay the price for our mistakes? Nor were we going to use them.

Their father and I remained very close for decades. He remarried years later, as did I. Of course he and his new family spent all the holidays with my new husband, me and our children. I know this sounds like Mother Goose Land, but it was the only way we could do it. In fact, we became the best of friends and I miss him, still. We lost him just over two years ago.

A month after I remarried, (the children were with their father) I spent two weeks with them. My former husband had under-gone foot surgery and I stayed with them to help. My new husband came for dinner almost every night. We didn't do everything perfectly, but what we did was in perfect love for our two children, and what you would do for a friend. He and our children needed my help. I was there for him, just as he would have done the same for me. Again, I said we were never perfect. We both had to work very hard on our relationship, for the children's sake, and it was well worth it.

Of course, I was angry with my former husband. I felt I worked harder at our marriage than he did. I was angry that we would not raise the children together, in one house. I had to harness that anger, accept reality and go forward. Anger and bitterness is like a cancer, it will eat you alive.

One day, watching my children play in the backyard, I paused and thanked God for them and their father. They were his too. I didn't conceive alone. He and I brought these two precious children into the world! I was released of the anger, being driven to watch them grow as healthy, functional, cherished children that they were. I couldn't be more proud of either one of them! We did some things right. Both children are Christians. My son is an Author/Actor/Model/Producer/ Director, with two beautiful girls, Honor roll every year. My daughter is about to receive her Masters and begin her Internship to earn her Ph.D. She too has a 4.0 GPA She has two children also, a daughter, an Honor student and a first grader son. Both have huge new homes. Yes, I am so very proud.

I cannot accept any parent using a child to wage war or use them as a pawn. I find it disgraceful and in no way will I condone it. Sue is a woman using her children against the only father they knew. Does the fact of her being a victim justify such behavior? To an extent, perhaps. But that's simply not enough for me. I know too much, saw too much and heard too much to enable me to view her as a good mother, but deep within, I refused to accept the fact that she truly didn't love them. As I told Bill Jr. "She loves you the best way she knows how."

It's no wonder we have so many troubled, rebellious children in this world. In so many cases, they are just a product of a product, having been reduced to their parent or parent's defects. We are living in a toxic world. Toxic? Yes, being taught first hand, life has no value. Desensitized by just about every TV show, news, video games and schools! Yes, schools. I'm going to step in it now, but I would love to see the NEA abolished! Does anyone, other than a teacher, believe they care about our children? Politics has penetrated yet another Union. Our children cannot go to the school library and find a Bible, yet, have access to all books on Witchcraft, anything about satan, including the satanic bible. (refuse to capitalize his name) sorcery and trash. They are taught Evolution, with a concept full of holes, big enough for a another planet, and no one can prove it. More on this subject, later on.

Political Correctness is nothing more than secularism, erasing the true history of our nation, wherein there exists no separation of Church and State! Nowhere in the Constitution will it be found! Children are being taught in elementary school to turn the parents in for abuse. Thus, an angry child rebelling against the rules of the home and faith, are given a way out. I find this detestable and too similar to Communism. Students are not taught the history of America! This is being prepared for the future? Instead of getting angry at me, pause and think about it.

Correct me if I am wrong, but, did not being "Politically Correct," increase after 9-11? I ask why? I have spent so much time being offended, that I no longer care about such nonsense! It's just another ACLU gimmick to oppress and pursue their agenda, with the Dems falling right into it. Please understand. I first contacted the ACLU about this issue, upon Rick's request. I knew it was a waste of time, as we had so many strikes against us. First we are Christians. Second, Rick's a white heterosexual male. This case merely involves the rights of a innocent man, falsely accused. If I had claimed to be a witch, a homosexual or an Atheist being denied my rights, they would have jumped on it! They exist to stand against anything Christians find unacceptable. I received a very brief letter stating, sorry, we cannot help you.

CHAPTER 19
THE MYSTERIOUS NEW SON

I finally got the details on the new baby! The baby had come a little prematurely. It was a boy, with many health problems from the beginning. This was their second child together. They were not married at the birth of the first child. (I am against living together without marriage, but I was happy they hadn't married) But, two children, born in the same hospital, yet very different this time. Sue asked Rick to go home and get her vitamins. Home? Over forty miles away, why not just run to a drug store and buy them? No! That wouldn't do, Sue insisted he had to get those from the house, so he did.

Upon his return Sue was not in her room. There were two nurses, one male and one female cleaning the room. Rick was scared, asking where Sue was. The male nurse told him the baby needed a blood transfusion and they had a hard time finding the type necessary. (That particular blood type is not medically possible for them to have produced a baby with.) Before the male nurse could finish, the female told him to shut up, that he didn't know what he was talking about and gave Rick her new room number. The female's attitude was disturbing, leaving Rick with pity for the male. What was the female so mad about?

Rick worked the morning of the day of Sue's release. Rick went home early to clean up before he went to pick Sue and the baby up. While Rick was showering, Ellie left for over four hours saying, she had errands to run. Rick had no choice but to stay home with the children, until Sue's mother returned, four hours later! Why would Ellie do this to him? She knew Rick's plans!

Rick entered Sue's hospital room. He was sure Sue would be perturbed with at him for being so late, but before he could say a word, Sue said she knew why. Her mother had been there! Why? She told Rick she had to run an errand and would be right back. Yet, she drove that far to see Sue? We are certain her mother knew about the plan and tried to get Sue to change her mind. We can't prove it, but I told him it was the only logical rationalization I could come up with.

In her room, before he could even ask about the baby, Sue took over. She told him the hospital would not release the baby until they got married! What? It's dark outside. It's nighttime. Oh, not to worry, she had made all the arrangements at a Funeral Home, just down the road and all he had to do was sign a piece of paper, stating they were married. He did so, without even reading it. Drove back to the hospital to get the baby. Nothing in life would ever be the same again. This time, there were no threats of him not seeing his son again, if anything happened to them.

Why on earth, after close to nine years and a previous son, did the same hospital refuse to release the baby until they were married? Now, the fact of the unusual name, the blood type, the absurd request for her vitamins, (obviously to get rid of Rick for awhile) her mother being there and now having to get married. This is to appear normal? What was she concealing? I asked Rick, "Are you truly willing to accept this as rational, without any questions?"

I saw was mass confusion cover his face. As usual, he began making excuses, always giving her the benefit of a doubt. I love him, but often I just wanted to shake him until his teeth rattled! What would it take to get him to face reality? This charge was as serious as it could get. He well knew, Sue would never back off or even apologize when she was wrong, nor would she do anything without a motive, for herself. "Brother, what's wrong with this picture?

"Rick, in less than three months of your signing that paper, agreeing to being married, you are attacked three consecutive nights. You were accused of having an affair, being gay and then of molesting your son and you don't hear sirens, see any flashing lights, nothing?" He was silent for some time. Was it conceivable that he was finally beginning to see through open eyes? Perhaps this was indeed a well-planned scheme that he fell for, hook, line and sinker? Dare I believe he was awake now?

By this time I felt we had so much on Sue, yet could do nothing about it. Again, I suggested an attorney. No! Okay, how about a private investigator? No, can't afford one. I did speak with two investigators, only to learn much would be public record, but to be very careful. I was told, do not go to the school, the hospital, the neighbors or the IRS, as it could backfire and we would be sued! Is this a great country or what? Our hands were tied.

Much of my mental state was shock. I was raised in the Midwest, without racial prejudice. Yes, I even got mad at God some times. I stayed in Church, but again, I was in shock for a very long time. I was so terrified at the thoughts I had toward Sue. I knew I had to stay in Church so as not to act upon the truly ugly ideas I had. Ideas and plans I knew God would never approve of so yes, I guess you could call it my safety zone. But, one of my goals was to never do as Sue would do. I refused to lower myself and all I stood for, to come off looking like her clone. Had I not already suffered greatly, learning to think like Sue. That was bad enough. Call it a crutch, whatever, but God and my Church kept me going. I do recall demanding God smite her, more than a few times.

Since our experience, I'll witness a segment on the news where someone yields their self control of wrongs they have suffered, going on a killing spree. I do not condone such behavior, but it frightens me, as I recall how close I had come so many times. I found I had compassion for them. I would go back in time, sifting the awful memories, as well as the battle we were in. I asked my heart what all they must have endured, in order to arrive at such a destructive ending. I sensed how easily I could now relate to them.

And yet, Rick had still not been charged or arrested for anything. I knew the battle was far from over. I could only imagine what was in store, keenly aware of the unknown rearing it's ugly head at anytime. I prayed to be prepared for whatever was to come. Constantly reminding Rick, we were not dealing with any rational, mature, stable person here. Fear factor! Who can predict the next move of an irrational, unstable person. It was much like being held hostage of my own worst fears for Rick's life. With so many possibilities of what she might be concealing, in doing this, the options were very limited. How do you go to battle unarmed? I was positive war had been declared, Rick was not.

I asked Rick again, if he considered the IRS, with all that money going through her mother's account? He didn't know. How about her drug dealing friend, the school, her counseling, another man? Or perhaps her mother, brother? He had no idea. I knew she got caught or was about to be, the way Sue was going all out to protect herself from something quite important. Rick simply had no idea. How does one protect another, when they are oblivious of the facts in their being in such jeopardy? I cannot tell you, I never figured it out.

Suddenly, Rick couldn't locate Sue for a few days. Nobody seemed informed as to where Sue was. We would learn in a couple of years, not only where she was, but what she was up to! I knew the clock was running, I just didn't know it was the twelfth hour!

CHAPTER 20
DIVORCE DATE ARRIVES

The end of July, Sue had gone by the shop, telling Rick she had given much thought to all he said. Sue, now claimed he was right and she was going to get some help. And, oh yes, "Rick, don't bother to go to Court, I dropped the divorce." Sue vowed she would seek help to save the marriage. The divorce date was set for August.

BB was there and heard it all, telling Rick not to believe it! BB couldn't stand Sue. In fact, BB swore that Sue was totally crazy. (Remember, BB moved out soon after Sue had moved into the house he and Rick shared) BB was furious with Rick for considering he could believe anything Sue said! BB warned Rick he had better show up, regardless of what Sue said.

Sue had been going to the shop more than ever. She appeared friendly and concerned for Rick and her family. Rick said he felt she was really listening to him, about all of them needing help. He truly believed she was actually considering it. She made many calls to Rick at Lori's. Sis would see red every time she heard her voice, but vowed to be kind.

At this time I was staying with Randy, who lived farther south, in the country. Randy had just undergone surgery, due to the accident. I stayed there with him, helping in his recovery. Randy wasn't able to drive and it was difficult and very painful for me, too. I had to switch clinics in order to continue my therapy. Randy had a Blazer (truck) loaded with options, which enabled me to drive short distances. It worked out quite well, yet I would soon learn how it couldn't have been better. In truth, it would soon become a blessing.

I wasn't aware of the court date, but I wish I had been. I think I would have thrown Rick in the car and forced him into that Courtroom! In no way would I have ever bought into her chicanery. Suffice it to say, by the time I became aware of it, it was too late. I don't recall ever hearing a word of truth pass her lips. I'm sorry for such harshness, but as I said, I would never have believed she dropped the divorce! But, hindsight they say, is 20/20.

.

I am confident Sue had a plan, but I'll always wonder how it might have ended, had Rick gone to the divorce hearing. In reality, this blame belongs to Rick. He should have gone, regardless of what Sue told him! Rick trusted and believed Sue's proclamation of, "No divorce." What a setup! Sue's plan worked perfectly. Sue knew Rick far better then Rick knew Sue.

I received the phone call! My brother had been arrested! He was in the county jail, which was the same county I was in with Randy. Believe it or not, that was such a blessing, in being so close to my brother. It was also nice to leave Rick and return to Randy. Thank God, I had a friend in whom I could vent my feelings. Randy is a fine Christian man. He knew Rick and, as anyone knowing Rick, loved him. Randy loved him dearly. I was doubly blessed in having Randy to turn to for as much support anyone could ask for. Above all, Randy knew Rick was innocent. I found the common equation was simple, no one liked or trusted Sue, but all loved and trusted Rick.

Sue finally made her biggest move yet. I knew things would continue to worsen, now that she appeared to be in the driver's seat, so to say. Only God knew what tomorrow would hold. I did good just to get through one day at a time. Now, we had a declared war!

CHAPTER 21
THE PRICE IN BELIEVING
IN GOVERNMENT AND LAWYERS!

Rick had believed Sue's proclamation, "No divorce, I'll get help." I have to admit, she is good. So, Rick didn't go to Court, but you bet she did. When the Judge asked where Rick was, she said, "I don't know your Honor, he molested our son and I ran him off, I have no idea where he is." I can see it so clearly, the poor helpless, timid, scared little woman, standing before the Judge.

Three days later Rick was arrested at his shop, for Aggravated Sexual Assault of a child! He was arrested on a one million dollar bond, asking for ninety-nine years in prison! No, the county he was arrested in had no official officer from that county. But, this is Texas. We make our own laws as we go, and as circumstances are deemed necessary. Remember, this is Texas! Rick was also told by one of the officers, that Sue had just left divorce court. A lie! The divorce was three days earlier!

Now was the time for an attorney! I contacted my former husband, (Lee) with the news and a request for help in finding an attorney. Lee was overwhelmed, (to put it mildly) he and Rick had always been the best of friends. Our divorce had nothing to do with their friendship. Also, Lee, who never disliked anyone, disliked Sue fiercely. Now, I had to call mother with the news of her baby being in jail.

I went to see Rick daily, though I was not allowed to visit. I would park on the street and sit for hours and wait to see his face in the window. I pray none of you ever have to go through this! Remember, our mother was over a hundred and fifty miles away, in bad health, sick about her son, which I could do nothing about. I was doing therapy all the time and not able to make the drive to see our folks, even on weekends. Plus, doing what I could for Randy in recovering from surgery! So, if I sat there for hours before seeing Rick's face, it was worth it!

I felt like I was not living, merely existing, telling myself to breath in and out. I functioned more like a robot. Caring for Randy helped me keep busy. I noticed my therapy was far less painful, or was I simply so numb I couldn't feel it? It was the longest twenty-four days in my life. If there exists a feeling worse than helplessness, I have yet to discover it.

The folks came to town immediately, but no one had the bond money. A million dollars! Do the math, ten percent of that is $100,000.00! Rick would spend twenty-four days in jail, without being charged, with the detectives announcing, they knew Rick was guilty and they would get a confession one way or another. They didn't, though, and they never will.

Lee, found the attorney. Mother, dad and I retained him, while Rick was still in jail. Again, his twenty-four days in jail, for us, was hell. I can only imagine what it was for Rick! As I said, he was released on $20,000.00, costing us $2,000.00. Rick had nothing to come back to, not even a car. He didn't know it at the time, but would learn in such a cruel way, what Sue had done.

Lee, me, mom and dad met with Max. Max first told us very few attorneys would go into that county, we needed an expert, like him. Max said he had been the Chief Prosecuting attorney for seventeen years. He was foul-mouthed, overweight, arrogant and nasty. Max was loud, rude, obnoxious, crude, and came off as a very tough guy and spoke with such profanity. I actually felt confident in thinking, "No one will push this guy around." So confident, I briefly felt a tinge of pity for Sue to go up against this guy! Nobody liked Max, but we felt he was what we needed to go against Sue and that county.

Max told us up front he wanted $5,000.00 and another $7,000.00, if it went to trial. Since Rick wouldn't consider anything less than a trial, we gladly agreed. And of course, additional small expenses for a private investigator. No problem. (I thought) Randy also helped to pay for this attorney, over $3,000.00. Lee and many others contributed. Anyone and everyone that knew Rick, never questioned his innocence.

Are you getting the picture yet? Max was retained for $5,000.00, getting another $5,000.00 in the next four months and none of that went towards a trial. No interviewing any witnesses, nor did Max investigate. Although, I paid mightily for two Private Investigators. After all of this and we had another sixteen months to go before we got into a Courtroom! A total of twenty months to go to Court! Giving Max more money on most every visit!

I told you he was foul, cruel and arrogant, by now I learned he was also greedy, a liar and an alcoholic. If that's not bad enough, I would continue to learn worse things yet. I spent the next two years being sexually harassed, but this I never allowed Rick to be aware of. That nasty, foul, disgusting man never quit hitting on me!

All Rick's sisters are older then he is, but he was always very protective, like a big brother. If he knew what Max was putting me through, well I couldn't afford to let him find out, so I kept quiet.

Due to my accident, Max insisted I should move in with him, as he had a whirlpool and everything I was in need of, and would take real good care of me. I asked him what he would do with his live in girlfriend and he replied, "Hell, I'll throw Judy out." I believed he was dead serious. I tried to keep my distance from him after that. No way, he would call me repeatedly, till I had to remind him that I was not his client, Rick was. For what good that did, as Max never let up on me. Remember the name Judy, as it will become very important later!

Another a real problem was Rick's immense dislike for Max. I was forced to attend each and every meeting, as the mediator. I would stay between them, such a clash in personalities. Rick didn't like or trust Max. By now, I felt the same in my growing dislike for him, but the bigger picture was the fact, he was Rick's attorney! We were dependent on him and I still felt he could do the job. Max always expressed his belief in Rick's innocence. That meant so much to me.

I had to tolerate Max and his advances, for Rick's sake. However, I did soon have to draw the line, regarding his habit of taking the Lord's name in vain, with every other breath! It took some time, but I finally broke him. If I was in his office, I would announce I would not take it and walk out into the waiting room. If he called on the phone, I simply reminded him of my feelings in his use of God's name, then hang up on him. Finally, he caught on and even apologized a few times.

After the accident, I wasn't able to make all of the meetings, so the case was largely done by mail and the telephone. Rick only met with him about three times without me and it wasn't pretty, so much so, Rick refused to see him, alone. Rick swore the guy was a liar, not worthy of trust and positive he was not qualified to handle his case, regardless of his credentials. Rick and I finally agreed to disagree. It was very tough on Rick, as he felt in my debt for hiring Max, but I needed to know how he felt. Honestly, I knew his feelings had some merit, but also, I was so aware of Rick's personal feelings towards Max. I wish I had listened better, but again, what's done is done and now I have to live with it. Yes, I hold myself largely responsible for the final results. Another purpose for this mission!

CHAPTER 22
WHAT A MESS TO RETURN TO

While Rick was in jail, Sue went to Rick's shop, sold all of his tools, parts and all nine cars, at the house. If that wasn't enough, she went through his files, calling Rick's customers, telling them what Rick had done. From his own shop! Most didn't believe her. Those that knew her hung up on her, and the ones that knew Rick told her she was crazy! But, there were some new customers that really didn't know either one of them. It mattered little later, as when Rick was able to return, he had no tools to work with anyway! He began pin-striping vehicles. I said he was very gifted and can do just about anything in that field.

She told everyone that Rick had molested the basketball team he coached at the YMCA and all of his nephews! When this accusation got back to us, having five sons and nephews, we were quite disturbed. We talked and prayed about it for days. We finally decided as much as we were convinced of his innocence, we didn't want to be one of those with the attitude of, "Our loved one could do no wrong!" We knew without a doubt Rick was innocent, but elected to gather our sons together and ask them. Their expressions alone were enough to assure us, but their shock and fury that we would even consider such, stunned them.

It was a great move! It certainly had a downside though, as the boys became so angry, they wanted to go to Sue's house, right then! We couldn't have that. My son Roy, actually yelled at me, "Mother, who the hell does she think she is, that's my Uncle she is accusing!" The others joined in, making plans to go out there and straighten her out. We could see the anger and understood it too, but that was no way to handle it. It took hours to calm them down. They finally agreed they would wait to take the stand and testify against her credibility. At least we had our answer. We knew it all along, but had to do it. And Rick didn't need more problems.

They never got the opportunity to take the stand. Rick never got his trial, but Max sure did get his money, and then some!

I was overwhelmed at the loving support Rick received from so many. Just recently, I ran across a couple of letters from two strangers, to me, but

80

obviously friends and customers of Rick's. One letter was sent to the jail. A man said he was so sorry to hear what had happened to Rick, stating that he knew Rick was innocent. He apparently knew Sue also and had nothing good to say about her. Rick had this man's car inside his shop, apparently he was working on it when he was arrested. The man went on to say how he didn't want to hurt Rick, but the shop was locked tight and could he give him the Landlord's name and number, so he could contact him.

The letter was dated the day before Rick was released, so the problem was solved. But that was how Rick learned of what all Sue had done and taken.

Rick asked Max, if she could do that? Max coldly replied, "Hell yes, it's called Community Property, get over it." I asked, after being married for three months? His comments were it didn't matter, she could do whatever she wanted, she wasn't charged with anything, Rick was. Okay, suffice it to say he was right, how was Rick going to support the children, let alone himself when she just stole his lively-hood. And all those cars, even his shop was in his name, how could she legally sell any of them? It didn't matter, we had other problems to deal with. Cold, callous and maddening! Max told Rick he had better find something to do in order to pay his bill. Yes, Max was a real jewel. We need so many more just like him! As well as more Governmental Dept. idiots and Judges that are fools!

CHAPTER 23
SUE V. GOVERNMENT INTELLIGENCE

Obviously this greedy woman had to have other plans, as bad as she would need finances. Sue had something going, but what? Christian or not, can you imagine how I felt for Rick? I've spent years praying to forgive her and to not retaliate. I have to ask, what would you have done? Yet, it was only the beginning, and we actually thought it couldn't get worse. But, why would she take Rick's livelihood if she expected child support? Trust me, she would always expect that! I have the divorce papers and am shocked at what I see. I will print the divorce papers exactly as I have them, as well as the Affidavit of inability to pay court costs. In short, the taxpayers picked it up. **Allow me to expose the brilliant minds involved in this farce!**

The first date is less than fourteen days after Rick's departure, wherein Sue filed an **Affidavit of Inability to Pay Court Costs**. It contains several questions regarding her income. One question is about her **Governmental entitlement**. Sue wrote **NONE**, scratched through it and put in what appears to be **$781.00**. I have to assume that was for Bill Jr. As for the **two middle children, Sue received child support.** .....**But, it is listed nowhere!** Furthermore, I must now state, the fictional name I first used for her oldest son, had to be changed. To my shock, in the midst of these papers, I became aware of his actual name. I stand amazed! Every time I go through the papers and documents, I find error upon error and more suspicious evidence. Therefore, I had to go to the beginning and change his name throughout the entire book. What are the odds that I would come up with the actual name, I thought I had fictionalized? It never ceases to amaze me.

She answered her **spouse had no income for her**. He did at the time! Rick had his shop. But, Sue would soon see to it, as time passed, that her statement would come to pass! She lists the five children by name, saying she is responsible for them. **She owned nothing and had no checking or savings accounts**! Could be, she did write the checks on her mother's account. Did anyone ask about the father of the middle two? How were they being supported? If they did, it's not noted and this really provokes me. Yet, typical of law and Government. I especially love the #10 question, asking what her **debts** were. Sue listed that **she owed Montgomery Wards $300.00, JC Penney $300.00 and the Hospital $6,500.00 and $7,500.00**.

Under monthly **expenses,** Sue said she lived with her mother, who provided most of the essentials, adding Sue received **$374.00 in food stamps!** No, I did not error. It is as I said.

I asked Rick if he was aware of Montgomery Wards or JC Penny? He was stunned! How can you owe a company like these without a credit card? Rick feels the cards belong to her mother.

Sue stated, she and Rick agreed to be married, eight years prior to the ceremonious wedding, three months earlier. (the Funeral Home was a Ceremony?) Rick, I assure you, was not aware of this. **This fact enabled Sue to sell the nine cars.** Now, let me share Sue's Grounds for Divorce; "The marriage has become insupportable because of discord or conflict of personalities between Petitioner and Respondent, that destroys the legitimate ends of the marriage relationship and prevents any reasonable expectations of reconciliation. The request to divide assets was entered also. I wonder why Sue went ninety miles and Counties away, for her attorney?

Sue did tell the truth in the beginning, as to the conflict and discord in the marriage! But, why would she not tell them Rick molested their son until the divorce hearing? (four months later) I know I would have! I can't stress how she easily fools people, but dear Lord, are all brainless?

Just picture this, if you will, all these offices, with Degrees hanging on their walls, but not a one intelligent enough to discern or see through this woman! Doctors, Lawyers, Judges etc.

Sue requested a name change, but at that last minute, declined. She still continues to use all four names, which makes it so difficult to track her down. For all I know, she has another, already. As for the oldest son, who is not named what we were told. I cannot find him or any evidence of him being in the service. I am beginning to see why. It's obvious why I haven't able to find him. I have no clue to his actual last name! Could it possibly be that he is the son of that Realtor, where Sue attended college? Pure speculation on my part, but we are talking about Sue, with anything possible.

Rick and I always wondered why Bill Jr. received such huge checks. Sue said that they were from the Government, because the father had become addicted to drugs while in the service. That he lived in a western state where the state would have him in a program and supply his needles and such. We had a problem here in thinking Gov. checks for such a huge amount and that they would cease upon Bill's sixteenth birthday. At sixteen most are still in school. Very suspicious! Bill's sixteenth birthday came in 1989, which is the same year of Sue's accusation towards Rick. Sue was about to lose a lot of money. Were her false claims to establish or compensate for this loss? I have no idea. Rick wondered if perhaps by the father leaving the program early, it would have stopped the checks. Or, could it be that it came to someone's attention of other resources? Just another enigma.

Rick recalled about two months prior to Sue's wild and false accusation, she mentioned to Rick that the father of Bill Jr. wanted to return to Texas. Rick said, " Sue had the gall to ask me if the father could move in with us!" Rick says he thinks Sue got herself in such a jam that she couldn't see daylight. Rick said back then everything was so crazy, that at this point, he could believe just about anything.

Now, we have to ask, had the father already returned when Sue pulled off her scheme? Problem here is that, if that were the case, then how could Sue have sent Bill Jr. west, to be with his daddy for a year? With Bill Jr. loving Rick and being a threat to Sue, we felt she had to get Bill Jr. out of the picture. Sue swore she sent him to his dad's. Rick says anything is possible and he is not positive Sue ever married the father of Bill Jr.

Rick also said that Sue told him one evening, that her mother wanted Rick out of the house. I always felt, (as well as Rick) that Ellie was very fond of Rick. Sue ran the house, not Ellie. Did Ellie really say that? Was the dad back and Ellie liked him more? Rick was the main source of income, so this is really quite wild, but again, it's Sue. God only knows.

I am still determined to find out where the father is and the real name of the one called Bill Jr. I shall say it again, there is no telling anything with Sue. All the theories and no proof.

Speaking of schemes, plots and plans, exactly what was really going to become Max's role in this event?

CHAPTER 24
ATTORNEY'S REQUIREMENTS IN TEXAS!

Allow me to inform you of Texas law. In Texas, an attorney has two simple steps required by law, that must be done. (1) Any attorney, hired or appointed, must interview witnesses. (2) He must investigate the case. If one cannot afford an Investigator, the state will appoint one. Yet, I personally paid $2,500.00 for two Private Investigators, without one word of any results. No reports and no further contacts with either one of them. Upon demanding something, anything, I was told by Max, "Hell, it don't matter what they found, she's not charged with anything, Rick is." Okay, so why did I pay for them?

As for interviewing witnesses, not one. Not even the members of her family that called, saying they knew she was crazy and if they could help, don't hesitate to call on them! Did he? No! Max did speak with mother, dad and of course me, as well as Lee, that first day, when we retained him.

He did call our sister, early the next year wanting money! No questions except for what did she own? Could she get him some more money? She hung up on him. He never even spoke with BB, who was a witness to Sue telling Rick that she had called off the divorce. Sue had said not to bother going and that she would seek help. Again, I cannot blame her for Rick's decision. He should have never believed her. Again, Rick should have gone to Court.

Max swore the issue was too hot. We'd need to wait and let it cool off. (this brought about filing one continuance after another, without our knowledge) After we shared what we did know with Max, regarding Sue, (in the beginning) he said if half of what we told him was true, it would never go to trial. He constantly reminded us, "If only it were in another County." I quickly got fed up at this remark, asking him if this other County was above the law? He would only reiterate that few attorneys would go into that County. I was still naive enough to believe our system worked, no matter where it was. I would learn better. Max said he would call in a private investigator, Ed. (real name but, cannot find him.)

Rick and I met with Ed at Max's office one night. We really liked him. He appeared to be very intelligent and experienced. Having heard our side, he smiled and said to give him one day, two at the most and he would blow Sue out of the water. He had seen this more than once. We hired him. However, that was after he left and I gave the money to Max. Huge mistake!

Soon after Max called in another Investigator. Why? I have no clue, since the first one never did a thing, (that I know of) no report, nothing. Rick met with the new P.I., at Max's, without me. Generally, Rick and I were together at least 95% of the time. My car accident messed things up. As passive as Rick was, Max could infuriate him within seconds of entering his office. Rick didn't become violent or curse at him, he would just clam up. Leaving Max's office one night, I tried to tell Rick that he simply had to start cooperating more. I heard again, how he couldn't stand Max, didn't trust him, thought he was a crook and asked me what I had seen Max do about anything, so far. He said it was a total waste of time in talking to him. He finished with, "Sis, I'm sorry, I know you like him and hired him. I hate being so ugly, but you asked me how I felt." "And by the way, I love how you shut him up when he uses the Lord's name so rudely." Rick could cuss, but would never take the Lord's name in vain around his sisters, out of love and respect in knowing how we felt.

I reminded him that Max believed he was innocent. Rick said, "Oh yes, he told me that, but after you left for the ladies room, he told me prisons are full of innocent men and, if it weren't for you, he would drop me." I saw fire! I enlightened him to the fact that I couldn't stand Max either.

Perhaps I had made a bad decision in hiring Max, but did so because he was so crude, mean and not vulnerable to intimidation. Rick chuckled a bit and said I probably was right about that.

I confessed to Rick how Max called me too often, and that "I had to remind him numerous times that you are his client, not me."

Max would curse about Rick not cooperating with him. I knew this indicated Max wanted more money. I finally told him "Perhaps Rick would, if you weren't such a jackass and could greet us one time without asking if we have any money for you." With God as my witness, Max is just as greedy as Sue is toxic! What was he doing to justify a dime we gave him?

He got huffy saying he filed all these motions etc. I asked him when we could see just one of those documents? I'm serious. We had yet to see anything. We gave him his retainer fee before Rick was even released. Why were we expected to give him more every time we saw him? What was he doing to earn anymore money? Even the retainer fee!

I am the one that contacted the Bail Bondsman, made all the arrangements and did the paperwork. Max did go out there the day Rick was released, but for what I am still not sure of. I decided it was time to see some action and I informed Max of this.

He became very defensive and again I heard about all the motions he had filed but now I heard something new. The Grand Jury was about to meet and Max wanted us there! "Are you sure of this?" Was this the normal thing to do? It sounded rather mysterious to me, according to what I knew regarding law, which pretty much was based on what I had gleaned from TV.

Oh yes, Max wanted us there. He wanted Rick to go before them and testify. He said Rick was so delusional about the charges he was facing, he needed to do this. I warned you that we knew nothing about criminal law, but I would later learn, to my horror, that we should never have been in the same County the day the Grand Jury met.

So, Max convinced us that Rick needed to appear before the Grand Jury! Every attorney I have spoken with couldn't believe this fact! I was there. Scheduled time was 9:00 AM. I saw Ms P. (Human Services) come out of a room laughing and hugging another woman. When she saw us, it was obvious we were not expected to be there. She spun around and back into the room. Max leaned over saying, "I wanted you to see what I am up against. The woman she hugged is the Grand Jury Forman." Aren't we supposed to trust and depend on our attorney to look out for our best interest? Only a fool would believe that!

We sat there until 2:00 PM. Then Sue, little Rick, and the drug dealer showed up. Little Rick saw his daddy and ran across the room, stopping dead in his tracks when Sue stood up and yelled his name. The expression on his little face was such disappointment. He turned, walking back to his mother, with his head down and shoulders drooping.

God forgive me. I did enjoy seeing Sue so stressed and actually shaking. She looked as though she just came from the IRS office, very unruly. I felt sure Max knew what he was doing. He did, but not to our advantage. It was obvious they weren't expecting to see us. I thought this good.

Later, we learned Rick had been indicted. I was amazed, not only at the news, but the fact that Max seemed to have enjoyed being right. He told Rick, "See, and you were so sure if you could take the stand and testify, you could end it. Well, it didn't work, did it?" He reiterated about the hug from Ms. P. and the Forman, how it ran so late because we were there, unexpected. How they ran to the phone to get Sue there with little Rick. Again, "Now you see just what I am up against." Whoa, meaning what? Was Max indicted too? Just who was having to fight for their life here? Was that a test, a scheduled appointment of doom, in his quest for more money? So, were we to feel sorry for Max?

His point was well made as far as Human Services was concerned, but to what degree? We would learn later. Rick was charged with Aggravated Sexual Assault of a Child, thirty-two days after he was released from jail. This, after having spent twenty-four days in jail, prior to the charge. I have yet to understand that aspect of it. We still had not seen anything on paper. All we knew was what Max shared with us.

In retrospect, I realize the Grand Jury would have met without any of us there and perhaps our chances would have been much better, had we not been there. It's speculation yes, but a good question, I think. Now, I feel we were ambushed by our own attorney. As you continue to read this, you too will not only highly suspect Max, but become aware of just what a criminal he is, and yes, I am prepared for you to ask how we could have been so stupid. I don't blame you, we live with it daily. Another purpose of this book is to help you!

No wonder there are so many cruel jokes about attorneys. I receive them daily on my PC, with the majority of them coming from attorneys. I will not tell you that every attorney is a crook, but I will state, emphatically, the vast majority are worthless! Time for a break. Seeing how there are many "others" that feel the way I do, I thought it fitting to share my favorite jokes.

"What do you call a lawyer gone bad?...................... A Senator."

"What do you call fifty skydiving lawyers?................. Skeet."

Oh well, I may as well share a few more, I'm on a roll here;

"What do you throw a drowning lawyer?....................... His partners."

"What do you get when you cross a pig with a lawyer?...... Nothing, there are some things a pig won't do!"

What do you call a bus loaded with attorneys at the bottom of the river?............. A good start!

Last, but not least,

"How many lawyers does it take to change a light bulb?.............. How many can you afford?"

No, I don't have much use for attorneys. Most of them. I do know a few Christian ones, and a couple of just really nice ones, with morals, ethics and values. I especially like the part in the Bible where Jesus "jumps" them good. He tells them how they put burdens on people's backs that they couldn't carry. Is this not true? However, the Book of Titus exposes Zenas, a Christian lawyer.

So, as I said, they are not all crooks, but you will be hard pressed to find a good one! I told you I still have some sense of humor. I apologize right now to all those out there that do sincerely care about law and their clients.

CHAPTER 25
WE GET TO SEE THE BOYS

We were now able to see the two boys, under supervision, at the cost of $67.00 per visit. We were allowed to visit twice a month. I paid because Rick had little funds, thanks to Sue. Recall, upon his release, Rick had nothing left, Sue saw to that. We could also see CPS, Human Services and Social workers in action. I paid for most all of the visits, gladly, knowing he had to see the boys, myself included. I had yet to see the baby, which was close to a year old now!

Upon our first visit, the baby was screaming and the workers, (visibly distraught) were delighted to see us. We were running a little late trying to find the place. The second I took the baby, I was bewildered. From the moment I saw him, I knew he was not Rick's son! But oh, how I loved him! I was amazed at how calm he was, as long as I had him. I wondered if he knew I was a grandmother and that I truly loved him. He was always screaming, not crying, but literally screaming uncontrollably, when we got there and when we left. I've always wondered about that. Children are so much smarter than we give them credit for. The baby is an innocent victim. How could I not love him?

On that visit, the first thing little Rick said was, "Daddy, why did you put sugar in mamma's tank?" A four year old using the term tank instead of gas? It was extremely obvious, he had been programmed to say that. Rick dropped his head and replied, "Ricky, you know daddy would never do anything like that."

As I sat there, holding the baby, I watched little Rick walk over to his daddy. He placed his tiny little hands on each side of his daddy's face. With his face maybe two inches from Rick's he said, "Daddy, I know you never hurt me, but mamma says if you get well, you can come home." Out of the mouths of babes! Using this child that worshipped his daddy, to say what Sue told him to say with the promise if he did, daddy could come home!

Now, the whole staff was all over Rick, yelling how he couldn't discuss that with him! Rick nor I had spoken a word! Boy, did they jump all over him. I had remained quiet until then. I stood up declaring how I would bet every dime in my account, that on a witness stand, they would never recall what they had just seen and heard! The next time we saw them was in another county. I met a young lady there that appeared to have some sense. I even shared the story of what little Rick had said to his daddy about if he would get well, he could come home. She was moved to the point of almost saying exactly what I already knew. The child had been programmed.

So much for that. It seemed to make Rick's life more painful. I never brought up the subject of the baby not being his. He loved him dearly. I just couldn't bring myself to ask him if he thought it was his son. Lori is the only one I discussed it with. Lori hadn't seen him, therefore she had no idea. I told her I would get a picture of him, and then she would then know. She was amazed, asking me, "You really think he is not Rick's, don't you?" I sure did! I honestly had not thought of the idea, until I saw him. There was no way to deny it. Parts store guy? Forced marriage? Do I hear bells and sirens going off here?

At the same time, I had to remind myself it was none of my business either. I knew the day would come when Rick would be able to talk about it. I recall when we started seeing the boys, there were times we would run late or not be able to make it. I didn't know any better, so out of what I felt was consideration, I would call Sue to inform her. Huge mistake on my part!

Oh how wrong that was! I got a nasty letter from her about never calling her again, as though I were a neighbor borrowing a cup of sugar! How Rick ruined their lives and when I called, they were being abused all over again. I was to call the Center, not Sue! I got a real song and dance about all they were going through, losing their father, her husband and such. That perhaps one day, after they recovered, we might be able to chat again. Sue went on to boast about her Grant of $150,000.00 <u>because Rick molested ALL the children</u>! Oh, now it's not just Rick's own son, but all of her children too! Each and every time, it would be another story.

So, why with four other children, was he only charged with one? Why not charge him with all five and put him away for life, opposed to a ten year Deferred Adjudication Probation? I know if it were my children, I would go for the maximum to insure he could never see life outside of the prison! I find this absolutely ludicrous. Allowing a criminal on the streets, if he did in fact sexually abuse all those children, then <u>Sue</u> should be in prison for not holding him responsible.

But, again, I know her. I could easily see through the letter and what she would expect from me.

I refused to play into her hands. As a Christian, (yes, even we have ugly thoughts) I couldn't react. I refuse to allow my life to be ruled by fear. I have seldom known real fear, before I met Sue. I feared her to the extent, that when dealing with a crazy person, you cannot predict what they are capable of doing. I did know Rick was right, in that she would take her anger out on the children. That knowledge was how I refrained from responding to her letter.

I recall the ghastly thoughts running through my mind. They were so ugly, I was ashamed of myself. I was a Christian, but for a short time I forgot that. I was feeling very human, but still couldn't bring myself to put those thoughts on paper. Just thinking them was bad enough. It was just as difficult not calling her to share my opinion of her remarks, but again, I knew I couldn't afford to risk it. I knew I had enough on her to get her undivided, attention, but that would be the same as being a Sue, not a Christian. I do firmly believe 'what goes around will come around' I have to be able to sleep at night.

Even Rick had several friends that sincerely offered, to eliminate his problem, Sue. I was so proud of him. He didn't hesitate. Shocked yes, but he immediately said, in no way did he want her touched! Well, then how about we put the fear of God in her? He actually laughed at that, saying, "She doesn't even believe in God."

These were not Rick's friends, but more friends of friends, that hated Sue. They were convinced Rick was being falsely accused. Fact is, people we didn't even know came out of nowhere with these offers! That is scary, isn't it? What's worse is when you begin to think you might be capable of such! I can assure you. Until you walk in the shoes of the masses, being falsely accused, you don't have a clue as to how far you might be able to go. Imagination has no limitations!

In the late eighties, the entire city area consisted of less than fifty sex counselors. Last time I checked, (couple of years ago) there were over five hundred! The sexual molestation accusations have become a huge business. I know many are not false! My heart breaks for any and all that suffer from this. But let's not assume that just because one is accused of such, they are guilty. With our experience in this, when hearing one accused of this crime, my first natural instincts are, to defend them, fearing it may yet be another false allegation. In other words, I'm not quick to judge them at all. Fox News stated that Texas has the second highest sex offender registration. How did that happen? Texas thrives to be number one in all things. With the fact you are forced to register, either legally or illegally, I can't conceive them settling for number two in any area!

I know that 67% of molestation's occur with juveniles. These horrific crimes are occurring far too often and appear to becoming more frequent. I find this worse than appalling. The facts are nauseating and difficult to even think about. But, we must!

Our children have become "prey," in any environment. I blame the Supreme Court to a large degree. Again, under the guise of the First Amendment, which guarantees our protection of freedom of speech. Former President Clinton, in his desire to "take care" of his funding buddies in keeping the colossal porno enterprise prospering, is incomprehensible. A billion dollar industry, in which the "Coalition," would have greatly suffered, financially. Which in turn, would have cost Clinton and the "the Party's" gigantic funding. Placing legal child porno over the safety of the lives of our children is, to me, completely unacceptable.

The United States Attorney General John Ashcroft, in an attempt to protect the children, took on the "Child Pornography Prevention Act." I'll cover this topic and every Supreme Court Judge and their voting record later on. But, for now, let's face reality and ask, "Why is this happening?"

Our children are exposed to pornography and drinking everywhere they turn. They can go into any Public Library and no matter what they are looking for, before they know it, they will be cast into a form of pornography. Without seeking it, they will be faced with thousands of these filthy sites. No matter what their parent's wishes are. They see naked bodies on television, in books, magazines, in the movies, video games and on the computer, being forced to deal with this trash.

I see it as being brainwashed and programmed into believing that one cannot play or enjoy sports, shop, listening to music or even going to the park without drinking beer and having sex. Let's not eliminate drugs either or date rape. Children are being taught that it is "expected and accepted."

Otherwise, they do not fit into this toxic society. Our own Government labeled our children, the "Generation X." With a label such as that, what future do they have to hope for!

No one wants the responsibility of being a "role model." Parents fighting and at times killing another over a game of sports! Professional athletes are acting like thugs as they slug it out with each other, the officials and sometimes the fans. Britney, Madonna and Janet Jackson, to name a few, dress and act like hookers. We are allowing our children to live off the <u>FAD</u> of the land. The results are school drop outs, drug and alcohol addictions, date rape, teen pregnancy, STD's abortions, runaways, suicides. Mix all of these with acts of violence and see how they have gone off the scales. God forbid, any child or an adult should be exposed to the Ten Commandments. Where is the harmful threat or danger in being instructed not to lie, steal, fornicate, cheat or to love your neighbor? I do not believe the children are as much against these things, as the adults!

"Just say no?" What a joke. The parents should be saying no! But, schools have been given authority over the parents. Students, at a very early age, are being taught to "turn their parents in." Thus, an angry, rebellious child is presented with a "get even," pass, should they be punished or grounded over grades, the wrong friends etc. Many parents have become so dysfunctional they cannot help themselves, let alone their children. When did we hand over our children to the state? The state or Government can't regulate it's self, let alone raise our children!

Our priorities are so twisted. NASCAR is no longer the "<u>Winston Cup Circuit</u>," because that represents cigarettes. Have you ever witnessed a cigarette smoker go out and rob, rape or cause an accident while under the influence? I am not implying any should smoke, but get real! Many of the race cars have alcohol all over them. The message we are sending is, **<u>"It's okay to drink, try drugs, have casual sex, (risking your health, mentally and physically) and have an abortion should you become pregnant, but do not smoke a cigarette!"</u>**

The statistics of men and women addicted to porno, drugs and alcohol are staggering! Family units are broken and divorces are at an astounding rate. Television, computers and libraries as well as the streets, are saturated with nudity, drugs and alcohol. Each encouraging promiscuity. I am repulsed at most all commercials. Commercials are inundating the young with messages of eat, drink, be merry and consensual, as "Self" and pleasure are all that matters. There are no lines that have not been crossed. Most commercials enjoy insulting one's integrity and implying that respect for one another is not expected, in fact, it is antiquated. Exposing the body, mind and spirit of the need for morality, ethics and loyalty, is in truth destroying the very fiber of their souls.

Our streets are flooded with filthy pornography, but the most heinous porno is that of children. The smut filled magazines and web sites solicit the weak and create monsters, roaming about, seeking the helpless children. This so-called First Amendment's "freedom of speech," should be a crime in itself, when used to prosper the perverts and the elite.

We have nine year old children in jail, teens on death-row. Failing schools, failing students and failing parents, but the NEA, ACLU and the Politicians fail to see a problem here? No child left behind? Behind what? Behind closed doors, hard hearts, hopes and dreams. We are burying our children daily. If not in the grave, we are losing them mentally, emotionally and psychologically in denying them the ability in loving themselves and others.

Our daughters want to look like their false idols, Spears, Madonna etc., but unlike these stars, the young fans have no bodyguards to keep them safe. They don't realize they are walking targets and prey for the sick vultures.

We have allowed Darwin's theory and Dr. Spock to leave some awful scars on our lives! I do not wish to attack Dr. Spock, but if he truly had all the answers to raising children, why did his son commit suicide? As for Darwin, he knew just enough to be dangerous! Without any proof, his theory has replaced the truth of creation in our schools, history books and obviously the Supreme Court.

We did not evolve from an ape! The only "BIG BANG," is our inability to accept that there is a Creator. I shall quote Carman from a song called "There Is A God." My favorite lines are; "If there is a design, there is a designer, if there is a plan, there is a planner and if there is a miracle, there is a God!" Atheism is the wedge under the foundation of our faith trying to topple our relationship with Christ. Atheism has never given an answer to our existence, peace to a troubled mind or even dried a tear."

Recently, it has been discovered that we have approximately twenty-thousand more suns and fifty billion more galaxies. Science has also found the "empty black hole" in which the earth sits, as stated in the Bible. Why then, are our public schools not teaching the alternative? Could it be that answering to God might just be too fearful, for too many? We need truth and justice to heal our land. We cannot accept any substitutes.

The children are our future! Just how do we expect to be treated when their time comes to care for us? I have not, nor will I write them off as "Generation X." I have faith, hope and give them my love and prayers. Look back and search the statistics. We've had over four generations of no prayers and God not being allowed in schools. If anyone takes the time to do this, I think we can agree that we need God in America again, especially in our schools! I am very passionate about my faith! Now, back to Rick's issues.

CHAPTER 26
INADEQUATE, CORRUPT AND DRUNK

I was now with my old roommate, Lida, in a suburb about fifteen miles from Lori. Rick was there at every opportunity. We still spent hours every day going over all the events we could think of. I asked him so many questions. At times, he just went brain dead from exhaustion in trying to recall the events. He worked seldom, having lost everything. We could do nothing about it.

Rick was so impressed with the latest Investigator. It was so refreshing to see him excited. He couldn't recall his name, but we knew that he had cracked a huge case in Ellis, CO. A woman was accused of killing her wealthy husband, the owner of a fiberglass company. The Investigator broke the case wide open and she was eliminated as a suspect. I assume that is why I spent so much more on him. Again, I gave Max the money.

Less than a week later, Rick and I were out doing some Christmas shopping and got back to my place about midnight. Lida met us in the yard, so excited, saying Max called and had great news. If it wasn't too late, we were to call him back. It was too late!

Lida couldn't stand Max either, mostly because of his profanity, and because he was usually drunk and even more belligerent. Rick was thrilled, thinking the investigator found something, but upset at the hour, as we would have to wait until Monday morning. That made for a very long weekend!

When we finally got Max on the phone, Monday afternoon. He denied calling, said he didn't have any news whatsoever! Actually, he was cruel and expressed anger over it! He was angry? Lida was and is, still furious, saying he made her look like a liar. She knew his voice, having heard him take the name of the Lord in vain and other words I will not include. Max denied it just the same! I still don't think that mysterious phone call was about the investigator. I'm convinced we never had one! That phone call still haunts us, I know he made it!

Since then, I have been informed how an investigation works, or should work. Investigators are regulated by the state of Texas. The investigator

97

must keep itemizations, report to me, show all the expenditures, where they went, for what, their findings, then either give me a refund or bill me more. Not only do I have Rick's Power of Attorney, but I paid for them, and by law, they had to report to me! I feel such a fool, paying $2,500.00 for two investigators with not so much as a word. Why? Because in my lack of knowledge. I gave Max the money. Cash, which he pocketed.

Max had a less than professional way of giving receipts, I have several, but most are on pieces of yellow legal pads, his business cards and even a napkin, to name a few. One day I met him at a bank, giving him $2,000.00, on a holiday weekend, I did not get a receipt! He was too just too busy. Max wanted to go out of town, on vacation. I do have a witness, though. Randy was there with me, giving him $500.00 also. I had taken an advance on our suit regarding the accident, paying 12.50% interest on it. Randy was most uncomfortable about the lack of a receipt. I told him, that Max did that to me all the time. Another signal I excused.

The mysterious phone call for Rick, was unbearable! His depression had become more severe. In short, he was completely lost. The holidays were almost here, again, and he still bought every one of the children gifts, which remained in the trunk of his car for years. Heartbreaking to say the least!

Rick discovered he could scarcely live a life without his sons. We were scattered. Rick with sis, me with Lida and the folks were not around.

Much like me, he went to the country with the folks. A place to try, not so much to heal, but at best, to be able to function again. He stayed there for a few months. He then decided to go to truck driving school. I knew it was for survival, enabling him with a valid reason to be gone at all times, without accepting the reality of not seeing his son. Also, the school was not far from me and I saw him almost daily. Our talks resumed.

I was especially inquisitive about the baby. I asked him for every detail he could come up with. It took some time, but he began to recall some strange incidents that I insisted were there. It was time to ask him if he was sure the baby was his. His reaction was such sorrow. Rick sat in silence for some time. Eventually, he asked me if I was sure. I responded with my own question, "Are you saying he is yours, without a doubt?" No, he couldn't say that. In fact, he recalled a remark he had made to Sue shortly before the great explosion. The baby was crying and Rick was trying to tend to him, to no avail, and being frustrated he asked Sue, "Sue, what is the problem with this baby?" "Why can we not bond, like I did with Rick?" She instantly became defensive and angry. Sue grabbed the baby out of his arms, and stormed out of the room.

We went over the details again, of how her mother had left him the night he was to take them home from the hospital. He was seeing the conspiracy theory now. The mounting evidence and actions left us nothing but comprehensible. As he left that night, he confessed he felt the baby wasn't his, but he loved him just the same and the baby was innocent. My thoughts and feelings, precisely. What a brother! Can you see how much I love him and how proud I am of him? And you haven't heard anything yet!

By now, a year has passed and nothing to show for it. Rick gave up on his visits with Human Services, with Ms. P and Mr. J. He still couldn't get a polygraph, screaming for any sort of tests to prove his innocence. Finally, he was told to see a man in Ft. Worth. Sounded easy enough, but I had spent three weeks just trying to reach the guy.

I finally got him in to see a type of "examiner," Tim. It took me over three weeks to arrange it. It was a test, (I can't name it) consisting much like a polygraph, with the wires attached to the penis, then watch pictures of children in order to gauge sexual arousal. Less than a third through the test, Tim jerked the wires off, asking why Rick was there. Rick told him the entire story and Tim went right to the phone, called Human Services demanding to know why they were wasting his time and the tax payers money sending Rick there. Rick wasn't able to hear their response, but heard Tim speak in a louder tone saying, "Then I think if you are that convinced that there is a problem in that house, I suggest you look in another direction!" This made Rick feel so good. I did too, but later Rick would get into trouble because he didn't complete the test!

Just like another test Rick took. There must have been over three hundred questions, Rick said, but the examiner told him, "Not all the questions will refer to you. In that case, just skip them and answer the rest as honestly as you can." He did and because he saw a picture of two attractive young women standing in front of a huge picture window, he might be a peeping Tom! It's called Voyeurism and once gain, because he didn't answer every question, he looked bad.

Rick was diagnosed as being in denial! The games people play and the price we pay!

It was a Phallometric and an Able Assessment tests. I recall and Rick passed both......but. It would all come back to haunt Rick and make him look bad! One test alone consisted of three hundred questions. (But, not all applied to Rick).

One specific question was basically about attractive women and would you cheat on your wife. Rick answered no. This reply exposed him as being too honest, again, Rick was in denial! Apparently, no one is that honest or faithful I guess! Who are these morons? Rick's sex counselor was more upset about his fees of $150.00 than his patient. Nor was he qualified enough to even diagnose Rick. Rick needed to be more cooperative. My question is, exactly how does one go about the rehabilitation of a non-offender? Exactly what is there for one to learn, when he's not guilty of any sex crime to begin with!

As stated, the tests would come back to not just haunt him, but would be used to make him look guilty as charged, <u>years later</u>, in a Revocation Hearing!

Getting ahead of myself again. You can most likely tell that I am very passionate about what I believe in. I am seldom ever at a loss for words. I am painfully aware these sex crimes do truly exist! I am dedicated in seeing these offenders punished! But, let's be realistic before we prejudge.

The term "Penitentiary," derives from the old word, repentance. A place you were sent in order to repent and learn to become a better person. Prisons, at least in Texas, are nothing more than a huge enterprise! They involve nothing more than money! You don't get help. You will merely be dehumanized.

Guards are hired, many at minimum wage. Many, too many, are there because they can't get any other job. Most, (this does not mean all) are on power kicks, suffering with a "God complex." They become superior by treating inmates as less than an animal. Yet, in their defense Rick says many of the inmates speak terrible to the guards. He told me not only were they despicable words of choice, but how so many would do it to their backs, as the guards walked away. He said the guards had an awful job and he didn't envy them. When I asked if he ever did such, Rick said, "No, sis. It's not their fault I am in here."

He also told me not to listen to how "Everyone in prison is innocent." He says the guilty boast about their crimes, but that he, (Rick) was not the only innocent man there.

I must tell you I have had the pleasure of meeting some incredibly good, devoted employees.

Many, I have actually learned to love and respect. Unfortunately, as time would pass, they would no longer be there on one of my return trips. I go out of my way to be kind and respectful, not just because I was raised that way, but largely due to the fact that anything less, might be taken out on my brother.

By habit, I automatically treat people the way I want to be treated. I have never succeeded in being a "brown nose," or "sucking up" to anyone. I spent more than fifteen years in management. I had to eat a lot of crow, often. I had to learn to acquire a taste for it. If any one of my offices would mess up, I would accept the responsibility. I was responsible for every office, as well as all the employees. I was the mediator. I had to keep our Corporate accounts, at all costs. You have to make allowances for errors, but also, I had to be able to assure my accounts, that it wouldn't happen again. Since I was also in personnel, having trained them, I had to stand by them too.

In short, kindness and understanding goes a long, long way.

CHAPTER 27
A LITTLE PHILOSOPHY OF MINE

I spent many years in upper management. I had numerous rules. For example, no one was allowed to call me Boss. I never asked anyone to do anything I wouldn't and didn't do. My goals were, in today's terms, extremely unorthodox. I worked in Personnel, Management, Public Relations, Corporate sales et. all. Hiring only employees that wanted my job! Inconceivable? Not in my book. I was the best at what I did. I worked very hard to be the best I could be. I was very secure, knowing the better the employees I hired, the better I looked. I would tell them, "I want you to want my job, as I am not going to stay in this position." I never ceased to be amazed at those frightened at my attitude. I wanted a team, not competition. I wanted ambitious people!

I especially sought the younger ones. I found them easier to train and I simply loved giving them a chance at a career. I kept jeans in the office and wouldn't hesitate to throw them on and help do whatever needed to be done. In seeing me back up what I said, they would become a team member, which led to more of a family effort.

Another rule, they would be told this is the way it is done. Why? Because it works. It was my way. However, if you can come up with something better, I want to be the first to know. I often took them to my home over weekends, to swim, cook out and play water volley ball all night. I was called mom, when no clients were present. I had many employees that worked for me all through college. A lawyer, Nurse, electrical engineer and such. I always encouraged education.

I was gifted with discernment. Many, which I knew had dabbled in drugs, or had a record and such, I sent for pre-polygraphs. If I saw potential, I hired them anyway. I wanted them to work with me, opposed to for me. I abhor power kicks and cut-throats. Once, my son was hired at one of my companies. I had no problem with that, but I did have a problem when he was sent to my office. How do you tell your own son, that when he punches the time-clock, he is an employee, not your son? He was young and had the attitude that mom was the boss and he was her son. He went too far one day. After a couple of warnings, I fire him. He had to respect the rules, but he didn't.

Eventually, I hired him back and he became one of the very best employees I had. He learned the hard way, and the other employees were overwhelmed when he was fired. The reward here for both of us is, he now is living in a huge new home he built for his family. The first time I went to see it, we stood out on the drive. I told him how proud and happy I was for him. He replied, "Mother, because of you, I have been able to accomplish all this." I was stunned, immediately remembering I had fired him once. He knew exactly what I was thinking of. He put his arms around me and said, "Mother, when you fired me I deserved it. You were the toughest boss I ever had, but the most fair one too." He went on to say I taught him that if he wanted something, he would have to work hard and earn it! Yes, one of my fondest memories.

Memory also recalls the time I hired a troubled young man that I knew could be a problem. I saw his potential, convinced he just needed someone to give him a chance and believe in him. He was from a broken family and living with three other guys. I hired him and within the first three months I bought him a battery for his car and paid his rent. The third month, I had to fire him for drinking on the job. It broke my heart, but he had been warned. All were special to me. I had to be firm and abide by my own rules. Thank God, he came to me two weeks later with such genuine remorse, and an apology, asking if I would give him a second chance, like I gave my son? I did. When I left, he was still there as an excellent employee.

Eight years later, while in a sports bar with my boyfriend, playing pool, Gene asked me why a young man was watching me so closely. I wasn't aware of it, but Gene pointed him out to me. I didn't recognize him, but noticed he was much younger than me and told Gene, "I don't know him, but maybe he thinks he knows me. Don't worry about it, he seems harmless to me." This often happened with me. I had worked all over the area for years and more people seemed to know me than I was aware of. Many times it might have been a child of an employee of mine or perhaps one my former husband's. I was not uncomfortable, in the least.

Later, with Gene elsewhere, the young man approached me asking if my name was so and so. "Yes, that is me, do I know you?" It was that same young man I had fired for drinking and rehired years ago. He was so handsome. Neatly dressed, well groomed and such a gentleman.

When I asked what he was doing now, he blessed me so. He was self-employed, owning his own company, making a hundred thousand dollars a year! I was so happy and proud of him. Then he asked if he could hug me. Of course he could. He whispered in my ear, "I owe it all to you, because you believed in me and gave me a chance. I made it." My heart smiled as I thanked the Lord for allowing this to come to my attention! What an investment!

This defies words. We never know the impact we can, and do, make in one's life! When we treat them with value, giving them a break can be such a blessing! I'm not bragging. I'm in awe and very grateful for the opportunity to touch a young life, in a positive way. How many of you have done such a thing? I told you, we were brought up with the proper staples. This was back in the early eighties. I still believe and my husband and I practice the same thing, to this very day!

My point is simple. Let us return to the basics of life. In the midst of our nightmare, I still have faith, hope, love and charity. I know, one day this hell will pass. My concern is for those having to experience this cold, toxic world without these gifts. Some things cannot be purchased, such as the gifts I just shared; faith, hope, love for humanity and charity!

CHAPTER 28
BLIND SIDED BY THE ATTORNEY!

We had a Court date, actually a pretrial date, with the trial date eleven days later. Rick was so excited. Little did we know, Max sold him out the year previously!

We were offered a Plea of Deferred Adjudication with ten years Probation. Rick was furious, refusing it as quickly as Max got it out. Max was visibly unhappy. He said, "I have never known that County to make such an excellent offer!" In stereo, Rick and I asked at the same moment, "Well, then why did they, if they are so convinced of the guilt?" I reminded Max of his own words, asking, "Are they not, still, out to make an example of him." Does this not indicate the case is weakening? "No, hell no," said Max

Rick walked out of the office, leaving me behind! What a golden opportunity I had. I seized it as a gift of precious time, in order to express my fury at Max attempting plead my brother out. We made it perfectly clear, he wanted to fight. He wants his day in court! I asked what part of that could he not comprehend? I then informed him of exactly what he could do with that Plea, even making suggestions as to how he could go about it, with a possible destination.

I yelled at him, "If you are not capable of fighting this in a Court of law, tell me now!" On my departure, I reminded him we had already covered the extra money for the trial, so he best get off his butt and earn it! Wow. I hit a nerve I guess, because the mean, obnoxious Max backed off. I wondered if he had heard the stories about redheads and their tempers. I had jumped Max before, but not like this.

He had never seen that part of me. I was furious at allowing him to get me so riled, as I well knew how ugly I could be when I lost my temper. That's why I seldom revealed it. I didn't want anyone to see me that ugly, but he crossed the line messing with my brother's life! He didn't like it, but agreed to inform the DA that Rick refuses any form of a Plea.

Rick was waiting for me by the car. He was angry. His body was ridged with head hung low. I placed my arms around him and just loved him, as he tried to apologize for leaving me back there. I laughed, telling him he didn't need to apologize to me, and that I was grateful for the time alone with that slime ball. He stood back with big eyes asking, "What did you do, sis?" He knew quite well the temper I had, when necessary. "Sis, what did you do to him?" I was still laughing, even harder. He was more serious than ever now, asking louder, "Sis, what did you do to Max?" I couldn't stop the laughter. I was reliving his expression, with the scene in my mind, of how I must have looked the day I killed that <u>killer rat,</u> (figuring he was doing the same thing) and I couldn't stop laughing.

Rick finally joined in. We laughed so hard we were borderline hysterical. I finally regained my composure and told him, that I didn't physically hurt Max, but I did make it crystal clear as to what he could do with that Plea. He laughed and said, I had scared him and he sure hoped Max didn't have a whisk broom in his office. I was right. I knew it, he remembered too! I told him, "No, he didn't, cuz I looked for one." Laughter is so good for the soul! He felt much better now, and his attitude improved even more when he got me to elaborate on what I said to Max. So often, I look back and marvel at Rick. I knew the hell he has suffered, for so long. I honestly wonder how I could have withstood, under the same circumstances. Yes, I am very, very, proud of Rick!

CHAPTER 29
AS A THIEF IN THE NIGHT!

We were notified that the pretrial date was canceled by the DA. Needless to say, no new Court date. Max said he refused the Plea offer and that must be the reason for the canceled Court date. What a liar and thief! If the pretrial was canceled, why did Max show up, that day, with the forged **"Application for Probation?"** Not only was Rick's name forged, but the date had been altered to the original Court date. The one that was canceled!

Unfortunately, it would be years before we would become aware of this! Almost seven years would pass and then, it would be too late.

The audacity of this flim-flam-man! All this time wasted and we were still giving him money. For what? If that's not bad enough, I would find another Court date scheduled a month later. It would be years later before I would learn of this and the fact that, once again, Max was there with another forgery, which appeared to have been done in a Courtroom! Details later.

Suffice it to say, Max called constantly, demanding more money. Still the only papers we ever saw were Motions Max had filed. I am cognizant, now, in seeing the Motions, but never seeing the results or the Judge's decisions. This includes denials or grants by the Judge.

One day, when Max called me at Lida's, I jumped him about his ability to call me at any time, and how I had to walk through hell if I wished to get in contact with him. I informed him that if he wanted access to me, then I demanded the same in return. I got his cell phone number, that day!

I wish I had done this earlier, but I wish a lot of things now. I can't go back. What's done is done, for now at least.

Another Court date for April, but it too was canceled. I do not know why. I can't recall why, but I have found many continuances Max filed without our knowledge. This was not one though.

I have located the "Waiver of Arraignment," with Rick's name forged, but also, with the signature of the Judge on it.

Questions and more questions without any answers. If only we had known then what we have come to learn since Rick's sentencing, it would be an entirely different story. I am convinced that Rick would have never even gone on probation or have been forced or coerced to cop a "Plea." Even so, I would still, most likely, be writing a book, but with different goals. There are just too many fighting the same battle to "let it go." Never forget, if it could happen to us, it could happen to you.

Excluding our ordeal, the law is supposed to be the law! Equal justice for one and all. The meaningful lesson here is simple. You cannot trust the system to work. Life has no meaning in a Court of law, anymore than being guilty or innocent. Actually, the guilty appear to have more rights than the innocent. While the accused tries to clear their name, the attorney is thinking nothing but a "Plea."

CHAPTER 30
IS THERE LIFE IN SPITE OF SUE?

Rick finished his schooling and got a job with a huge company. He was now an over-the-road truck driver. A great job, with great benefits. Naturally, Sue immediately sued for child support and coverage for the boys. Rick had no problem with that. But, as usual, it didn't stop there. Sue was constantly suing for more and more.

However, he would not leave town until I had a car. I went against the Doctor's orders and got a job in a new field, Optics. Since I could only stand for twenty minutes and sit for the same amount of time, it was a perfect solution. I would be up and down. I excelled quickly and was offered a management job in Oklahoma. No thanks. Not only did I not wish to leave the state, but I knew I wasn't physically able at the time. Plus, my daughter was making her Wedding plans. With my elderly folks and my family, I had no desire to relocate. I would stay put for Rick, for now.

I moved to the city and took over a store there, managing it. I loved the business and with Rick pretty well situated at the time, I felt I could finally take care of myself. I lived alone in a one bedroom apartment, where the Manager became my new best friend and I slowly began to socialize.

I rejoiced in defying five Doctors. It wasn't easy, but I am very stubborn and couldn't bring myself to file for Disability or early retirement. I truly loved working.

Rick, bless his heart, would stay out on the road for months at a time. I finally had to ask him for help with my car. As always, he was right there for me. He took my car and had a brand new set of tires put on it and fixed the electrical problems. I had purchased the car Rick picked for me. One I said I would never own, a Cadillac, loaded. At first I was very unhappy at the size, but as Rick pointed out, it had eight-way power, split bench seats, velour, telescopic tilt and cruise. I mean loaded! I could not only drive it, but it didn't hurt nearly as bad as other cars. It had belonged to a friend of his and I got it for next to nothing.

I could tell that Rick loved his job. I knew a huge part was the escape of him not seeing his boys, but I felt he was doing what he had to do. We all deal with things the best way we know how. He was still drinking, but never on the job! He loved being alone, out on the road. He too, had made several friends now. He had his music and pictures of the boys in front of the truck. I was so thrilled to see how far he had come, but we still hadn't resolved any of the legal problems yet.

Eventually, he would have a female team driver Ann. That took some getting used to. She literally chased him across the country. She worked for the same company and amazingly, after months, she managed to get Rick's attention. This brought about mixed blessings.

Rick finally told Ann the story. Ann had been abused too, so she had great understanding and confessed she didn't believe Rick could do such a thing. This was very good for him, for a time anyway. As I said, mixed blessings. At times, our "good intentions" or our desire to help, can actually hurt the already, injured party. In Ann's defense, with Max putting her on the witness stand, did far more injury than help. For the defense anyway.

CHAPTER 31
A PLEA UNDER DURESS

Twenty-seven months later, the Plea is renewed and we had another Court date. I have a three page letter from Max. On the first page he begs Rick to accept the Plea. The second page he urges him to accept it. On the last page, I saw it as a threat, that if he didn't accept it, Rick would likely get ninety-nine years and if so, Max didn't want to hear him whining about it! Max said to accept, "The excellent offer he had never known that County to offer before." Which was the ten years Deferred Adjudicated Probation. Max swore it was no admission of guilt!

Sounds good? First, why were they willing to come down so far from where they began? I was sure the case had fallen apart, but no, Max assured me, if Rick refused it this time, they would go all out to make an example of him, seeking ninety-nine years in prison. That's life!

This was the second time it had been offered and the last. The problem was, Rick still didn't want it, but insisted on his day in Court. This infuriated Max. Why? I don't think he was capable of such a trial. After all, isn't this Rick's right, to have his day in Court?

Before I saw the "letter," Max called me and managed to instill the horror of Rick's possibility of receiving the maximum term. Did I want that? Could our mother live with that? I didn't sleep for three days. He urged me to convince Rick to accept it. Yes, I was horrified when he reminded me of the Grand Jury Foreman hugging the woman from Human Services. I had to accept the terror of, perhaps, having Rick sent to prison for life! By now, Max reminded us daily, how prisons are full of innocent men and women. Dare we risk it?

I was working when Rick arrived in town and he went to see Max. Rick told him to shove the Plea. He still wanted to fight it, willing to take his chances. He went to see Max before he came to my place! Neither of us went to bed that night. We talked all night, with me begging him to accept that darn Plea, "Rick, why did you go see Max without me?" This was exceptional and surprising. Rick said he wanted to have what we, his sisters, called, "A come to Jesus meeting," with Max. He said Max pointed out Rick could still be a part of his sons lives, continue paying child support and pay for their insurance. Max asked if Rick didn't want to be a part of their lives and to be able to pay support and insure the boys. Of course Rick wanted to. Finally, Rick relented, but not based on those issues. I thought he did it for mother and me, basically for the family. I learned later what Max pulled on Rick and why he really accepted the blasted Plea!

Rick told me that Max had promised him, he would even get him off in about five years and have his record expunged. A lie, I now know, not in Texas anyway! Texas state law prohibits such as this. But, everything Max said was a lie. He is a chronic liar! And, I am being kind. Max wouldn't know the truth if it fell from heaven, written on a scroll! But, what options did we have left? We had to trust him to keep his word and rely on him as our attorney, to do that which he promised and was paid to do! As for now, we had nothing concrete to accuse Max of. He had a degree. We didn't have any legal experience or knowledge, beyond television.

Therefore, the decision made. Coerced yes, but again, what were our options? So, off to Court we would go, walking into a trap that would seal Rick's fate.

CHAPTER 32
THE ONLY THING DEFINITE, IS NOTHING IS DEFINITE

Rick and I were at the Courthouse waiting for Max to show. Five minutes before he was to go before the Judge, Max comes running down the hall, waving papers, saying, "Rick, I'm sorry I am running so late, whatever the Judge asks you, just say **Yes Sir** and I'll explain later." OOPS! We fell for it! Yes, I am well aware of our ignorance!

Max, I thought, used me to convince Rick to accept the Plea. Max operated with the "fear factor," reminding me of mother's health. Could she handle her baby going to prison for life? No, I knew she would never be able to accept that. He said Rick couldn't pay child support or insure the boys from a prison cell. I allowed him to use me in this fashion.

I kept my word, in getting Max off his butt, although Rick didn't get what we wanted, which was his day in court. He never received his Constitutional Rights. Max knew I had money coming and he already had his heart set on getting it, which he managed to do. It was obvious to Max, that our family was very close and we knew, without a doubt, Rick was innocent. Max was keenly aware of the especially, close relationship between Rick and me. He's not an idiot. Max knew I would do anything I could to help Rick. He used the entire family.

From where I sat I couldn't hear everything, but I did hear the Judge say, "But, I think you are guilty." I saw Max having Rick sign papers and noticed a change come over Rick's face. Then I saw the rage in his eyes as we were leaving the Courtroom. By the time we got into the hall, Rick was in a state I had never seen before. The anger, the fire in his eyes with his body trembling all over.

He was yelling at Max about being a liar and other remarks I didn't understand. Rick's abrupt behavior continued to increase to the point I had to stand between them. Never, ever, had I seen Rick in such a state. I tried to get one of them to inform of what had just happened. Rick yelled at me that he could have no contact with his son, that he had just been screwed and he wanted out of there before he hurt Max! My brother, threatening Max? Rick even called him a damn liar to his face! I grabbed his arm and said "Let's go." As we headed down the hallway I could still hear Max's words, "Well, at least your not in prison." Rick yelled back, "Small compensation." A part of Rick died that day. You don't have to be behind bars to be in prison! How dare he say such a thing. No, Rick wasn't physically in prison. This was far worse than prison.

Outside at the car, Rick's body was still trembling, so I drove. There was total silence for several miles, then I noticed Rick's tears. I knew what those tears meant. He was on the edge. I couldn't stand it anymore. I took the next exit, found a place to park, and asked him what had happened. The details were unbelievable. In short, Max sold him out. He was so upset. He just wanted me to take him to the terminal, so he could hit the road. He had basically given away any rights he had as a father. It was a nightmare! He wanted to get out of town, now!

At the terminal, he hugged me and told me he loved me, but that he didn't know if or when he would return. He gave me some numbers to call in order to reach him, if I needed him. I was so perplexed and distraught, I had to make several corrections to finally get back to my place. I was still living in the city, alone, and took the rest of the day off to try to regroup and put the pieces of the puzzle together. I held myself responsible for everything that happened that day. I was the one that talked Rick into that damn Plea. I folded and didn't work that day or the next day, either. I kept asking myself what I had done to my brother?

The third day I returned to work. Being busy helped in not having time to think and imagine how Rick was doing. I decided to leave him alone for the time, allowing him to come to grips with the situation. I kept hearing that Judge say, "But, I think you are guilty." I wanted to stand up and scream, "Then why are you allowing this to happen? You are supposed to be the Judge."

Okay, then obviously Rick didn't confess to anything, or the Judge wouldn't have been angry enough to make that remark. I needed a few more days before I felt I could talk with Max. I prayed nonstop for Rick to forgive me for what I had done to him. Little did I know it wasn't me.

When I did get Max on the phone, he was very defensive. Max vowed he got Rick such a great deal. A great deal? I asked max, "If you got him such a sweet deal, why is he not allowed to have any contact with his son, when you told us wouldn't happen? In fact, by you swearing that you would enable Rick to continue being a father and seeing to it that Rick could pay child support and insure the boys, if he accepted that plea and now what does Rick have to live for?" Max replied, "Well hell Clar, I'm not responsible for the Judge deciding that and I did keep him out of prison." In my angry, I ended the conversation with, "Yes, Max, you did keep him from going to prison and you are not responsible for anything more than that but, I assure you, he is already in one hell of a prison, compliments of you!" As I was hanging the phone up, I could hear Max, in a loud tone yelling the same o same o, "Well, I kept him out of prison."

Lord, when would I see my brother again? Well, that request came about quite quickly! Still a mystery to this day, as to why. The only good thing about it would be seeing Rick again! Rick would be called back into court in exactly three weeks. For what? As I stated, we still aren't sure.

Seeing all the records I now have, I think I know why. The Judge had messed up and even calling Rick back, the Judge still messed up, again. Speculation yes, but as time passes I think I have found the proof. More later.

CHAPTER 33
ANOTHER COURT DATE!

I have the letter from Max, stating, how he had gone over everything with the Courts, the DA and all was in order, but Rick would have to return for another Court date. Exactly twenty-one days later, following his Court date. For what? Max said, "It's just paperwork I guess. It happens all the time."

In all of my records, the only difference I can find is the, "<u>Admonishment to the Defendant.</u>" Not only is it the law, but a requirement! Apparently, the judge screwed up and failed to get one. All the other records are dated with the first date, scratched through with the newer date written above the old one. I've since learned, <u>no Judge in Texas can allow such a Plea without a Judicial confession</u>, which I could not locate. In short, the Courts screwed up and tried to cover their errors. I assure you, the full fifteen years are running over with error upon error. Again, the Judge repeated the very same words, "But, I think you are guilty."

Poor Rick went through hell on probation. Not at first, **I remind you that he only had forms to send in monthly, until he was assigned a probation officer**. It took about two years! I used bold font for further consideration in his revocation hearing, whereas the assistant DA would lie, under oath, telling the Judge how Rick had refused to report.

For the record, all attorneys and the DA are under oath!

I could still hear Rick telling me, "Sis, they will never let me go. Max screwed me and I'll never get out of this." He swore something was wrong, all along. I can't say I was comfortable, but I couldn't see any other way out. Max appeared to be the "necessary evil."

Once again, all Rick wanted to do was get in his truck and hit the road. I was confident the only peace he had was being alone on the road. I wanted to give him time to come around, to the best of his ability. No one could be capable of knowing what Rick was going through. Unless you have walked in those shoes, you couldn't possibly know.

The only thing I was sure of was the guilt I was having to live with. Me, in convincing Rick to accept that Plea. The fear of losing him was too great.

I felt guilty and selfish. My only source of comfort was in knowing he was not physically in prison and I could call him if I needed him. Plus, the prayer that Sue would come forth with the truth. I am always open to miracles and I knew one was desperately needed here!

I spent years living with an unnecessary guilt. Only after Rick went to prison, would he finally tell me the truth, facts and all. I was not the reason Rick accepted that plea. No! It was good old Max that did that and in such a way that Max should be doing time. This is why I say Rick was coerced into that plea!

CHAPTER 34
JUST WHEN YOU THINK YOU CAN BREATH

About three months later, I had car problems, bad tires and extremely low finances. Much as I hated, I had to call on Rick. Part of me longed to see him and know how he was doing. Naturally, he rerouted and arrived in just over twenty-four hours!

He stayed with me for three days. I had moved to the big city. Oh, how I enjoyed having him all to myself. We had such a wonderful time, with all new surroundings, for Rick. No one knew a thing about what was going on in his personal life. Rick really needed that. He met most all of my new friends, hitting it off right away. I spoke of Rick, always, so all my friends felt they already knew him.

But, I never told anyone of the story. Not even Dean, who was my Doctor and best friend, for over twenty years now. Rick never had to worry about that, I vowed to protect him and protect him I did!

Dean knew Rick and cared very much for him. It would be nine years before I confided in him. With the stress and my guilt, I broke down and shared the horror story with Dean. Dean had been down on me about my stress level and weight loss for years, now he knew why I was so stressed. He couldn't believe I had kept it to myself for so long. I only confided in him after the sentencing. I told you how I protected Rick. I never wanted him to feel uncomfortable in meeting anyone. Dean, didn't understand why I wouldn't have trusted him with the issue. It was because they were around each other so often and I just couldn't risk it. I promised Rick, all along, that Dean knew nothing, which made it easier for Rick to be around him. I told Rick that nobody knew a thing, which helped. Dean then told me horror stories of the same thing with many of his patients. Do what? Really? Yes, really. His next statement was, "It's like an epidemic, these false allegations." He really could appreciate it and like he said, "Your brother isn't capable of that!" Of course, he could never give me the patients names, because of his oath. What he could tell me was enough to assure me that our family was certainly not alone in this. That helped greatly. The knowledge was a mixed blessing. I was relieved to know we were not alone, but I was filled with sympathy for the other victims. As for my feelings regarding the system, it only served to renew my anger!

I was so glad I had finally told Dean what had been going on for nine years. Now, I had someone that would be so supportive and not have to conceal it any longer. I hated the fact though, of so many others going through the same thing. Comforting? Yes! But, anger too.

I never kept silent about Rick because of shame! Absolutely not. I remained silent for other reasons, like how so many are too quick to judge. Dean knew and loved Rick. I had someone outside of the family I could now turn too. Aside from Lida and Randy, both now back at work and with the distance between us, I needed Dean, badly. What a blessing Dean was. I now had unconditional, loving support.

Also, I feared my reactions if I detected a questionable expression. It would take nothing to lose control in my defense of Rick and I decided I couldn't afford the risk involved. It was just easier to remain silent and take in the joy of those first meeting him and liking him right away. Plus, I was painfully aware of many friends and acquaintances that did suffer of such crimes, asking myself if they would believe in Rick's innocence? Thank God, I have never been sexually abused. I know this must be so traumatizing, therefore I would never wish to minimize it in any way. I found that my being silent, was the only solution, for all concerned.

CHAPTER 35
IS LIFE WORTH LIVING?

I looked back at all those times when nothing was being done. Before Rick went to school, before his Plea. When I was living with Lida, I was awakened very late one night. Knowing Rick was contemplating suicide, I dressed and drove over there to do whatever I had to do to prevent it. He was thinking about it. I didn't ask him, I simply stated my case. I told him, "Brother, I know what you are thinking about doing. You're thinking suicide and I'm here to stop you!" I caught him completely by surprise.

At first he denied it. I wasn't buying it, I knew better. Finally, he broke down confessing it was true, but how did I know. Simple I replied, "The Lord woke me up telling me what you were going to do." Then laughingly asked him, "Or would you prefer I tell you, I just wanted to take a drive at 2:00 in the morning, for my health?" He knew better than that and went limp, for he knew that I really did know!

He didn't dare question that. We cried together and talked. He was hurting so badly and no, he didn't want to do anything that might make it appear he was guilty. Then his son would live with the possibility that what his mother had told him was true? That thought made all the difference. He never wanted his son to have any reason in believing his daddy would hurt him in any way!

I could never fully describe all the awful, ugly memories of the pain I witnessed, first-hand, for so many years. No book would hold them. I don't even have the vocabulary. All the tears and humiliation he suffered. I used to lay awake half the night, praying and trying to picture him out on the highway. What music was he listening to? What was he feeling and thinking?

When one you love and believe in one, as deeply as our family does with Rick, there is never just one victim. Our whole family has suffered in ways you can't imagine. Our lives have never returned to normal, nor will they. Ever! Knowing this, I can only pray that since things can never go back, the future will be better.

It's worth repeating, there are many forms of prison. Every member of our family has been in a form of prison. From the first day Sue falsely accused Rick, we have each done "hard time."

It has never gotten easier. Fact is, it continues to worsen. Since Rick has been sentenced, we have lost three family members, mother is failing rapidly and holidays are extremely difficult. It is common, I have learned, that the statistics say, after the first two years family and friends lose interest. Apparently, many settle for accepting the situation or just go on with their own lives. Perhaps, for some it is the only way to keep going.

I truly believe that the state, that County, the Judge and the State Bar expected the same thing from us. Well, I told you, this family is not the average family! We are too close and loving to be able to "just go with the flow," not when an innocent member is in prison. I vowed to Rick from day one, we would never accept his situation and "live with it." So far I have kept my word and I have no intention of ever giving up. Not as long as I breath and God is on the throne!

CHAPTER 36
THIS CAN'T HAPPEN IN AMERICA!

Two years later, Rick lost his job. Being a truck driver, no company can employ a Felon. Rick was not a felon, though someone in that County Court, called his company informing them, Rick was a convicted felon. Naturally, the safety department had to release him. The owner himself spoke with Rick, very disheartened, telling Rick he was considered an excellent employee, with a flawless record, but as he said, they had no alternative.

Rick called me with the news. I called Max immediately, demanding he find out what happened and fix it now! It cost me $500.00 for a letter Max wrote to Rick's company. Rick did get his job back, but we couldn't get any answers as to how and why it happened. Apparently, according to Max, a Government employee made the call. She also had to call and apologize for the error. When we attempted to track her down, she had either resigned or had been transferred. No one knew which.

In Max's letter he stated unequivocally, that he felt Rick was falsely accused by an angry wife, and how he planned to get Rick off probation early, and again, have his record expunged. That in Texas, with that type of plea, Rick is not a convicted felon! (I have the letter) Rick told me again, "Sis, they are never going to let me go, you wait and see. It's never going to be over, until they send me to prison." He was right! Things just kept spiraling downward, and as bad as it was at the time, the worst was yet to come.

Rick had transferred to the County where the folks and I live. He was assigned to a wonderful probation officer, Cary. Cary went out of his way to work with Rick, so as to keep him out on the road at longer periods. He sent him to a Counselor, Jan.(female and great person.) The problem was, Jan was not a Sex Counselor and didn't know how to treat Rick, realizing that he was not a sex offender, so they would talk about the weather, life and events.

I spoke with Jan on the phone several times. I had taken over Rick's bills, appointments and such, as he literally lived on the road. He jokingly gave me his address as something like, 5900 Kenworth Ave. (his truck). Rick might get caught in a winter storm in Canada, on the east coast or perhaps in Colorado, he never knew, so I would notify Jan and the Probation Officer.

The Probation Officer, Cary, came to the folks place often. We always enjoyed visiting with him. Better yet, he appeared to believe in Rick and cared very much about him. I have a letter from him stating, Rick's family was very nice and extremely supportive of him. You bet we were.

However, between Max, the County and the sex Counselor, Cary got caught up in the midst of the bureaucracy. Along with the appearance of Rick not being truthful and moving here, because Ann reneged on her promise. After her pending, legal (medical) settlement was finalized, Ann had agreed to move the mobile home to the county Cary was in.

I cannot blame Cary. Having put myself in his place I could understand how and why he felt that way. Cary had to go up against that corrupt County and Max. Max even tried to use me to get to the poor guy. Cary tried to help, but Max threatened Rick, saying if he so much as returned the call to Cary, Max would drop Rick! I cannot fault Cary nor say anything derogatory regarding him. One day he will know the truth.

CHAPTER 37
SUE FRACTURES ANOTHER LAW!

I had taken over all the bills and business for Rick and Ann, (team driver and girlfriend) as they were on the road constantly. I got a letter from a Judge near Sue's home. The letter was a demand that Rick had to pay $526.00 for insurance bills to Sue, for Doctor bills on the boys.

He had ten days in which to do so, or else! I noticed the medical bills were especially high on the last born. I received all the bills from the Insurance Company, through Rick's job. At first I was astounded and very suspicious of them, with good reason.

I got my records out and sure enough, two checks had been paid. One had been deposited by a Doctor and another deposited by a Clinic in Austin! Austin was so far away from her. I had to wonder why in Austin, with another hospital and Doctor much closer, where she usually went. Who else, but Sue, could use a Judge to <u>collect twice on Insurance checks</u> and get away with it?

I was furious! Sue had already gone through Austin to collect more child support, even back support for the time that Rick couldn't work, because Sue had stolen and sold all his cars, tools and called Rick's customers. Now, she wanted all of the money that wasn't available while Rick was in jail and for when Rick wasn't able to work, prior to becoming a truck driver.

I contacted Rick with the information. He told me to just pay her. But why Rick? Two of them have been paid. I have copies of the Insurance checks that were paid. Don't you realize she is collecting twice on them? That, legally this was fraud. A Federal crime by her using the Postal System in doing so. He told me it didn't matter. He said one or two of the smaller checks Ann had deposited in error. He had to see a Dentist in Arizona, and Ann thought they were his checks. He told me he felt sure he was responsible for the two small ones, but to pay the full amount and let it go <u>or</u>! I knew the "or." It meant she would likely take her rage out on the children.

I paid the amount. However, since then I reported her fraud to the White-collar Crime Unit as well as the Postal System. I also reported Sue to a child abuse Hot-line. I have never heard one word from a one of them.

Big deal, never a word from them! It's as though she can do anything she wishes. Yes, this angers me. Does it not bother you? Sue missed her calling. I think she should have been a Politician or an attorney!

No matter where I looked, I could never see any justice for Rick. All I have ever seen is a gross injustice. **Let the Jury go, set the sinners free**. I do know that one day, she will have to stand and account for all her wrongs. I still pray she will awaken to what she has done. I have learned that no matter how trivial something may appear, for every wrong done, there will always be someone that will pay the price for it.

I am reminded of the late, great, singer/songwriter Rich Mullens. His Christianity was so very practical and simple. My favorite thought he shared was, "I know that the business of vengeance belongs to our Father, but sometimes, I would just love to go about my Father's business." I confess, I know how he felt. I, too, have been tempted. Often.

For the record, I had married again, to a wonderful man. He lived just over two miles from the folks. A good man that completely believed in my brother. What a blessing! The love of my life, and I was able to be very close to our parents!

And Sue was not close to stopping yet. Rhea finally found us, with another horror story!

CHAPTER 38
ANOTHER SUE PLAN>>>A< B OR C?

Apparently, when Rick couldn't find Sue for a few days that summer, no one knew where she was. It's because Sue was not in town. Sue made an unannounced visit to see Rhea. (Rick's former wife)

Sue appeared at Rhea's with only little Rick, so DeDe could get to know her brother. Oh, yes, Sue had another motive. (I hope so, having driven over two hundred miles to recruit Rhea to cover for the lies Sue told her attorney)!

It seems Sue had informed her attorney that Rhea wouldn't allow Rick to see their girls either, because she did not trust Rick with them! Rhea said she had never said such a thing! Rhea asked Sue where she ever came up with such as that. Sue actually tried to convinced Rhea of an old conversation that had transpired between the two of them. (Mind control) This time Sue picked the wrong person to play that game with.

Rhea told Sue, if she told her attorney that, it was not Rhea's problem, but Sue's. Sue then began begging Rhea, saying she would get into trouble with her attorney, should Rhea not back Sue's story up. Again, Rhea said, "If you told your attorney that story, you lied and you will have to deal with it. Rhea added, "If Rick has changed that much over the years, he should be punished and get some help."

Rhea tried to contact us, but wasn't able to. I was in the country, Lori and our other sister Lea had moved and one divorced etc. However, Rhea said she was so disturbed and uncomfortable with the situation, in the best interest for Rick, she decided to have a Notarized letter written in order to help or protect Rick, and for the girls I believe.

Rick's daughter, DeDe, was very upset and asked Rhea if she thought her daddy could have done such a thing. Rhea told DeDe, "He was not a perfect husband and always had an eye for a pretty woman, but I can't see him as a pervert or a child molester." Thank you Rhea! I told you this was not only a good mother, but one with such integrity too. Fact is, Rhea wished Rick had spent more time with the girls.

I have the Notarized letter. I love the way she closed it. **"If this story is a fabrication, like Sue's memory of a conversation that she and I never had about the girls, this should end."**

Just another reason for the case to have never gone as far as it did. But, we didn't get the data from Rhea until the last minute.

Sue was living on food stamps, yet had the money to make that long trip to recruit Rhea into her scam. Yes, our tax dollars at work! I would love to know how she got around that one with her attorney!

For the record, at the "Revocation Hearing," the Judge refused to read Rhea's letter and two others. Again, I thank Rhea for being so wise, thoughtful and kind. Sue's mind-control was of no help this time. Sue picked the wrong person for that.

CHAPTER 39
KEEPING ON KEEPING ON

Ann, I stated earlier, became very ill and could no longer drive. Diagnosed with carpal tunnel, (having had surgery for) and a rare disease I cannot recall, and fibromyalgia. I suffer from the latter too. I consider it a trash can term, (for a lack of actually knowing) and overly diagnosed.

The disease was caused by a job she worked at in the east, having been exposed to toxins. She filed for disability and with her Insurance, a settlement was forthcoming. In not being able to drive she bought a mobile home. She hadn't had a real home of her own in decades. She told Rick as soon as the settlement came, they would move the home. (to the county where his Probation Officer was) Rick found a lot, less than two miles from the folks. He had mother and I calling around for information on a well. But, when the time came, Ann refused to move. This was a hazardous decision and selfish, not to mention the difficult position it placed Rick in. This is the reason Cary thought Rick lied to him. I admit, it did appear that way, on the surface, but I knew the truth. Rick never lied to Gary but, Ann took it out of Rick's control.

The next step she took was explosive. Ann filled out a change of address, for her and Rick! I know she wasn't aware of what all she had done, nor was it intentional, but Rick wasn't aware she had done it. It came to the attention of the Probation Supervisor in the original County. Upon Rick's awareness, he had to change his driver's license in order to keep his CDL license.

Before he knew what happened, he was ordered to appear in that County. This Supervisor was nothing like Cary, in fact, more like the Devil's advocate. Power crazy, like most, and took Rick off the road. This cost him a minimum of $17,000.00 per year in a pay cut.

Rick was sent to another sex Counselor, Brad, in the city. At first Rick was very pleased with him. He told me he was sure the guy believed in him. He said he was told, "Okay Rick, just work with me for a few months and we'll get this over with." That was in the beginning, before the County got to him.

For months, I was going back and forth, living on the Interstate, or so it seemed. I would go back there for weeks at a time to care for Ann, so Rick could stay out on the road. But now, he had to work locally, for the same company. Thank God, my trips were cut for awhile.

Later that same year, Rick was ordered to register as a sex offender! He read it and refused to sign it. He told the Supervisor, " If you look at my file, you will see that this does not include me, by law." The Supervisor leaned over the desk saying, "You know I can force you to appear here every day if I choose, then how would you keep your job?" As for Rick's file, he said, **"No, I have not looked at you files and I may never, so sign the damn form**." Rick was boiling. Still he refused to sign it, until his attorney saw it too. "Okay, then get him out here," said the supervisor!

Rick called me and I made a dash for the city, calling Max before I left. He said, "Oh hell, they can't do that to him." He agreed to be there first thing in the morning. Big deal, a waste of time, he said. They simply couldn't do that and he would "set them straight," Sure, Max, you set them straight!

As soon as I arrived at Rick's I asked to see the form. I am but a simple layman, but I can read and comprehend. On the very form he was expected to sign, the second page clearly stated three codes and dates. Not one applied to Rick. I laughed and told him, "Brother, this does not apply to you in any way, so calm down. Max will take care of this in the morning."

He didn't calm down, repeating how they would never let him go. Reminding me he had just been threatened by his Supervisor! He was hurt, angry and confused, not to mention scared. I really needed to return home to the folks, but agreed to call Max again. I would spend the night and leave early in the morning. I did just that, but I wish I hadn't. I don't know what I could have done, but I would have done something. I called Max, reading the entire form to him and again, he stated they couldn't do that and he would inform the Supervisor, first thing in the morning. I left for home about an hour before Rick went to see the supervisor.

Rick arrived finding Max already there! Max was never on time in his life, and he beat Rick there. Before Rick got to the Supervisor's office, he heard them laughing and joking. As he entered the office, they were drinking coffee. Max looked up asking, "Where's the form?" Rick had left it in the car, thinking they would have one too, unreasonable? Max said, "Well, go get the G-d thing." He went back to the car, very concerned at

Max's attitude, took it in and Max glanced over it, threw it at Rick saying, "Just sign the damned thing," and he left!

That morning, within ten minutes of my return, the phone rang. It was Max, yelling at me about Rick making a fool out of him that morning! What? I was astounded, I couldn't believe it. Blind with fury, I began yelling back at him. I asked if I understood him correctly, that he told Rick to sign that form, even though it was not applicable to his case, after we had discussed it? Yes, he did tell Rick to sign it! I honestly cannot recall my words to Max, but they were not kind at all. I was still yelling at him as I hung up the phone.

Since then, I have it in writing that Rick was not obligated to sign it, by law! It <u>did</u> violate the very codes on it. But, once you are in the system, there is no way of getting out. My dear Lord, Rick was right! They were not going to ever let him go! Max was an attorney, the form's earliest date was over two years after the date of Rick's so called, offense. Why, in God's name would he tell Rick to sign it, unless he was involved with the corruption with the rest of the County? It certainly appeared to look that way.

In signing that form, Rick couldn't go out on the road, he couldn't afford to move, he couldn't even come to the folk's place. Yes, they now owned his life. Each day he lived in fear. Even working locally, he couldn't go near a school, park etc. He became alarmingly depressed and I went back to the city for several days. Eventually, he would return to the road, only after a great loss in salary and sanity.

Rick convinced his sex Counselor to release him to go back out on the road. This saved what little sanity he had maintained. It was a blessing indeed, but it didn't last long. He would now live in his truck. No more Hotel or Motels, because they all had pools and children around. Still, he made the best of a very bad, chaotic situation. I marveled at him, even more so now. I took many trips with him, not as much as I liked. With the folks health being bad, I couldn't be gone longer than three days. My husband would stand in for me, so I could be with Rick, loving him and supporting him, as best I could. My brother, one of the nicest, most kind gentleman you could meet, suffering such humility in not being allowed to live his life to the fullest, because of a crazy woman and an inept, corrupt system. Having always stopped to help anyone on the side of the road, he would now possibly risk the rest of his life if he were to attempt to assist anyone in need. He would use his CB to ask another to stop! I would love our time together, but return home furious with this crap!

CHAPTER 40
YOU CAN'T FIGHT THE SYSTEM

Less than three years later, in November, I received a letter from the County Probation Officer, ordering Rick to come to his office. They were upset over a Birthday card Rick sent to his son. I was surprised at this, as Rick, (no contact or not) always sent him a card with money in it. Yes, Max was aware of this. I contacted Rick with the information. He was on the east coast, but came right back to town, by switching loads with another driver and went right in, expecting to be arrested.

He told me he was very surprised at the Officer's attitude. He was actually nice to Rick. Rick asked if they wanted to arrest him. He said no, they spoke about it and Rick told him he had always sent a card, every year, but that year he had no money to send. He asked the Officer, "So what happens now?" He was told not to worry about it, that they would get in touch with him. Rick returned to the road, but was amazed at the nonchalant attitude.

The following March, I received a letter stating an Arrest Warrant had been issued for him! Not a word since November, and now a Warrant? I think this time I contacted him on the west coast. He put in for an emergency leave and came right home. I had called Max. Yes, what else could I do as he had been on this for over seven years know. I told him Rick was coming to turn himself in. Max threw a fit. Yelling at me he said, if Rick turned himself in, he would drop him, that this was what he was for! Max claimed that was his job! Rick asked me if I was sure what Max said. I'd gone to the city to be there when Rick arrived.

I got Max on the phone to assure Rick of what he said. Yes, Max said just what I repeated and more. He said he had checked on the Warrant and it wasn't there, so he told Rick to get his butt back out on the road to make money to pay him! God as my witness, he did this. The weeks became months and Rick was still on the road. He had gotten several Court dates, but Max kept getting a continuance. Max told us, if anyone came to the door for Rick, we were to say he was with his attorney! Also, that if ever we got to the Courthouse and not see him or his car, do not go in!

In April, Rick finally, after nine years plus, would get his polygraph, with Ed. The problem was, there was a Warrant out for his arrest. Was this a trap? He went, sitting there for over four hours. Can you imagine how scared and helpless he must have felt? Every time a door was opened, he was sure he was about to be arrested.

Eventually, someone came up to him with an apology. They were just too far behind. He would have to make another appointment! Relieved? Not necessarily. Rick wanted it over with. Now he had to come back, as it turned out, the very next day.

He had gone all night without any sleep because he was worried about it being a trap. Now he had to return, tomorrow. Again, he couldn't sleep. He was also suffering with his teeth again and allowed Ann to give him something for his pain. He knew he was not to take any medication, but Ann assured him this medication would not interfere. What Ann gave him was not for pain!

Rick probably never took any prescriptions more than three or four times since being an adult. And then only for sinuses and recent dental work. He didn't do drugs. He knew nothing about them. He wouldn't have known anything other than an aspirin or Tylenol.

Rick took her word for it. He was hurting so badly and was so exhausted. Yes, another huge mistake. I felt Ann should have known better, but what's done is done. She had taken polygraphs, Rick hadn't. And, of course he told them what he thought he had taken. They immediately ruled it inconclusive and that didn't make him look good at all. This I can accept.

The next polygraph appointment, I took him. We only had to wait less than an hour. Rick and I talked about the importance of him passing it. The problem was, they said he was too angry.

This time I told him no matter what, just stay calm and answer the questions. I came up with a plan of what he should think about when asked if he molested his son. Instead of reacting, think back about when he and his son worked on cars together. He felt sure he could do that. He was called back into the office.

Within ten minutes he was in front of me in the waiting room, eyes the size of half dollars. I jumped up asking what was wrong? He wanted to leave right then and took my arm, practically dragging me out the door. I was angry, thinking surely he didn't blow it again. He sensed my anger and asked me to please hear him out before I chewed him out.

Remember, this was over nine years later. The examiner, Ed, asked Rick why he was so angry? Rick explained of being falsely accused of such a heinous crime. Didn't he have the right to be angry? The examiner looked puzzled, picked up a form, announcing he couldn't understand the anger at Sue, because she had refused to press charges, stating she just wanted him to get some help! Rick grabbed the form and read it. It was the first <u>Preliminary Report</u>. Flabbergasted, Rick asked, "Has my attorney seen this?" The examiner, (another friend of Max's) became visibly uncomfortable, stammering, how he didn't know if Max had or had not, but imagined he did. He then quickly suggested that it wasn't a good idea for Rick to take the test that day, because he could tell he was very upset.

On the ride back he was telling me what all it said. I quickly pulled off the road, looked him in the eyes and asked, "Am I hearing you defend Sue?" Well, yes, he was. He had read where she refused to press charges. "But Rick, think about it!" "This woman accused you of molesting your own son, your YMCA basketball team and all of your nephews. She was to have dropped the divorce, sold all your tools, nine cars, called your customers and testified before the Grand Jury, and she did nothing wrong?" I was convinced and concluded that Sue had finally, perhaps for the first time in her life, lost control of the situation and panicked. Then it hit me. When was this report dated? Nine years ago! I asked if Max ever showed it to him, "No." I had never seen it either. I said, "We're going to talk to Max."

I called him as soon as we got home. I was upset, speaking in an ugly tone, demanding he tell me why we had never seen it. He became very belligerent and angry, but not at me. He was grumbling about how they withheld information, using legal terms and announced, come Monday, he would have the whole thing dropped! Was it possible he had never seen it? With Max, much like Sue, the only thing definite is nothing is definite. But, Max did sound as though he knew what he was talking about, this time. Dare we get excited?

We dared. For nothing. I can't recall how Max phrased it, but in the end, it was only the Prelim, the Final Report was due within five days. I got to see that one over a year later. Rick has still not seen it. But, we weren't finished with the polygraph business yet. A week later we had to return for another one. This time I had to take the examiner $100.00 cash. Why, I asked Max, when the state is paying for it? Max said, "He is afraid Rick might be pulling the wool over his eyes." I was livid, saying "Oh, I see, the money will correct Ed's vision?"

What could I do? I knew I couldn't allow Rick to know this. When Rick had gone to the men's room, I gave the secretary the money. Rick came back as she was handing me my receipt. He was upset, asking what I was doing, giving them money? I lied to my brother! I was forced to. If not, I was risking his state of mind right before a very crucial test, so I told him Max owed Ed the money and he asked me to pay it for him, and he would reimburse me later. Rick bought it!

Rick finished the test, came out to the waiting room with a rather good attitude. I was thrilled. He said he thought it went well. Outside, we ran into Max, spoke for a few minutes, then Max went into the building. Rick said, "Sis, you forgot to get your money back." I had to run after Max and tell him I had lied to Rick about the money and I was playing it out. Then, I smelled the alcohol and asked Max, "What are you doing drinking this time of day and driving? Don't you know that is illegal?" He mumbled "hell with it" or something similar.

When I go back to the truck, I looked in Max's car and there, in plan sight, was his bottle. A huge one, a fifth I think. The man never ceased to amaze or appall me. And, why was he now with the polygraph examiner? Did Max get my $100.00, or what?

It crossed my mind to make a call to the police to warn them about the man driving such and such a car, while under the influence. But I didn't. I wish I had though. If you think he's gotten away with so much now, have I got a surprise in store for you!

I am so exhausted with the many that get away with so much! I know, according to the Bible, I am not to concern myself with this, but again, I'd often like to go about my Father's business.

Everything these "elect" do, leaves at least one person, to pay the price, endure the pain and fight the injustice, directly. Seldom, will there be but one of the elect to face this. The elect think they get off free, but I assure you, there is a price to pay and will, most always, be paid by an innocent person! Are we not all supposed to be created equally? Why should any one be above the law, or have the resourcefulness to do anything they choose, considering no one else.

I know I have already covered this, but it needs to be repeated! They should be held to the same rules, regulations and laws we have to contend with! No one should receive, "A free pass."

Max told Rick, "Hit the road, make money to pay me." Meanwhile, Rick's probation was being revoked? He was going to have to stand trial for sending a Birthday card, and $188.00 final fees, (in arrears) and not finishing his sex counseling! Max didn't care about anything but money. He had no real concern for Rick and his well being!

We were waiting for a Court date, so Rick did return to the road a couple of times, for the money, but brought that to a halt out of love and respect for his Company. It's a good thing and no thanks to Max! Fact is, Max was furious at Rick for refusing to return to the road! But, again, Max would get even for that decision.

CHAPTER 41
AN ESCAPE ROUTE!

The end of May Rick called me. I knew by his tone it was bad. I sat down, whispered a prayer and asked him what was wrong. He said Max had just called saying the DA didn't give a damn about that card. If Rick would confess to the crime, they would drop the Revocation and reinstate his probation. I asked him, "What do you want to do, brother?" A long pause, then a cracking voice said, "Sis, how can I confess to something I never did?" "I can't believe, after over nine years, they still want a confession to a crime I didn't commit." "But sis, Max says if I don't take it, they are going for ninety-nine years in prison, that's life!"

I fought for every breath I took. Neither one of us were saying a word, for minutes. Finally, I asked him when he had to give them an answer. "By noon," he replied. It was now 9:30 in the morning. Noon huh? "Brother, I guess you need to do some thinking and praying and I'll do the same on this end." We hung up. The last thing Rick said was, "Please don't tell mother."

Oh, what a morning! I did not tell mother. I was so torn up, I knew in my heart he would never do it to save himself, even if it was a life sentence.

At eleven O'clock, the phone rang again. It was Rick. Max was furious with Rick, for saying "NO!" He told me, "Sis, I would rather die in prison knowing I am innocent, than to give my son a reason to doubt me, even though I'm sure Sue has brainwashed him. I refuse to give that woman anymore ammunition. I'll take my chances."

I was right! I knew he wouldn't play their game! I was scared, of course, but so proud of Rick! He had a way out and chose his son over his own life! Is this a criminal, sick father and husband?

I told him I knew in my heart, the DA would not go for ninety-nine years anyway. He asked me if the Lord told me that? I couldn't say yes, but I couldn't say no, either. The best way to explain it was, in my heart, I simply knew it. They didn't either, asking for only five years!

I know, you are asking why would we keep this attorney? Well, Rick visited two other attorneys on two trips home. They each wanted the

case, but also a retainer fee of no less than $5,000.00, which no one had. I too, had checked with some. Like it or not, we were stuck with good old Max! Plus, Max had all the records, so we thought.

Each time Rick came home, either Max would check for the Warrant or have Ann and I to check the County Sheriff's Office, to see if the Warrant showed up. He even gave us the phone number to the Sheriff's Office, but the Warrant never did come up, outside of the county. Rick tolerated this for a while. Never was he pleased with the situation, nor any of us, save for Max, all he carried about was money! Never concerned with how we came about it.

I still thank God that Rick was never stopped by the DOT. His timing was perfect. He knew when to terminate placing his company in such an awful and potentially expensive situation. I know our prayers covered him. The hazardous position Max kept Rick in, all for that almighty dollar!

CHAPTER 42
A HEARING WITHOUT THE ATTORNEY

Finally, we had a Court date. For all the good that would do! Max was at Rick's place with us until after midnight.(the night before). Yes, Max was drunk and demanding more money, after I, alone, had given him $1,500.00 and Rick well over a thousand, but Max claimed Rick still owed him another hundred dollars.

Rick had a min-pin dog that Max wanted badly, offering numerous times to buy it, but Rick was nuts over that dog, taking him on every trip. That night, Max pressured Rick into settling his bill for the hundred, with Max giving him $200.00. This meant the bill was paid and Max gave him ninety dollars, saying he owed Rick another ten dollars. Rick was devastated when Max left with his dog, asking me, "What else could I do?"

I walked out to the car with Max as he was leaving. I did somewhat threaten him about the hearing the next day. I felt in my heart he was not prepared, and that he was in over his head. All along, I was to be the number one witness. He said he was ready. Was I? "You bet I am." But, he didn't want to talk about the hearing. No, he wanted to know why I had remarried? My reply was, "That's none of your business Max. You have bigger problems than my state of happiness, be it single or married," and went back inside.

We were to meet for breakfast, fifteen minutes from the Courthouse, at 7:30 AM. We arrived ten minutes early. We waited, waited and waited. At 7:45 I began calling Max. I never received an answer, just a machine. Okay, he's running late, never on time, but my stomach told me other-wise. I called four times, to no avail. It was now 8:40. We had to go ahead. Perhaps Max was running so late that he would just meet up with us at the Courthouse. Wrong again!

Upon not seeing Max or his car, we remembered what he told us about not going in. I parked three blocks away, telling Rick to stay in the truck. Ann and I would go see what we could find out. It was shocking and we overheard the discussion. No more continuances. Issue the Warrant. We then recognized many that were there. It looked as if we were walking

139

into an ambush. We saw the Sex Counselor, the Probation Supervisor, both Human Services/CPS idiots, MR. J and MRS. P. And Sue with her drug dealing friend. One of them recognized Ann and asked where Rick was. Ann replied she didn't know, that she was looking for him, too. We got out of there quickly.

Back at the truck, we jumped in, yelling at Rick to hit the floor, so he couldn't be seen. I was a basket case all the way back to their place. I took several different roads in case we were being followed. I wasn't sure if they knew my truck or not. Poor Rick. He had to wait for all the details and it was so arduous with both of us talking at the same time.

I hit the door grabbing the phone, calling Max, this time he answered! I was not kind. I was not in control. I had just left what appeared to be a lynching mob. Where the hell had he been? Oh, poor Max. He had spent the entire night fighting with his common-law-wife! He was so exhausted! But, not to worry, he would call his buddy, the Judge, and fix things. I told him I didn't think so. I had heard his buddy say, "That's it, no more continuances." I told him who all was there to Max's amazement. Max told me, "well it was a good thing I wasn't there. Now I know what I am up against and I can be prepared!" If that was how they wanted to play, he would play the same game! Was this a joke? What had he expected to begin with, a tea party?

I asked Max just what Rick was supposed to do now, after hearing about the Warrant? He told me to call and check on the status of the Warrant. I screamed, "No, I will not. Do your own job." I hung up on him. Max called back in less than ten minutes saying, "There is no Warrant, tell Rick to get back out on the road to pay me." This time I didn't say a word, I simply hung up on him. I told Rick what Max said with Rick's face turning ash white. Rick said. "Sis, I can't do that to my company. If I get pulled over or even go through a scale and a Warrant comes up, the DOT will impound the truck, a $1,000,000.00 truck, with someone having be dispatched to get it, costing my company a fortune. I cannot put them in that position." In short, Rick refused to go.

I called Max, informing him of Rick's decision. Max didn't like it and came up with another idea. Max had another buddy, Sam. The top-dog in the field of sex thearpy. Max had made an appointment for Rick that evening.

I took Rick to this meeting to seek my own satisfaction. I didn't want him driving and I wanted to see for myself, if this Sam would come through. I met him upon arrival and conversed with him a bit before we left. Yes, he agreed to take Rick on and to testify on Rick's behalf. As we were leaving, Max said to me, "Okay, see what I've done? Now you can go back home. All is under control and Rick can get back on the road." He was sure, that should this man take the stand for Rick, all would be fine.

I left late that night to return home. A long, long, drive home. Many questions were eating at me. Could we possibly trust Max again? Yes, I had to confess, the man we met appeared to be very professional and kind. I admit, a couple of times I was tempted to turn around and go back, but not sure why. I felt needed in both places, but came to the conclusion, that was impossible.

I knew I was needed at home. The folk's health, my husband, who always covered for me, but this was a busy time for him. Okay, I would come on home, praying that, for once, Max could back up one thing he said, with positive results. He did seem quite confident and with my confronting him, perhaps he could pull this off. Only time would tell. I wasn't aware time had already run out!

I was awakened by the phone. It was Rick. The Police had just left their place. Ann had answered the door, saying exactly what Max had instructed us to do. Ann told them Rick was with his attorney. Rick was scared, but added how happy he was that he had not gone back out on the road. We agreed we had no idea what would follow, but I asked him to keep in touch with me. Rick promised he would. But, I wouldn't hear from Rick again. I would hear from a very hysterical Ann, about fifteen minutes later, while Rick was being arrested!

On my second cup of coffee, the phone rang and I knew it wasn't going to be good. At first I didn't know who it was. The voice wasn't audible, but I quickly figured it out. I knew in my heart what was happening. Ann was crying so hard, and I could hear remarks in the background. Rick had just been arrested. They were still there, hammering Ann about what a criminal Rick was. They were angry with her for not believing Rick guilty. I heard some of the cruel remarks made! I was appalled to say the least. I truly believe God didn't want me there for this! What I could hear was bad enough!

I asked, where is Max? Ann said the Police told her they went there, to learn that not only was Rick not there, but Max responded, "Hell, he ain't here. He's at home packing, to go back out on the road." Max then suggested the police search his own house for Rick! Yes, this was our fine, experienced attorney! With all his buddies down there. God forgive my thinking, "with attorneys like this, all you need is an AK47 and no witnesses!" God forgive me, I know. Terrible talk for a Christian, but remember, I am human too. This was my brother's life! Christianity doesn't mean you will not have hard times, like being angry and human, but it will get you through it! My only consolation is that God hates injustice also!

In short, Rick was arrested because Max failed to show for Court! Our crime was accepting some really bad advise from an inept attorney. Because of this, Rick agreed it made him look guilty, in that he didn't turn himself in, as he had planned on doing. And for not returning Cary's phone call, with his offer of help!

Cary, here where I live, tried to help Rick and called him. Rick wasn't home but Ann took the information and said she would see that Rick got it. Rick did get it, but unfortunately, he had spoken with Max. Max threw a fit saying it was a setup, threatening Rick to not even return the call! I did not believe it, then, and I don't believe it, now. Cary is an upright guy. Max and I had words over that too. Max actually attempted to pit Cary and me against one another. Now I know why.

Max told me that Cary was hurting Rick's case. I argued in defense of Cary and Max didn't appreciate that. Max wanted me to call Cary, and request he write Max a letter for the Court. Max actually insinuated how I was to dictate to Cary what he was to write! In a very ugly tone, Max said, "I know you think this guy is so great, so call your buddy and get this done, now!"

Cary had already written one letter. But Max said it wasn't good enough. I read the letter and it was not bad, vague in some areas, but honest. I feel in my heart, Cary felt Rick betrayed him. I understand from his point of view, why he would feel that way. I have told Cary, repeatedly, he would one day come face to face with the truth. I so long for that day of redemption! Meanwhile, I cannot say anything derogatory about him.

I am as convinced today as I was then, that Cary truly attempted to help Rick and not to hurt him in any way. Again, Cary got caught up in a nest of hornets. Cary had to protect himself also.

I know he has a few pieces of the puzzle, but those pieces missing will on day come together.

CHAPTER 43
A JUDICIAL CIRCUS!

A couple of weeks prior to the Revocation Hearing, I wrote several letters to Cary and Max.

Each letter I wrote to one, I sent a cc to the other. Max had pitted me against Cary. Max swore Cary had turned on us. I wanted so badly to make Cary aware of what really happened. I blasted Max with threats and informed him of my suspicions of his inadequacies. In retrospect, I truly believe in writing those letters and threatening Max, I am sure I hurt Rick's case. Max was too afraid to put me on the witness stand, seeing it as too big a risk. I knew I had intimidated him to the point he couldn't afford to risk what I might have said.

However, having been there in the Courtroom and seeing Max's aberrant defense. I can't believe I just used the term, defense. There was no defense and I mean none! Only after arriving for the hearing, did I learn, I would not be taking the stand in defense of Rick!

My husband took three days off in order to attend the hearing with me. Excuse me, the Circus! The day before the hearing, my husband and I paid $260.00 for the late fees. (fine and probation fees) We didn't think it would hurt to get that off the books. Only to learn during the hearing, the amount was $188.00. Yes, I was over-charged and no, I will never see the money.

The hearing opened with the reading of the charges, the Birthday card, his final fees and Rick's refusal to report to his Probation Officer, that he didn't have for two years! Then Rick was asked how he would plead, true or not true? Max leaned over and said something to Rick. Rick then said, "True." I came out of my seat and Max immediately leaned back over, and said something, when Rick spoke, "I'm sorry your honor, "Not True." My husband and I just looked at each other. The writing was on the wall!

What really infuriated me, was how the Judge was nasty enough to make his remark, (during the hearing) "Apparently, your mother came by and paid your late fees." I wanted to stand up with my own remarks of, **"Rick's mother paid nothing. She isn't physically able to be here. I paid the fees, over and above the actual amount, so if you like, you**

big-mouthed, arrogant, prejudiced, inept Judge, I will gladly accept a refund, which I highly suspect, is already in your pocket!" Yes, again, I confess to anger and the temptation to retaliate.

The DA opened with a lie, in that Rick refused to report for probation, for almost two years! <u>All in a Court of law, are under an oath</u>. Max didn't even object. Rick didn't have a Probation Officer. He had forms to send in, until he was assigned one. I have the forms!

What about the expert witness? Well, the hearing ran very late and at a break period, Max informed me the expert witness, Sam, was losing money by being there. I had to write a check for $200.00 and was to send another $150.00 when I got home! When Sam did take the stand, he basically testified against Rick! You think I sent Sam that extra money? Not on your life.

When Tim, the Probation Supervisor was on the stand, Max jumped him about Tim forcing Rick to register as a sex offender. The egotistical witness leaned over, with a sarcastic grin, with a reply, "MR. Max, you told him to sign it." That was true, Max did order Rick to sign it!

When Brad, the Sex Counselor took the stand, Max accused him of being more concerned with the fees Rick owed him, than Rick's well being. Max argued how the Counselor did allow Rick to go back out on the road, didn't he? "Yes, he did. Brad claimed that Rick needed the money!

Max should have beaten Counselor Brad into the floor with his own words. The guy wasn't qualified to make any decisions or to even diagnose Rick, let alone treat him. Max never dealt with that fact! And, if Rick was such a menacing danger to the public, why would he be allowed to return too driving across the nation?

Ann took the stand to verify Rick's signature! <u>The Prosecution's best witness was the witness for the defense! Max's witness</u>. While Ann was on the stand, Sue was sitting just down from me, and pretty much right behind me. I heard her saying to her drug dealing friend, as she ran her fingers through her hair. "Oh my God, forty years is such a long time, but I just want him out of my life." Have you any idea what went through my mind? I wanted to grab her and choke her until she told the absolute truth!

Then, Sue took the stand with an Academy Award winning performance. She was great, I have to admit! I especially appreciated her nervousness when she was asked to speak up. Her reply, "Oh, I'm sorry, I'm just very nervous," in such a fragile tone. Sue's best line was in her telling the Judge how she got a call, on her cell phone, from the children, saying there was a card from Rick. (my thoughts) Good Lord, Rick sent cards every year for nine years! Rick had always put money in them, but that year, he simply didn't have it. Why was Sue not frightened all those other years or wait until little Rick was almost fourteen years old before she cried, <u>WOLF!</u> Why was she not frightened previously? Why didn't she file a complaint sooner, when the children were younger? Jeff was now twenty years old! And, Max was aware of the cards being sent all along!

Poor Sue, frightened and appearing very reticent. Sue continued to testify of her fear that Rick was there at the house with a gun, perhaps. And how desperate she was to get home to the hysterical, frightened children. A gun? Rick never owned a gun, but Sue sure did. Remember?

This woman, bold as any man I've ever known. Remember, Sue held a gun to Rick's head years earlier? Sue accused Rick of a crime she knew he never committed. Now, she sat in Court looking like the most frail, frightened, meek little mouse you would ever see. I looked at Rick's face and witnessed utter defeat. He knew she beat him and I saw him give up.

Rick chose prison over confessing to a crime he was innocent of, to spare his son. He took the fall. He was found guilty and sentenced to twenty years, consecutive. A setup for the three strikes and you're out in Texas. Max did ask for the jail days credit and got it, but didn't have enough sense to Appeal! Really! I have the document. Appeal: NONE. This would disable any newly hired attorney, drastically, in seeking any type of appeal! Max did see to it that without seeking or asking for an "Appeal," making it an almost impossibility, for sure!

I don't recall much after that except for two incidents. One was Max asking me if I realized he had done his best. As I recall, I told him, "Max, not only are you fired, but I suggest you grab your butt and run. I am taking over now."

At the elevator I saw Sue with the Probation Supervisor, Tim and her friend. I had heard rumors of Sue being involved with Tim, intimately. I was furious and couldn't resist what I was feeling. I spoke up, "Sue, I know you think you just won, but I am informing you that I just fired Max and I am taking over. Now you will be dealing with me and it won't be pretty. This is not a threat, but a simple promise." The next thing I heard Sue was trying to go to the South Pacific. It's been very difficult to track her down, as she continues to use all four names she has had. But, I will not give up!

I had to come home and inform our mother that her son was sent to prison for twenty years!

That was as bad as my trip, two months ago, to tell Rick that mother is dying. We tried to spare him as much as possible, but when it came down to the Doctors giving her four months to live, sis and I decided we had to prepare him. For months we had been getting letters from him stating his fear was that she would die before he got to hug her again. That was heartbreaking enough. I pray I never have to go through that again.

As I said, I returned with the bad news and spent every minute I had just to be there for her. But, I was not going to accept the gross injustice I had witnessed. I would find another attorney. A real one and fight back!

The day after Rick's revocation hearing, he fired Max, demanding his files. Max showed up the very next day with the files. They consisted of <u>five pages</u> of the revocation hearing, having had defending Rick for <u>nine years</u>! Rick's total worth amounted to <u>five pages</u>?

The next day I caught Max on his cell phone. I began yelling and demanding Rick's files. His response was, "For God's sake Clar, I'm on my way to Court and my client killed himself last night." I hated hearing that, as I had met him a couple of weeks earlier, but as I told Max, "I'm very sorry he is dead, but my brother is still alive, sentenced to twenty years and I hold you to blame for that. Now, I want those files and I want them now!" I'll never forget his reply, <u>"Well hell Clar, it's going to take me some time. My God, they are in my archives."</u>

Wait a minute, <u>he just represented Rick in a Court of law two days previously, but Rick's files are in his archives?</u> It certainly explained his complete incompetence and lack of knowledge! Of all the nerve! In his archives? Hello, is this BR-549? What audacity. Wait. I am being too kind here. What an idiot! Was this man capable of anything more than handling a traffic ticket, if that?

Max never put him on the stand, nor me. He didn't object when he should have and in reality, Max placed the case into the hands of the DA, as though it was a gift!

In retrospect, I feel so stupid and naive, but that is in the past. Now I'm learning more daily. I have written so many letters and spent so much time on my computer, I am no longer an idiot! But, did I ever pay a price for my ignorance! Please understand, we didn't know the first thing about Criminal Law! We never had a reason too. Whoever said "Ignorance is bliss," must have been an attorney, because that is a lie from hell and I can testify to that!

I watched the hearing on Capitol Hill. C-SPAN broadcast the nightmare of that poor man that spent thirty-three years in prison with the FBI and the Police knowing he was innocent. But, they all chose to protect a real criminal, a drug informant, other than sparing that poor innocent man from prison! I cannot recall his name, but the faces of him and his wife will forever be engraved in my mind. All those years he was denied of, seeing his children grow up. I am overwhelmed with the loving devotion, he received from his wife. Wow, she's so incredible. I feel for her and admire her, immensely.

Another abomination and it doesn't stop there! It continues to worsen, but until you are directly involved, or one of your loved ones, you tend to keep your heads in the sand. Are we to believe this seldom ever happens in America? What will it take to awaken you to reality? Wake up, before it's too late! It is happening daily right under your nose. The injustice and corruption will continue until we do something about it.

CHAPTER 44
LET'S LEARN MORE ABOUT SUE!

Bill Jr. was extremely reluctant to believe Sue's accusations. Rick had stopped at a store near his shop and ran into Bill Jr. Bill Jr. sure expressed joy in seeing Rick, but kept turning to look for his mother's whereabouts. Rick asked him what was going on, but before Bill could reply, Sue was right there. Sue was very upset, grabbing Bill and all he could do was shrug his shoulders as he looked back at Rick. Less than two weeks later Bill Jr., was sent out of town, to his father. Sue had to get rid of him. Apparently Bill Jr. had refused to testify against Rick.

When I say this woman is obsessed with mind control, I know of what I speak. After the joke, better known as the "Revocation Hearing." I called Sue's house about a month later. I wanted to know and I had promised Rick, I would find a way to check up on the children.

I spoke with Bill Jr. He had been in the service. He sounded so grown up. I asked Bill Jr. if my call would be a problem with Sue. I simply wished to know how there were doing. Bill Jr. said he felt it was all right for me to call, knowing I didn't wish to upset his mother. He said she wasn't home and that he was happy I called, because he wanted to talk to me.

Eventually, Rick's name came up. I recall Bill saying something to the effect of, "After Rick did that." I wasn't going to listen to such and told him he knew better than to believe that crap! I asked how he and his mother were getting along. He replied great! Great? I had to ask him, "Is this the same young boy that I would console, listening to threats of anger, wanting his mother dead, for the way she treated him?" He actually thought for a moment and answered, "Wow, Aunt Clar, I had forgotten all about that." I said she is good, but possibly all the counseling helped too. I want to believe she has changed, especially improving in motherhood! But, I wouldn't hold my breath.

As for the Policeman's car door, Sue claimed she kicked in, on I-45. I have found nothing. And, as for the woman she said she ran over in college, I came up empty, again.

I checked the town where Sue attended college. I called every Realtor listed. I spoke with every one I could get on the phone. I spoke with two gentlemen and one female, and they gave me two names, saying both had left the area many years ago. There did seem to be questions regarding each one of them, but of course, they would not elaborate. All stated, how many years back, this might have occurred, how several had died and some had retired. One, seemed to me, to be too uncomfortable and although kind, he hung up on me.

I tried going through the college to find her, but because of specific information required, I had no access. I was unable to complete my search. Therefore, I must stress at this time, these issues must be considered as speculations or possibilities only.

Need I tell you how seriously I take false accusations? I cannot accuse her of any of these events. I have to be honest, in that I cannot prove them, yet. Another reason I have attempted, with such determination, in locating her first and second husband is, that I know the first husband was directly involved with Sue at the time she ran over the woman. When Sue lived with her girlfriend, prior to Sue sleeping with the Realtor father, in Las Vegas, then thrown out. I want that data!

I know the hell she had placed the second one in. I know he has information that could be invaluable in my efforts to expose her. But, I can't blame him for not wanting to be found. I feel, in my heart, I would want to stay as far from her as possible, too. Sue is the type of woman that goes out of her way to burn her bridges. Sue would put a snake in your pocket, then ask you for a match!

I did find Sue's marriage and divorce to the second husband. I still cannot find any data on the first one. I am beginning to think there was no first one. I still question who the oldest son's father is, as well as his real name! Next, I did an in depth search on Sue and those residing in that house in 1998. I found two new names. An Alan Jr. I found the Sr. in a small town about forty miles away! Did Sue really send Bill Jr. to another state or perhaps to this small town? Could this Sr. be Bill's father? I called, only to learn the phone had been disconnected! I wrote him a letter and it was returned with no forwarding address.

It took me five years to find the second one. (Wendy and Jeff's father.) Finally, I found him! He was now living in a suburb outside a large city in TX. I called repeatedly for two weeks. I never got an answer nor an answering machine. So, I wrote him a letter. Another letter returned and no forwarding address! I was so close, for nothing. I will not give up. Somewhere there <u>has</u> to be one willing to stand up to this woman!

The other unknown person was a female, according to the name. She has a valid Texas Drivers license, but height, weight, eye color and race were <u>unknown</u>! That is a full house. At least eight people living there and I am not counting Sue's brother. I have no clue as to his whereabouts. I did hear that the AWOL charges were eventually dropped.

I heard that little Rick left home a couple of years ago. DeDe tried to find him, but without succeeding. That leaves the youngest one, about fifteen years old now. I honestly pray when Sue's number comes up, that none of the children will be around to witness it. I can only imagine that!

As of this writing, as far as I can ascertain, Sue and the children no longer resides in that house. My husband took me by the house a little over a year after Rick's conviction. I was astonished and confused. The house I saw had been remodeled and certainly not an eye sore. It was quite nice, with a long running porch all across the front and a nice sports car in the drive. The house was so beyond recognition that I was sure it was the wrong place. The area had sure grown and I was convinced that I was on the wrong road. After three drive-bys. I finally walked up to the mailbox for assurance. It was the same house! Ellie's name was on the mailbox. That once plain ugly, dark, trashy house had become so pleasant to the eye.

Immediately, my shock turned to fury. Where did they get the money for such a renovation? I thought it too coincidental that Rick had been convicted and they had come into some money! A lot of money! That renovation was expensive and no one in the family had any skills in which to do such!

One day, Sue will mess with the wrong person and I want to be informed. I hesitate in saying, I want to be that person. I don't wish to be "the wrong person," but, I do want to redeem Rick. I don't wish to hurt the children and prefer to keep my hands as clean as possible. I do find relief in all of the children being so much older now. I would really rather see Sue hang herself, than my doing it. I've always heard, "Give a person enough rope and they will hang themselves." It's been fifteen years now and I am still waiting.

CHAPTER 45
IT'S MY TURN NOW!

I got on my computer and began pulling up web sites by the dozens! I had no idea of the many that are falsely accused. It does tend to look like the new <u>National Pastime</u>! Check out Al White's THE- FACTS. (Falsely Accused Citizens in Today's Society.) He is a Vietnam Veteran in California. Al had set out to put the accused away for life. But, a funny thing happened along the way. He would learn of the startling facts of the enormous accusations that proved to be false. California Politicians hate this man. They hate him so badly, they have tried to make his life hell. You see, Al is now a Crusader, fighting for the rights of those falsely accused. And, for the children removed from homes only to be sent to unsafe homes. Al has learned what an enterprise foster child care is and how corrupt it too has become! This man collects aluminum cans for funds to aid those in need! He is a real Hero to me and I'm sure many others. You go Al!

Then, there is Dean Tong with his site and his story of the hell he suffered. Praise God, he was one of the few to win! However, he paid a tremendous price legally, emotionally and financially. Bravo, Dean and thank you for all your help. His book is "Ashes to Ashes: Family to Dust." His plight began, as with my brother's, when Dean's wife wanted a divorce, accusing him of the same thing. I strongly encourage you to read his book, or at least check out his web site. He finally won, but check out the price he paid!

I found a Consulting firm in N. Y. I spoke with them for several days and hired them. I was sent an attorney, Tom, from Annapolis MD. He flew in the last of July, (on a Friday) for three days, to evaluate the situation and help me find an attorney here in Texas. (However, I had already found Gerald, an attorney in Texas.) I had spoken to Gerald before Tom arrived. I had a good feeling that he was indeed, a good man. Gerald didn't appear to be a typical lawyer and I was right.

Tom went to the County where Rick was, the same day he arrived. He went to the Courthouse requesting any and all records. They were remodeling, files in basement, scattered and yada, yada. Tom leaned over the counter asking, "Where is the DA's office?" They told him where it was, he then said, "Thank you, I will be back in one hour and you will have the records!" The DA wasn't in, so we checked out a couple of attorneys. We were not impressed, feeling the town too tightly bound. That didn't bother me at all, as I was still leaning toward Gerald, and he agreed to meet us at the Airport the next day.

We returned to the Courthouse and sure enough, they were able to find a lot of the files. Tom and I then went to the jail to meet and visit with Rick. Rick and I really liked Tom. Tom couldn't work Rick's case on his out of state license.

Saturday, Tom and I met Gerald. We spend hours in the Airport, going over all the records Tom had managed to get. I saw files, letters, motions and documents. I couldn't believe it. I hadn't seen any of them prior to that day. I sat, listening in awe, to these two Professionals.

Tom agreed Gerald was the man for the job! Now remember, Rick had just been sentenced twenty-two days ago. For some unknown reason, Sunday night, in the wee hours, he was sent to a transfer facility, by private van. Not on a bus like others. In fact, he left the other cell-mates, that had been waiting four to six months to be transferred! Why was it so imperative that they get Rick out of town, again by private van, using the tax payer dollars, unless they had something to hide? Plus, once Rick was in the system it would take years to get him out! Texas knows exactly what they are doing!

The prison was one hundred fifty miles from me and of course, I had a waiting period before we could visit. By phone at first, with a glass between us. It would be months before we could have contact visits.

Rick chose to go to prison rather than confessing to something he didn't do. Something he was not capable of doing! Max said that the County would drop the Revocation Hearing and reinstate the probation if he would confess. He wouldn't do this, but choosing to leave his family, job and ailing mother, to go to prison, rather than to confess to something so awful!

After his sentence, two detectives went to the south unit, where Rick had been placed. They said they wouldn't leave without that much desired confession. Rick told the investigators he hoped they had packed well for their trip, because they would be there as long as he would! Why, I ask, was that confession so important after over nine years of their pursuing one? Rick had been given seven years probation and just sentenced to twenty years! They had tried everything they could think of, to get that confession. They didn't then, nor will they ever! But, why is it still so important?

Sadly, many children are sexually abused. Little Rick wasn't, at least, not by his father. I know this! I find it inexcusable! Not a child in this world deserves such a ghastly crime. To our horror, we do fear, most likely, little Rick was abused. We can only wonder who would have done it.

Now, somebody please tell me how Rick being imprisoned helps the situation any? I have prayed that all the counseling, Sue and the children received, has helped, but who knows? Did Sue's brother receive any counseling? Not to our knowledge. Rick, having been in prison almost six years now, has had no help offered! Were he guilty, what good would twenty years in prison do for the potential victims that will be out there, upon Rick's release?

Thank God, Rick is not a threat. What about the guilty ones that are released, only to repeat the same crime, generally within six months? Again, prison does no good, (other than to enrich the state, provide jobs, generally for unqualified employees and line the pockets of the crooks!) As Rick says, "Prison is where you come to learn how to be a real criminal!

Combine this with the "three strikes you're out" ridiculous law. I say ridiculous, because when you put a man back in prison, based on this, it is often an absurdity. These are the prisoners to be feared the most. They are given the message they do not count any longer, therefore, they feel they have nothing to lose. Not only are they a greater threat to other inmates, but worse yet, to the guards that work there. It places the guards and the very public in an even more hazardous environment. Example, the Texas seven!

The state has laid off teachers, guards and cut back on meals, actually, omitting them. With the state receiving anywhere from $37,000.00 to $39.000.00 per inmate, per year. Where is the money? The inmates have no a/c, or hot water. The prison no longer offer pictures being made, at $3.00 each. They used to offer meals, prepared by inmates with the money going to charity. It was great sharing a meal with Rick. All exists no longer, because the money has been mishandled. Always follow the money trail. Thieves in prison and thieves working in the prisons! Rich mix!

The Texas Prison system was so profitable (all through the nineties.) They led the nation's industry! The prison system in Texas is a huge enterprise!

CHAPTER 46
MAX'S LIES, FORGERIES AND EXTORTION!

There are far too many attorneys, out there, doing the same. I strongly suggest that you be very careful! Investigate them before you retain them. Texas, and I suspect every state, has attorneys that should not only be prohibited in being in a Courthouse, but should be in prison themselves.

Actually, many are, but not enough. Yet.

I've been getting a crash course in law, the last two years, since receiving the files from the latest attorney, Gerald. We hired as soon as Max was fired. Bless his heart. He cared so much and tried so hard. With Max's utter failure of not Appealing the Revocation Hearing, refusing to release any of Rick's' files, with no Appeal by Max, Gerald's hands were tied. The first Appeal went back to the same Judge that sentenced him, and it was <u>DENIED!</u> The next one was in the Tenth Court of Appeals. <u>No Jurisdiction</u>. The Writ was denied, because we waited too long in claiming <u>"inadequate"</u> counsel!

I wanted to go Federal, but they just handed down the "sleeping lawyer law." This is when any attorney can sleep through a Capitol Murder Case in Texas, and it's up to the client to keep the lawyer awake! Of course, he is not allowed to take a pillow and blanket into the Courtroom! Gerald felt it would be a waste of time. He is a good, honest, ethical man and stopped the clock with a balance of over $400.00 that he never billed me for. He truly believed it was of no value, at the time. Many attorneys were furious at this and several appealed the ruling.

We came to a point of helplessness. Eventually, Gerald sent me the files. It took me about two years to be able to comprehend what I was attempting to figure out. I finally broke down and prayed that my eyes would be opened.

Then it happened. I began seeing things I hadn't noticed before, with a greater understanding.

I found the first forgery! Gerald couldn't possibly have noticed it. He is very upset over it, though. I am, yet today, convincing him he is not responsible for it.

I began finding all kinds of very suspicious documents and now it was coming together. Pieces of the puzzle I had questioned for so long, were all coming together in a very ugly picture of. no less than, blatant corruption!

I endeavored to not be too hopeful. After all, what did I know about Criminal Law? I am but a lay person. I am capable of comprehending legal documents with forged signatures of my brother. I could no longer camouflage my delight at the findings. Yes, I dared to be excited at what I had in my possession. I was convinced, beyond doubt, somebody would have to deal with this! I held the hammer and Max was the nail! I could not withhold my exhilaration, after all these years!

However, Rick finally informed me as to <u>why he really accepted that "Plea."</u> The night prior to the first court appearance Max told Rick, "If you insist on a trial, then your folks will have to mortgage their land and give me $50,000.00." What a man! Max never did a thing to earn the thousands we had already given him. Max knew Rick would never allow the folks to do such a thing! I thank God Rick finally told me this. I was not to blame, but I could have choked Max! All those years I lived with guilt, thinking I was responsible for Rick's decision!

CHAPTER 47
WORTHLESS FOUND TREASURES

I again read the, "**Application for Probation**." It's a three page document, but I have only page one and two. I had seen it numerous times, but one day I read each page closely and noticed Rick's signature! This time Rick's signature jumped off the page, right into my heart! It was a forgery! He is a lefty and it's very obvious the person that signed his name was the opposite! I know Rick's signature and I don't think anyone could professional forge it. It was not his. Upon further inspection, I noticed the date and alarms went off! Flashing lights, bells and all!

I noticed the date was <u>Feb, but altered to Mar,</u> which was fifteen months prior to Rick ever finally accepting the so called, "Excellent Plea." The name of the Notary was **Judy**. Why did I feel such a connection? Why did it look so familiar? A very common name, but there was something about it I couldn't shake. It continued haunting me for days, to the point I was not able to sleep. I realized this was too big for me. I prayed the Lord would give me the answer I needed and fell asleep.

The very next day it hit me! Max said he would throw <u>Judy</u> out, if I would move in with him! I'd heard that often enough. I knew exactly who she was now, but I had to prove it. I got on my PC and went through the State of Texas Notaries, requesting help in tracing her. I had her full name and expiration date. (From years earlier). After two days, they found two with the same full name, in two other towns and counties. I knew neither of them was her and asked them to please do another check. They were very kind and helpful.

The very next day I got a very nice letter saying they were very sorry, and they did locate another. YES! Bingo! It was her, listed at the same exact address as Max. I was right. She is his common-law-wife! I immediately filed with the State Bar again. Finally, I received a package to fill out and I was now allowed to provide evidence I had. I filled out their forms and was allowed to send attachments of receipts, statements of facts and copies of my documents! I think I sent eleven pages in all. Now, I had to wait, watch and pray.

Just over a month passed by when the letter came. I had "Provided information that alleges misconduct on the part of the lawyer. An Investigatory Counsel has been set up, the lawyer had thirty days in which to respond to me and them, if not, they would provide me with his response. I would be notified of the hearing date." Of course, it was highly confidential. I could only discuss it with my attorney and witnesses! Glory hallelujah! Dare I hope?

No! I was informed, at the last minute, the lawyer appealed my classification, and they would get back with me. About a month later, the State Supreme Court ruled against me on that "four year statue of limitations." No hearing date and no response from Max or them. The letter said "Case closed," "Files destroyed!"

I replied with two nasty letters and two e-mails. Another letter, from them arrived. This time I was told, I "Could Amend my Complaint, if you wish!" Are you kidding? I wished and filed again, asking how I could do this, with the "Files destroyed?" Wouldn't I need to send them duplicate copies of everything? What is an amended complaint? No reply.

Meanwhile, I found additional evidence which included even more errors and questionable documents. My concern was, would I have any chance of an honest investigation or any hearing if the files had been destroyed?

We had to place our parents in a Nursing Home. I had to sell the land. In clearing out the place, I found more papers. A letter from Max with an old court date. Plus, a letter from the DA with a new Court date, the next month. The March date, we were told by Max, had been canceled, by the DA. Wait a minute! I rushed home to check the "Application for Probation." It was dated the same day! We were not in Court that day, but good old Max was and very busy! Was this where the idea of Probation came about? From our expert lawyer?

I noticed two different Cause numbers and was told by the MD attorney, Tom, the case had been dropped in March, of that same year. It was picked up again by Human Services/CPS. I see. The case was dropped at the same time of the "Application for Probation," that Rick never knew a thing about, or signed, because we were told "no Court."

I found a "**Waiver of Arraignment, and Reading of the Services and Indictment Cause**." From what I could glean, it had to be done in a Courtroom. Another forged signature! I knew it was not his signature, either, and the date was now April. The old Cause number was scratched through and a new one written above it. This document had the signature of the Judge on it!

I had already filed with the **State Commission on Judicial Conduct**. They had no finding of guilt on the Judge's part, however, if I had any evidence, please submit it. I sent them a copy of the <u>Waiver</u>! The Commission on Judicial Conduct will take forever, to get any results on.

I did another search on my PC and found a web link for TX attorneys. I learned that Max was on probation, for two years, in the midst of Rick's revocation hearing. No, he did not have to inform us! A week later, I found another site and from it I learned that Max is no longer eligible to practice law in the state of Texas!

I sent the form to Rick, asking if he had seen it before. Did he sign it and did he know Judy? To no surprise, Rick was furious. No, he had not seen it. No, it was not his signature. Rick stated that he didn't meet Judy until three years later! He was asking me to look at the date? Like I hadn't noticed. So, I asked him to send me a letter of verification.

It got better. I found a letter from the Judge, to Max, stating a Court date of April. Actually, it was a letter from Max, to the Judge, regarding a motion Max made. Max asked the Courts to conduct a competency hearing for little Rick. The Judge circled the request and wrote, <u>Denied</u>. Then he initialed it. The date matched the date on the "<u>Waiver!</u>"

We were unaware of the date. Unlike the first time, Max didn't bother to inform us of this date. Once again, Max was there again and quite busy, with several other documents all dated the same day! I fired off copies of every piece I had. In fact, I faxed it right to the State Bar. Okay, another letter of, <u>information that alleges misconduct on the part of the lawyer</u>. I asked about the "<u>Two Year Discovery of New Evidence</u>." A month later, same thing. Another Counsel set up yada, yada. Max has thirty days in which to respond to each of us. Wait! I heard that before and have yet to get any response from him. The State Bar promised if I didn't, they would get me one. Not so far. I don't expect to get a word from him. I don't want to <u>hear</u> from him. I want to <u>see</u> him in Court!

I sent a copy of the Waiver to Rick, asking the same questions. No, Rick had never seen it and furthermore, it was not his signature. He was shocked to see he was to have been in Court on that day. Rick sent me another letter of verification. I forwarded everything to the Office of the Chief Disciplinary Counsel.

CHAPTER 48
THE WORTHLESS STATE BAR OF TEXAS

I have held back on this book in order to allow the State Bar to do their job. Obviously, that's not likely to happen. I just received word Max, has once again appealed my classification and they will get back with me! The day prior to the last letter from the Bar, (with a new date) I faxed another eight pages to them. I didn't take the latest news well, at all.

Another sizzling letter to them, demanding to know, "On what grounds was he appealing now?" I have informed them numerous times of this book and that I intend to announce; **"In Texas, any attorney can lie, cheat, steal, exhort, forge and embezzle money, as long as he can cover his butt for the four year statue of limitations, with the Seal of Approval of the Texas State Bar!"** I want some answers, now! Gerald told me he would be my witness and that it would be far better. As an attorney, he can testify how Max refused all his phone calls, faxes, mail, (regular, certified and registered) in order to refuse to release Rick's files to him!

To their credit, I was awakened early Thursday Morning, the 4th, 2003. (having been up all night working on this book). It was female Investigator with the State Bar. Very kind, actually very nice, telling me Max was granted the appeal, due to health reasons. He has until the 9th, 2003! The Investigator, asked me if I would allow two or three more days following, for his response. Max's response? That's an interesting story in it's self. I asked if she received my fax, and she replied, "Just the first two pages." I faxed them again, the very next day. There were eight pages proving, beyond doubt, Max not only sold Rick out, but broke the law in order to do it!

This is cold, I know, but my first thought in hearing, "his health" was that Max is a very heavy drinker! Worse yet, I fear he will die before I can get anything done! No matter what, I have told all I have written to and spoken to, "I will not be silent and I will not go away!"

Both times I have "provided evidence to allege misconduct on the part of the lawyer," I was to give Max thirty days to respond to them and me. I wrote a letter a couple of weeks ago, asking why I was told this each time. I had yet to receive the first one. The Bar said, each time, if after the thirty days, had I not received a response, I was to inform them and they would get it for me! Still, I have not received one, from either. I was also to have a hearing each time. They have yet to follow through with anything that they have said would transpire!

The day before the Bar called, I was notified that Hospice has been called in for our mother! Yes, I am scared. I know we are losing her, but I know the Lord will get me through it. Not pain free, but He loves a broken heart and she is in such bad shape. I have to wonder if I am being selfish wanting to keep her. I want my innocent brother back home where he belongs! I fear what losing mother might do to Rick. He has written for over a year, about how he fears she will die before he gets to hold her again. That, I am trusting the Lord for. I could easily blame them for mother's two stokes, but I refuse to play that "Blame game," which I hate so immensely. It could possibly not be accurate. I could also yell VICTIM, too. I don't have the answers, but have seen her health and her pain, all these years and though I am angry, I will not play that "Blame Game," with them!

It just doesn't get any better. Now I am forced to fight the Board of Pardons and Paroles! For something I don't want, to begin with. Is there no shame? Doesn't anyone care if an innocent man is in prison? NO!

CHAPTER 49
FIGHTING FOR A PAROLE WE DON'T WANT!

Last spring Rick was up for Parole, **denied**. And set off until 2006! I received the print out form of why, with all their ridiculous codes! I read it and went into shock, then fury. Upon seeing terms of the code of 2d. "Violent, repeated crimes, brutality, with the use of a weapon!" Actually, I did begin to feel better, I was convinced they had gotten Rick's files mixed with another file. Okay, I can do something about this.

I began writing more letters, making phone calls and sending copies of all I was doing with the State Departments. I wrote Rick Perry, our State Attorney General at the time, and again, since becoming our Governor. Each time I received letters from each elected office. Apparently, they couldn't help me, expressing compassion and making suggestions. DeDe Keith of the Governor's office, twice, forwarded my letters to Gerald Garrett, Chairman of Parole & Pardons. As did the gentleman, MR. McElyea, TDCJ, in Austin Parole Division. McElyea informed me of his receipt of what I had sent to the Governor's Office. McElyea assured me they would be placed in my brother's file for review by the Parole Board Members. Upon firing off another letter demanding to know when they would be viewed, MR. McElyea called me to explain I was dealing with the wrong Department. I should contact Gerald Garrett, directly. I will explain the rest later.

Attorney General, Greg Abbott, couldn't help either, but had a wonderful employee call me, just for moral support! I was in awe, even though she said there was nothing they could do. She said my letter kept her up until 3: 00 AM. I assured her I didn't think MR. Abbott would see it, but she said I was wrong. She took it to him and he did read it. He was moved and told her to call me! I am including this in order to show my appreciation for such kindness. So refreshing!

Senator John Cornyn, (former Attorney General, now our Senator) having written both offices, directed me to the State Commission on Judicial Conduct, in which I filed a complaint with.

As for Martin Frost, he thanked me for "Bringing this matter to my attention, but since your problem is regulated <u>locally</u>, rather than by the federal government," he had taken the liberty of forwarding my letter to <u>Allen Polunsky, Chairman, Texas Board of Criminal Justice</u>. I wrote MR. Polunsky also, twice. No response, to date. But, it's only been four to five years so far!

Max Sandlin is my Democratic Congressmen who considered it as family law, and he could do nothing with state law. As a courtesy to me, he forwarded my letter to Representative, Teleford. I wrote him, never getting a response! I didn't expect one, though. Why do we have Congressmen, if not to help us? And family law? What a joke, it's called corruption of law! By the way, I love getting all of your re-election propaganda mailings, which are from two to four pages, but you never state which party you are with. Oversight or embarrassment, This also includes all of the e-mails I get, without the opportunity to reply. They are always undeliverable. Hit and run!

Senator Phil Gramm, who in turn, directed me to the Texas State Bar. Oh yes, that would be a smart move! But the man cared enough to answer, although he didn't have to. I spoke with a Margie in Austin, very kind and helpful, directing me to request an interview. In some cases, they will do this. Letters, too numerous, went out. Then I decided to contact MR. Garrett. I went online to find a physical address. To my shock, I learned he retired in August!

This was October! Hello, anybody know how to spell **C-O-N-T-I-N-U-I-T-Y**? Does the left hand know what the right hand is doing? Rissie Owens had been appointed. I must start all over.

I wrote McEylea, again, and others demanding answers to my questions. Everyone said the same thing, "The information I sent was placed in Rick's files." I wanted to know, for when? Would the file be seen now or 2006? I didn't think that question was unreasonable. I received a phone call from him, out of the Austin Division, informing me, yes in 2006!

I had a live person on the phone! I demanded an explanation for my brother's denial, and I must say, he was kind and patient, although not real helpful. I wanted this 2d code explained. I tried to convince him the files had been mixed up, but no, they hadn't. Shock, anger and astonishment! I was finally able to breath. With emotions finally subsiding, I demanded the answers to the awful terms I was seeing. A weapon? If any weapon was involved, then I said someone must have gotten a paper-cut from a Birthday card! I really appreciated no help.

Eventually, he confessed, **there was no weapon**. Great, now about brutal, violent, repeated crimes? **"Well, he did have a DWI in 1980 something**." I screamed, "Oh yes, as did President Bush." In other words, Rick is a number in a computer. Enter it and code 2d comes up? Yes.

Oh, and Rick doesn't seem remorseful either. Go figure that one out! Remorse from an innocent man is as easy as rehabilitating a non-offender! Everyone seems to agree Rick is angry! I wonder why?

I recall something I read in a magazine, Time or one like that, making an excellent statement, (I think regarding the WTO,) I found very appropriate and I noted it, but have forgotten just where I saw it. **"There is no shame in feeling outrage, and certainly nothing wrong with taking all necessary means to correct an Injustice, especially one inflicted on those that are truly innocent."** So, my brother is guilty or in denial, because he is angry about being falsely accused!

The man on the phone was kind, but could do nothing, including explaining my questions. Letters arrived with phone calls too, informing me of the same thing, "All my submitted files would be placed in Rick's file. For all to be viewed in 2006!"

I wrote Rissie, stated my case and requested another review of Rick's file. I expressed a desire for the gift of an interview, or to meet and discuss this issue. A total waste of time and postage! Rissie Owens sent me a letter and confirmed they would look at his file in 2006. No meeting, no interview, but did include, a bunch of worthless forms and prerequisites in order for a hearing. We didn't qualify. Although Rick is a model inmate, having earned, with work record and all, over an equivalent of sixteen years credit now.

Wait, what am I doing? I am begging for a Parole, which I don't want. That means an innocent man comes out of prison with the label of "Convicted Sex Felon." Desperate people do desperate things. Get him out, however, and get the case reopened then, or do something now, because our mother is at death's door! Fight, beg anyone, forget your pride. A man's life is at stake and the clock is running down.

I began my campaign over five years ago. I didn't go outside of Texas for any help. Why would I? Yet for some reason, John Ashcroft, while still in MO, received the e-mail of my cry for help and cared enough to reach out! I got a letter, regular mail, from him, with a desire to help. What a wonderful, compassionate man. Only to witness the Dems accusing him of everything but being the devil, incarnate, regarding his approval for the office our new Attorney General. I have found him to be such a gentleman, with faith, morals, values and ethics! In Washington, never! I can't believe he was finally confirmed!

I've written him again, since he has become our United States Attorney General, to no avail. How he knew anything about me is still a mystery. No office in Texas, but kind enough to write me, stating he could not help, but took the liberty of forwarding my letter to Senator Phil Gramm.

I had written every Innocent Project in the USA at the time. This was before I found all the new evidence. Most of them, at the time, accepted only those on death-row. OOPS, sorry. Rick only got twenty years. Many only deal with DNA, like Barry Scheck, and very well, but no help here. **The State didn't even have any evidence!**

To be fair, I had very little to go on at the time, but all nine responded to me. Now, having found such incriminating evidence, I have written them again. It's too soon to get a reply, so I stand in faith and hope that someone, out there, will be another Jeff Blackburn. He took on Tulia, Texas and won! Lord, we need so many more like him! Jeff exposed that crooked Cop of the Year in Tulia, where forty-six innocent people were setup! Court TV did an excellent job with this event. Governor Perry finally pardoned them. Bravo for him and I am so thankful and happy for each one of them.

I also tried to find Jerry Spense. I did, but never got any reply.

Even my first Grievance with the Texas State Bar, I had next to no proof! I knew Max had sold Rick out and embezzled money from me. I knew Max was inept and sorely misrepresented all of his credentials, as well as coercing that Plea acceptance, but I couldn't prove it. However, when you first file a complaint with them, you are not allowed to submit any evidence. This can only be done when they allow you to.

I must mention John, in Dallas. John is an attorney that has extended so much kindness to me, for nothing! He has tried to help, but with everything so old, and with his busy schedule, I can't ask for more. He has spent so much time with me on the phone, often on his own phone bill, in an effort to help me. He is Dean's attorney but, Dean convinced me to call him. I will forever be grateful for the care and concern, mixed with his distaste for such lawyers like Max and wanting them out of practice. To me he is another Crusader, just like Gerald and Jeff.

Does anybody out there believe the IRS would ever see an error or a forgery and say, "Oh well, too late to do anything about it now." Don't you wish?

I have spoken with other lawyers, all wanting between five and seven thousand dollars, just to evaluate the case, with no promises. Our finances are tapped, as well as my phone, (three months) Now, I want Rick's case exposed! I want it reopened. Now!

Remember Dan Morales, the former Texas Attorney General? The one that sued the tobacco companies and won. Dan used his so-called Bar Card as a purported attorney and a former associate to defraud the state, the United States and the tabacco company. He participated in a scheme to steal millions of dollars. He was indicted on charges of fraud, conspiracy and lying on a loan application. The lawyers in the settlement collected 3.3 billion dollars. Dan added his friend Marc Murr to the list of lawyers for 3% of the billions. Marc plead guilty. The Prosecution recommended Marc get six months time, probation etc. I don't know what Marc ended up with, but Dan Morales received only four years in prison. Yup, that is Texas for you!

CHAPTER 50
COMPLETE FAILURE OF THE TEXAS BAR!

It should be very interesting, should Rick's case be reopened, since there was no medical evidence. Sue, speaking for and through a child of four years of age, saying what his mother told him to say, so daddy could come home! I have to give up on the files Max had, if he ever had any, which I do not believe he did. Should he have files, I knew he would ride out the four year statue of limitations, as the files would be far too incriminating. Max would never allow them to be seen!

Rick was right about Max all along. He could not be trusted and we were both sure he knew much more than he would ever tells us. I have figured out just who to go after. Now, if I can get and keep the attention of the Texas State Bar, Office of the Chief Disciplinary Counsel, the State Commission on Judicial Conduct to uphold their end, I can finally get Rick his day in Court.

Oh, happy day! I just got my mail, a letter from the State Bar. They met the same day I was called, (the 4th, informing me, Max had until the 9th) **"No finding of misconduct on the lawyer and no further action shall be had!"** Again, they didn't do as they said. Having just sent another eight pages of evidence, proving Max lied about two Court dates. We weren't there, but Max was, with forged documents! A letter from the Judge to Max and other documents. Filing Continuance after another, without our knowledge or approval. I think I just got setup again!

I have tried, all day, to imagine a room full of educated people, (an assumption on my part) confronted with stacks of documented evidence I sent, (against the Judge and the lawyer.) None could find any misconduct! I have checked though, as of this day, Max is still on suspension! So, here I sit, in awe, like a fool, in believing that possibly, just possibly, I could obtain some justice. If I could have gotten Max on one thing, it would have forced the doors open for a trial that Rick never received. That must be it! Still "butt covering." What good is a State Bar? **What a Merry Christmas for our family!** Yes, I am angry, **"Righteously Indignant!"**

It doesn't matter now, **"Case closed." "No further action shall be had." "Files destroyed."** Well, I still have my files and will have to write one more letter to the Bar. Not a Christmas card either.

When I say endless error filled papers, that's exactly what I mean! No wonder it took so long in getting them. Myself and two attorneys worked for close to a year to gather what I have. I have to wonder what all I don't have! Just remember, I only received them after all legal steps had been denied. Gerald sent them to me early spring of 2001. It would take me almost two years just to understand what I was looking at. But, is that not the law? If we are able to understand anything, then it would be, they messed up, royally!

Here I sit with such outrageous forgeries! Legal documents, from A Court of law. I was told, "No Judge could give that type of probation to anyone without a Judicial Confession." There was none. Could this be why Rick was called back into Court, twenty-one days later. We both knew Rick would never have signed a confession, having made that crystal clear to good old Max. He warned him, more like threatened him the night before the Court date. Max assured him "Nolo," was absolutely no admission of guilt. But, now we knew more about Max, so we could expect anything. The case was keeping Gerald awake at night, saying repeatedly, he had never seen any-thing like it. But, he insisted the confession had to exist and he had to find it.

Searching each document, one by one for months on end and bingo, he found it. Well, it wasn't a real confession. He described it to me as a "Mousetrap, neatly concealed in the Stipulation of Evidence."

Now I have it and it is very suspicious to say the least. Remember, I told you I was there in Court with him. This document had three print styles in as many different fonts. I am convinced <u>Rick did not sign it with the finished wording</u>. I sent it to him and well, let's say he was beyond shock. He swore he didn't sign what I sent. He said yes, it was his signature, but the form wasn't filled in with those words. At the bottom of the first full, long paragraph, in bold font, the last three lines say, " I judicially confess to the following facts and agree and stipulate that these facts are true and correct and constitute the evidence in this case:" In a light smaller print it states what his son would testify, if called. Rick said it wasn't there, furthermore, he didn't know what his son would say! Further down, there are a couple of lines with a line running through the first one, both in another size print, but in bold font too. It is dated the first Court date, so this wasn't the purpose of him having to return. Finally, I think I found the purpose. The only difference is the Admonishment to the Defendant, which the Judge had forgotten to do. I realized this as I went over the Revocation Hearing transcript which I paid $486.00 for. I became angry when reading how the Judge "Admonished him and deemed him competent for trial." I was at that hearing and knew that wasn't true. When I went back seven years, I found the Admonishment dated <u>three weeks after</u> the first Court date. Also, I noticed that the Plea Bargain Agreement's original date was scratched through and the newest one written above it.

I think I now know why he lost his job, too. I found another document that was altered. Felon was marked, then scratched through with what appears to be "Nolo" out to the other side. Just one error after another.

The latest evidence I sent the State Bar, was that letter from Max to the Judge, stating the Court date and the motion for the child competency test. Again, we were never aware of that Court date, so naturally we were not present, but Max sure was with that other forgery. Anger, confusion and more anger!

This isn't even all of the evidence I have, yet it is worthless because we didn't find it sooner! This legitimizes lies and forgeries? What sort of statue of limitation will allow such as this to be sanctioned by any state or Court of law?

As for the State Commission on Judicial Conduct, that can take months to years. But, do you think I have any faith in that? I have now exhausted every idea and legal step there is left.

I am filled with a perfect anger and hatred for this injustice! The chick holding the scales, with the blindfold. Well now I think I know what the blindfold is for and I don't like it! I'm losing my sunny disposition. Perhaps, because Max appealed both times, (with the state bar). <u>I was informed that Max wasn't there</u> either, so I don't know anything, other than they never did one thing they claimed they would do. I am still attempting to learn their purpose, other than collecting Bar fees and covering up for one another.

I have not filed any type of a suit against Max. I could take him to small claims court or even Civil Court. Why Have I not? Once I initiate either one of these steps, "<u>it's case closed</u>." The door is slammed shut. There is no other recourse. I can never go back on Max again, for anything and I wish to keep the door open. I am not finished with Max. Not yet!

CHAPTER 51
TEXAS STATE BAR STRIKES AGAIN!

I stand amazed. I just received another letter from the State Bar, from the same woman. What her intentions were, I have no idea. Apparently, she felt she needed assurance in ruining Christmas this year. The letter was even shorter than the first, very blunt. The crook won his appeal and I have nothing left to do, "The matter is dismissed!" I was informed of this the first day of the week and again the last day of this week, "No further action shall be had." I have one more letter for them that I had faxed. I told them I was not wishing a reply. I knew it would make me feel better if I could express my extreme disappointment, expecting nothing from them.

It was a nasty letter to both Investigators. I stated that I did not seek a reply. I faxed it on the way out of town, Saturday, to see the folks, knowing it wouldn't been seen until Monday.

The telephone woke me up. It was one of the Investigators. I had a terrible headache and in no mood to deal with the enemy! I had just returned home late, the previous night. I saw my folks for two days and was still so depressed at their condition. I interrupted her saying, I thought I made it clear that I expected no response. Apparently, the fax messed up with them lacking a third of my letter, on the left side. If I wanted them to know what I had to say, I would need to fax it again. Nope, I decided not another dime would I spend on them. I mailed it instead.

She said she read enough to be aware of my anger, then proceeded to explain how great our system is. I stopped her right there, saying I didn't want to hear such deceitful chatter, as our system does not work! Not when a room full of lawyers and intelligent people sit around a table, with stacks of evidence I submitted, with forgeries in and out of a Courtroom, and declare no misconduct! I did thank her for calling me and I have already gotten the letter out. I had to send it, again, in order to include it in this book!

She confessed that many are not happy with the system and are trying to do something about it. Great, send me the list of these special, wonderful folks and I will gladly sign up with them!

I said contemptible things. I recall saying, **"I would inform them, when this is over, files destroyed, case closed and that further action shall be had, by me! I have my files!"**

Now, my problem is, she said they weren't there. Nobody was invited, because it was done in Austin. Wait a minute! What did that mean? When? I specifically asked that it remain in the same county. I had that option. Austin is not close to where I filed! Just like both times they informed me I had legal grounds for misconduct, I was to hear a response from Max, if not, they would get it for me. No. I never got it on the first one or the second one.

Also, there was to be a hearing, (they would notify me of the date). I could be there, with the attorney. It was very confidential. I couldn't discuss it with anyone but the attorney and witnesses. I had to save money to fly the attorney, both ways, in order to testify. I located witnesses and all of this at my expense. All, for nothing. I never got close to any hearing, either time. I was deprived of each step they said they would do!

Am I expected to just let it go? Maybe in another world, another family, another state, but not here! Not me, not our family. I will not back off. I don't care what THEY decide! The Law is the law.

CHAPTER 52
MOUTH TO MOUTH MANIPULATION!

I've come to the age of emancipation, in that I feel I have paid my dues and will no longer pay for grief. I abhor being "Politically Correct," meaning, I refuse to be secular! I have choices and I am willing to accept the consequences of such. We do have some freedom left, in order to make choices and decisions. I always taught my children they have the freedom to make their choices, but not the luxury or freedom in choosing their consequences or repercussions, so be careful. I think that should be a new law, if all are so determined in writing new laws!

Daily, I read statistics on those that believe in God. They all run anywhere from eighty-two to ninety-two percent. I am offended daily, (but that's okay, I don't count because I am a Christian) having arrived at a point I never expected. Being raised to love and respect everyone, regardless of race, faith, age or nationality. I have been offended too many times and now have the attitude, that the eighteen to eight percent should just sit down and shut up! Or as Jesus would have said, far more eloquently, "Hold thy peace." All faiths are protected except Christianity!

If I come off as a Republican, allow me to remind you I am a registered Independent. I can't help it if the Republicans have been the only ones to care enough to respond to me. I do not wish to single out Dems by name, regarding the Filibuster. But am reminded of a phone call during the Circus, with a lady calling, raising Cain about the Republicans. She had issues too and mentioned she had written letters to two Dems, Tom Daschle and Hillary Clinton for help. Before she could finish blasting the NRCC, the man asked her if she had heard from either of the two she had written,..... ....pause......finally answering, "No." I'm sorry, but I had to laugh. Are all Dems that brainwashed? First laugh I'd had in weeks! Don't think I don't have some Republicans to chew on also! I will not discriminate my disgust for both parties! I have plenty to spread around.

Now, like elected officials, I shall speak my mind, but unlike them, I will be happy to supply the explanations! I am appalled at what I have been witness to. Being Independent, I prefer to think I can be neutral. I do not hate the Democrats, not all of them anyway. We could use more Millers and Nelsons. I abhor what they are doing to this nation, at all costs, to take back the White House. Fighting Bush every step of the way and often boasting of their chicanery! To the point of risking our safety with all their scare tactics, generally with the minorities and elderly. Do you hear your message? I do.

If the likes of Schummer, Byrd and Biden, mixed with Clinton, Leahy and Daschle aren't bad enough, we have Ted Kennedy. What audacity, referring to the Bush nominees as, "Turkeys and Neanderthals," was just what I needed. Kennedy? Is this not the man with an alcohol problem, adultery, and the reason a set of parents are without their beautiful, daughter? All I recall were excuses and no apologies, yet standing in judgment of our President's, qualified, nominees!

Ted, has it dawned on you yet, how you managed to insult every voter that elected those so called, "Turkeys and Neanderthals" in their respective states, by huge percentages? You just told us how stupid we were, to have voted these highly nominated officials into office, in our state! I rest my point. If the Massachusetts voters wish to keep you in office, that is their privilege, but I am of the old school, "You don't throw rocks, when you live in a glass house!" This is difficult for me to say, as I so loved and supported both of your brothers! I often wonder what they would think of you now.

It's painfully obvious why the Dems are so concerned with Bush's nominees. The Courts are not qualified to rule, based on constitutional laws! They hand down cultural laws! The entire Judicial System has become a joke, without any humor.

When disaster strikes anywhere, I hear repeatedly, "Why would God allow this to happen?" Oh that's easy. God is a gentleman, giving us free will, not forcing us, so He removes the hedge and doesn't interfere with our requests! Could this be why we get such absurd Court rulings? Could this be why our public schools have become war zones, and is this the reason why we rate so poorly in education?

Why do Politicians, for the most part, fear Christians? In the Bible, some residents in Crete made a living off the gullible souls in the Church. (like you do off the country's tax payers) Paul had strong words about this; "These people must be stopped, because they are upsetting whole families by teaching things they should not teach, which they do to get rich by cheating people."

This goes for lies and scare tactics, too. Not to mention what our children are being taught in the public schools that we pay for.

I was not being derogatory about our President's DWI! I applaud him! At least he was man enough to accept the responsibility for what he did! What a rare commodity! No wonder so many hate him. Thank you MR. President. You restored my faith and increased, to a point, my faith in mankind! This is why you are not fit to be in the White House. You are pathetic! A man that loves and serves his country, reads the Bible, prays for guidance to do a good job, having compassion and standing by what you say! I do fear Iraq and Afghanistan under Islamic rule. No democracy there, I hate to say.

I never voted for Bush for Governor, but I did vote for him for President. I failed to realize that in Texas, he still had to go up against the Dems. I voted for his Presidency because the Lord told me to! I witnessed Pricilla Owens being ridiculed in such an ugly manner and with such repulsive behavior. All because she introduced her Pastor to Bush. Between her Pastor and Bush, the voluntary Bible study was created in Texas! Well, God forbid, that any criminal would have the opportunity to find the Lord, resulting in an incredibly higher percentage rate in not returning to prison!

Such open hatred for our Commander and Chief. Hal Lindsay said it best, **"If Bush walked on water, the Democrats would claim he doesn't know how to swim!"** The fighting and spinning has to stop. Nancy Pelosi, what a spin on Medicare! What will it take to convince you of your own statements? You think the public is smart enough to know? How many more offices are you willing to risk losing, before you realize, you are right? The upcoming election is critical to our future. Why all the hate speeches and scare tactics, generally with the elderly and minorities?

As a Christian, I represent both. I resent your scare tactics with the message, <u>I can't be a true American, a patriot or fit to sit on a jury, let alone be a Judge, if I have faith</u>? How dare you! Will my voting rights go next? <u>Don't give me any crap about Separation of Church and State</u>. Do your homework again! It's not there!

I am fed up with too much Government in my life! Instead of the hatred, get to the point. You are still referring to Bush as the illegitimate President. The Christians, (the enemies according to Al Gore) know better than this. We are <u>largely</u> to blame for the election! Wake up America! I'm just secure enough to know I don't need, nor want more, government in my life. And Rick of Fox News, you went over the line on Pat Robertson's statement of

Bush being re-elected. I feel and pray this will be so. But, your nasty, tacky remarks were tasteless and unexpected.

Does anyone really care who Gore or Clinton backs? I sure don't, but do to an extent. I do remember Al's book "Earth in the Balance," and how he blasted the Christians with his cruel, new age, untruthful beliefs, regarding us as threats to the greater good of the country! I also recall, during that endless period of filing appeal after appeal, to keep Bush out of the Presidency, that every Sunday, Al and his wife were either entering a Church or leaving one. He wrote, the most dangerous Christians are those that believe in prophesy! We eliminated "the Goddess religion!" Al, why don't you read that Book and see for yourself? Or, just sit back and note what has come, and yet to come.

So, Howard Dean wants Fox News off the air? Cable too. I can easily see why. They truly are your enemy, because they are fair and balanced. They give both sides and allow the smart ones to decide for themselves. However, correct me if I am wrong, but are we not seeing every Dem running for office all over Fox News of late?

Howard Dean wants us to return to values. Is he willing to start in Vermont? I am so weary of "Lip service." What values are you speaking of, Howard? Value of life? Any accountability and responsibility included? I watched the speech you gave while in your home state, when you were entering the Presidential race. I saw it on Fox News and I was overwhelmed with disinterest! Hot tempered Howard, flip-flop, in-out, up-down, where do I stand Dean? Does he even know? Is there no one to draw his attention to the many contradictions he makes? On the bright side, this guy could have a debate with no one but him present! A solo debate. That would keep him busy.

So, you think Saddam should remain in power? We shouldn't have gone over there to bring him down and give the people democracy. The country is no more secure now, than prior to 9-11? You may be right. I expect us to get hit again. I just pray Bush is still in the White House and not you! But wait, now it's acceptable to have faith! My, I sure remember the mockery and ridicule about four years ago, when Bush was so openly a Christian! I'm glad you were informed that the Book of Job is not in the New Testament! What a difference a day makes in Washington!

Dean and Clark think Bush allowed 9-11? How dare you! Clark, I know you were in a position to have known better than Bush. Where was your big mouth and patriotism then? And Dean, if you are half as smart as you tell us you are, you should have known and stopped it, too. Clinton wants Clark in. I wonder why? If this should happen or perhaps Kerry, look for Hillary to be appointed to a much higher post! Just watch who the Clintons back. At this point, I feel if any Dem gets in, we will be stuck with Hillary! What a legacy each Clinton will leave! I assure you, she is concentrating on 2008! I keep asking myself, with my constant working at home, how in the world does Hillary find the time for all those "book signings?" I thought she had a full time job in NY and Washington.

The Dems are upset with Bush's spending! I know and I understand this. It certainly does cut into your frivolous spending habits. Two million dollars to study Gay Indian habits? Good investment. I know this country couldn't exist without that information! Yes, I confess sarcasm!

If any Politician wants to truly serve, opposed to being served, start with our broken systems that no longer work to our benefit. Begin with enforcing the laws, already in the books, without writing new ones. Get rid of the inept, useless employees. Run out every bulging pocketed lawyer and see if they can make a living on their own, in this cruel world they helped shape. But, please back off of Bush and the fact we haven't found Saddam or UBL. **How many years before we found Ted Kaczinsky? Rudolph, took five years, and they were both in this country!** Can't any come up with something a bit more legitimate? We haven't even found the killers of President Kennedy yet!

NEWS FLASH. We got Saddam! Way to go! Oh no, I can hear the cries already from the Dems. How there are so many other things that need be done and how about UBL? Trust me, you are driving many voters to the Republican Ballots, with all your sour grapes.

Libya is coming clean? I have to wonder if what we did in Iraq had anything to do with that? Remember, our President gave out some strong warnings. He did what he said he would do in Iraq. Can it be that Bush is getting some attention? For once, we didn't hit and run, but stayed in two countries, vowing to finish the job! I don't know, but it appears to me, Gadhafi, might have thought he might be next on the list! I sure hope so, but another thorn in the side of the Dems. Look out George! Clark and Dean appear to be very regretful that we haven't been attacked of late. They swear we are no safer now than before 9-11. They are saying we went after the wrong ones. Yet, I see nothing the Dems did to prevent that awful day!

In 1998, Clinton said Iraq did have WMDs. No? We all know Saddam had them and used them! The Clinton administration could have taken care of Bin Laden. No one seems to agree on the spelling of his first name.

I may be a Republican at heart, I'm not sure yet. I know I like their goals so far. I do wish they would stand up to the Dems more! I never missed a chance in sharing my desire for that with every call I got at home. However, we were warned in the beginning, that the <u>Dems would make life impossible for Bush. That, they did not lie about!</u>

For those of you that are still in "shock and awe," with the last Presidential election, allow me to share this. God did place George W. Bush there! We Christians, spent years on our knees with concern for the direction our nation was headed. (the Clintonista years) We begged God to clean up the White House, receiving this reply, "When my children, called by My name, clean up their own house, I will clean up the White House." No, I did not care for Bill Clinton. No, I did not vote for him either. But, being a Christian, I was bound by the Word to love and pray for him.

We knew if the downward spiral continued, it will only get worse, and no Democratic win is going to change this, unless your views and attitudes change. Why not give the little guy a reason to hope and dare to believe we can return to our foundation, based on faith and it's freedoms. But, God forbid, that any woman would lose the opportunity of killing a baby, (in most cases) she doesn't want. I know there are extenuating circumstances. Yes, I am pro-life. I also care about health, but you will not convince me partial birth abortion is needed! Partial birth abortion is beyond description!

Life has no value in this new age. I'm sure President Bush is aware of this. Without ethics, morals and values, we have been on a downward spiral. No <u>"Ten Commandments,"</u> no <u>"Under God,"</u> in the Pledge of Allegiance. What's next, <u>"In God We Trust,"</u> being removed from our money? <u>It will be done if the ACLU gets their way</u>. Praise God, O'Reilly is making that difficult! Winter Holidays, just to remove Christ. Abortion on demand, without the parents having to be notified. When Africa sends Missionaries to America, we know we are in trouble! (And now with the likes of George Sorros, risking his billions to buy the Dems back into power. You scare me)!

No Nativity scenes, no prayers in school, at Proms, or ball games and now public schools are eliminating religious Christmas songs or substituting words, like winter. Don't offend anyone! The ACLU has them all too scared of law suits. ACLU was formed by Communists. Are you aware of that? (quote) I expect any day to see them going out to Arlington Cemetery and ripping all the crosses out of the ground! And they won't be happy until they get Christ out of Christmas. Why don't you go to France, Russia, Germany or better yet, go to China and fight for their rights!

Lori and I recall an Evangelist coming through our small town in 1963. It was right after prayer was abolished in public schools. The predictions he made seemed preposterous to us. He went about predicting that children would be killing children and their parents. Parents would kill their children and one another. Pregnancy would soon be seen as nothing and that it would become so common place. Drugs would abound every where and most children would be lost and suicide rates would soar. Lori and I really thought the horror stories were too unbelievable. Now, we see how truly wise he was. He certainly knew of that which he spoke. I won't bring up Columbine, Kentucky or the others.

In 1962, we, the Christians, allowed an over-weight, over-bearing Atheist to have school prayer abolished. I guess we all expected others to stand up. Look at the terrible ending she met with. To remain silent, is a bigger sin, that standing up for that which we believe. The blame game here is that we are guilty!

Parents would rather have their children read Harry Potter than anything of value. Teach them how to cast a spell on one, or conjure up demons and learn all about sorcery in a dark world. I have actually heard parents say, "Well, I think if anything encourages them to read, it should be all right." God, have mercy! Even children's diaries come with horoscopes! Our children are taught to tolerate unnatural life styles, regardless of how the parents feel. Even cartoons are outrageous and offensive. (parents, investigate what your children are watching, as well as their school books and I'm sure you will be shocked). Being a parent doesn't mean you are a good one. So snap out of it, before it's too late. Our children are our future! The conceived should not be looked upon as "a mistake."

How sick. Children are forced to learn evolution opposed to creation. Why not teach both and allow the child to decide? Our children are forced to learn about other religions but cannot use the Bible for any assignment, under the guise of "Separation of Church and State," which, I say again, does not exist! Define "fair and equal," to me, please!

In Texas, a teacher took two students Bibles and threw them in the trash can, saying they are "garbage." The school denies it, but one of the mothers saw her! Christianity won't be tolerated, but in California, students had to take on Muslim names and learn about the religion.

Why do I abhor the NEA? The NEA has become a political party and Union. Hear this, please, The NEA couldn't care less about your children! They teach subjects that they know are incorrect but, again, they do not care! Of course they are against vouchers! The results would be a loss of power, greed, control and the constant tainting of facts taught in schools, with a loss of funds in their Union and their pockets!

"OUR CHILDREN ARE NOT BEING EDUCATED BUT, BEING INDOCTRINATED!"

Again, this smells of Communist standards of decades gone by. History we seem determined to repeat. Will we ever learn? Will we ever care? We are rapidly becoming another Sodom and Gomorrah. Scientists have agreed both cities existed and were destroyed. They have numerous explanations as to how and when, but all agree with the destruction. There's a thought. Where did the term <u>sodomy</u> evolve from? We are being forced to accept "gay marriage" as normal. Marriage is between a man and a woman. This other lifestyle can not reproduce. It is wrong. Gays are not bad, they are simply wrong. I don't care who or how many try to convince me the Bible and God's love will accept it. That makes God a liar and I will not listen to such. Plus, it is in both Testaments. Our morals, ethics and faith are so cluttered in filth. A quagmire, more simply put. We have become so misguided. We should all be ashamed. What has happened to a system that once worked? We have allowed it!

I'm not eligible for a Federal Grant, but a couple months back, a Witch qualified for one. Now she can open her shop and sell her "mystic goodies." What an maladjusted country we are. What many will do for that almighty vote! I've always said, **<u>"Were it possible for God to make a mistake, it would be in giving us free will</u>**. We aren't capable of handling that. This is not my own personal opinion. The statistics are printed daily, the majority does not approve of this "new age" garbage. I truly apologize for any hurt feelings, which is not my goal. I do love every race, gender and color. I love freedom of speech, but not when it offends the vast majority and exposes the Christians as "haters." Christians are offended and ridiculed, for our beliefs. This is wrong.

There are too many teachers that should not be allowed in a classroom.

Preachers that don't belong behind a pulpit.

Judges that shouldn't be allowed in a Court of law.

Police that shouldn't be allowed on the streets, let alone carrying a gun.

Politicians that shouldn't be allowed in Washington DC.

And lastly, attorneys that should be barred from a Courtroom and especially in Politics!

In short, we need to <u>clean house</u> and start all over!

CHAPTER 53
THE STATE OF HEALTH INSURANCE

For over a decade I have witnessed Doctors leaving the field of medicine. Some have turned to driving eighteen wheeler trucks. Between the Medical Boards and the government, mixed with patients shopping for Doctors and Pharmaceutical companies, we are in a mess! Any HMO, Medicare, Medicaid and most all Insurance Companies, as well as hospitals, are on the take. Another example of mishandling funds. Workman's comp has become an enterprise in it's self. Disability? File for it and see how close to impossible, it will be to receive.

In Texas, the Medical Board suffers with a God complex too. Power hungry and out of control. Anyone can get mad at their Doctor and file a complaint. When this happens, it's a nightmare. I know there are bad Doctors, but it seems to be the good ones that are singled out. Malpractice rates are preposterous. Television is used to sell medication. We are informed at how great this product is, to "Be sure and ask your Doctor if you need it." Most often, we have no clue what it is or what it is for.

I know a Doctor who refused to prescribe Phen-phen. I was in his office, and twice, I witnessed two patients refusing to leave without it. Staying, literally crying and begging for it. He was not in favor of it, being Phen-phen so new and not having enough information on it. One of them finally wore him down to the point he granted her request. Naturally, she sued him for it later. The TX. Medical Board is much like the State. Once you are investigated, you can never get off of their Hit List. You are then reduced to taking their crap and dealing with it. In Texas, too many of our better Doctors have had enough. They are leaving the medical field, in droves.

You go in for a physical and you will not get one. Too often it will require further tests and insurance will not pay for it. However, they will give the Doctor a little kickback for not doing what the Doctor felt should have been done. I hate repetition, but again, follow the money trail. It's always the money. Hospitals rip off the government and insurance companies. Insurance companies are ripping off the government, hospitals, Doctors and the patients. Hospitals are charging five dollars for a box of tissues?

Everyone is pointing an accusing finger at one another, while loved ones are dying, waiting for the insurance to approve an operation, or needed care.

I was told by a Doctor that the day would come when the cheapest pill would cost one dollar each. Government wants full control over health! No longer is your health between the Doctor and the patient, but left to the obstructionists. It has come to the point of not being able to afford to live or die! I strongly suggest you watch the movie, "John Q," with Denzel Washington. This movie is so powerfully real it is frightening! A perfect example of the harsh reality many have to endure, regarding any so-called HMO. I have the movie and have watched it ten times. Aside from Denzel's powerful performance, the message is even more powerful and will scare anyone to the bone, because of the reality and what many are forced to do, for those we love.

Masses have been forced to look to Canada and Mexico for medication they cannot afford, in the USA. I assure you, our government will bring this to a screeching halt.

Do not assume you will have many Doctors left in a few years. Talk about extinct. Most people have no choice in choosing their own Doctor, unless it is from their list, already approved by your insurance company. Isn't that a warm, comforting thought? Do not believe the government or any hospital cares about anything beyond your insurance coverage!

CHAPTER 54
REPUBLICAN MANIPULATION !

You want to play politics? Time to pick on the Republicans! A couple of months ago, I received NRCC mail from Tom Reynolds and Dennis Hastert, (Tom DeLay's a week later) all requesting funding for the coming election. Not to mention all the phone calls and e-mails I get. The mailings simply expressed the goals and needs for this country, with some great ideas, mixed with concern for the future. The country is in such peril! Don't I know that? But, you asked me if I agreed with the issues you shared. I do, but I have some of my own issues.

Now is the time to expose some Republicans. I wrote Tom DeLay and Dick Armey first. Then I wrote to Tom Reynolds and Dennis Hastert, only managing to get on a mailing and phone list to give to the NRCC. I have given till it hurts! Why? Because I want change and so far I have seen efforts and a sincere desire to take this country back to where we once could be proud. I have written to many others, but have singled you out for a reason.

The more I read and thought how good it appeared on paper, thinking of all the money I have already given, seeing no change, I became disappointed and angry! So, in agreement with you, and the NRCC's goals, I decided to share some of my concerns, and in addition, several issues, just as important to many, that you failed to mention.

I made you a deal, which you may or may not have seen. MR. Reynolds and MR. Hastert, you should be apprised of what I am about to say! If not, I suggest you read your mail opposed to going to the bank!

I wrote to both of you, telling you I had taken the time to read every word printed, on all four to five pages. I refused to send any money. I chose to see if I could get any attention from one of you or the NRCC. I told you how to go about getting a donation from me. My request, **"I will make you a deal, since I have thoughtfully and thoroughly read every word you wrote, on every page and agree with you. However, I will ask you for the same courtesy. If you will just read my two page letter and call me, I will donate via the telephone."** I then proceeded to pour my heart out, regarding the pain and anguish our family has gone through because of the broken, abused and corrupt system, here in Texas. I begged you to apply some thought to this, as another very important issue, effecting so many in this country, as well as asking for explanations, suggestions, advise or anything you might have to offer.

Tom Reynolds responded over six weeks later, thanking me for sharing issues that are dear to me. Of course, an Express envelope was enclosed, to send my donation in.

I didn't get a call for several weeks and when I did, I chewed that poor young man out, for close to thirty minutes! He picked a bad night to call me, but took my fury with such kindness.

I had received mail from the State Bar and bad news about mother that day. I was on my PC writing another letter for help, when he called. I got so loud, my husband came in the room to check on me. He was able to hear me from the bedroom, quickly figuring out it involved Politics, for sure. Again, the young man knew nothing about my letter, but because of his sincerity, kindness, understanding and compassion, I did give the exact amount you were seeking. But, all I can say is, "Enjoy it, I don't know if or when, I will ever donate anything more than my feelings." I want change and that's not to be confused with pocket change.

As for MR. Hastert, I have two consecutive years of "The Speaker's Citizen Task Force," Member Cards, and an NRCC gold member card, but I never heard a word from you! All I received was more mail requesting donations, for a lot of money, at this time of year. What really riles me are the ones that come as bills owed! I have chosen to give you the same thing you gave me, nothing! I resent getting a "bill" for a minimum of $150.00, as though I owe you.

Senator Trent Lott is next on my list. Although, you begin at a mere $15.00. (I love him.) I am weary of the game, with my finances shot! Will any ever be reminded that "YOU WORK FOR ME?" All Politicians work for us, **"We the People."** You are to serve us, but you have it turned around. Wake up!

I have received a huge American flag, a beautiful Olympic like medal, a book, pictures of our President and the first Lady and a Texas Republican of the Year certificate. I hear my name was in USA Today and engraved somewhere in Washington amongst other items. Unlike you, I have nothing to show for all that money. I can't place a price on the waiting days, running back and forth checking my mailbox, hoping against hope, that someone out there would care enough to respond. A letter, a phone call and simple kindness goes a long way. I give and give, but see no change. I continue to deal with many that are suffering with megalomania.

I get e-mail from the Dems, blasting the Republicans, with warnings or scare tactics of how they are going to ruin my country. They are seeking my help to bring them down. On two occasions I tried to respond with my feelings, to no avail. Mail was undeliverable, except if I wanted to make a donation. Again, I have that luxury of communicating with the enemy. Questionable, at best.

The Dems complain about how long the war is taking.

It took less time to take Iraq than it took Janet Reno to take the Branch Davidian Compound, which was fifty-one days!

It took less time to find Saddam's goon sons, than it took Hillary Clinton to find the Rose Law Firm billing records.

The 3rd Infantry Division and the Marines destroyed the Medina Republican Guard in less time than it took Ted Kennedy to call the police after his car sank in Chappaquiddick, with a young girl in it.

Let's at least be logical and mindful of the facts! And finally, it took less time to take Iraq than it took to count the votes in Florida! Another good issue is the following; The Elected officials Retirement Benefit Plan, at our expense.

Perhaps we are asking the wrong questions during this, and each, election year. Since our Congress and Senate do not pay into Social Security, they do not collect from it. Because Social Security is not suitable for persons of their rare elevation in society, they felt they should have a special plan for themselves. Many years ago they voted in their own benefit plan. In recent years, no congressperson has felt the need to change it. After all, it is a great plan. For all practical purposes, their plan works like this; How many are aware that our elected officials pay no Social Security? Have you any idea of the benefits they will have until death? Even the death befits are staggering (in seeing what the widow will receive.) Yet, when we lost our father, a Marine Veteran that fought in WW II, we received $250.00. Can you not see accept that our governmental body is in such chaos?

Now, I will share some facts with you. You may or may not be aware of them, but I feel they have to be included in this book. It's an election year and we may have other important questions, like with the so called, Social Security Plan that our Congresspersons and Senators do not pay.

They reap enormous benefits, at our expense and lack of knowledge. It's got to be addressed and I will be happy to enlighten all! I do not mind being ragged on. I do mind being lied to, ripped off, taken for granted and being laughed at. All because I still desire to believe in the American dream! The problem with our nation is called **DIVISION!** We are so divided, we can no longer stand as a nation. We've become so divided we are about to fall! **<u>One nation under God is no more, therein lies the danger.</u>**

When these "elected official" retire, they continue to draw the same pay until they die! Except, it may increase from time to time for cost of living adjustments! For example, a former Senator and a certain Congressman and their wives, may expect to draw $7,800,000.00 (that's seven million, eight-hundred thousand dollars) with their wives drawing $275,000.00 during the last years of their lives. (data off Congress.com etc) If I'm off, blame the web site.

This is calculated on an average life span for each of those respective Dignitaries. The younger Dignitaries who retire at an earlier age, will receive much more during the rest of their lives. Their cost for this excellent plan is $OOOOOOOO, Nada.........Zilch.......

This little perk they voted for themselves is free. You and I pick up the tab for this plan. The funds for this fine retirement plan come directly from the General Funds: "Our tax dollars at work!" From our Social Security Plan, which you and I pay, (or have paid) into, every payday until we retire, (the same amount is matched by our employer) we can expect to get an average of $1,000.00 per month, after retirement.

Or, in other words, we would have to collect our average $1,000.00 monthly benefit for sixty-eight years to equal Senator Bill Bradley's benefits! Social Security could be very good if only one small change were to be made. That change would be to jerk the Golden Fleece Retirement Plan from under the Senators and Congresspersons. Put them into the Social Security Plan with the rest of us....then sit back and watch how quickly they would fix it!

Just another fact to keep me in an uproar, especially with their threats of Social Security going belly up before we know it and it will President Bush to catch the blame. Isn't everything his fault? Yes, spending is high, too high, but how else or who else, would have faced the price of 9-11 and our Homeland Defense plan? Perhaps had the awareness of danger from Saddam and Bin Laden been dealt with years ago, it wouldn't have come to this. Just a thought.

I have to wonder if Bush is seen inept, a war monger, an illegitimate President and a stupid cowboy abroad, were it not for the insulting, whining, cry baby Dems. They should be held fully accountability for this! Are they aware of aiding in the world's mistrust of America? How far will they go to bring our nation down, because they didn't get their way? We are not a nation, but a country, vastly divided. How long do you think we will stand as a nation, with this attack? This is too similar to Hitler's thoughts. The vast majority of the impure are in office. The Courts, as well as Washington and Hollywood are forcing us to believe we should be dependent on the Dems!

God forbid, any would hold them accountable or force them to face the one in the mirror, as being instrumental in our nation's moral decline. All we seem to get is more child porno, another Janet Jackson, Britney Spears, Madonna and sickening, frightening rap lyrics that lead our children to suicide, murder and cults. Brought to us by "unelected judges," based on freedom of speech!

CHAPTER 55
WHAT I BELIEVE

I am not only a Christian, but old fashioned too. I am acutely aware of not being special. I can live with that. I believe in heaven and hell. I am sick and tired of convenient, organized religion!

I love Bill O'Reilly. Not that I always agree with him but, at least he does his homework before shooting off his mouth! Why do so many hate Fox News? (mostly Dems and Liberals) Because it truly is fair and unbalanced. I read their e-mail accusing them of such conservatism, too liberal, too un-American, what a joke! I have to wonder if we just watched the same thing or not!

I admire and respect Neil Cavuto, but tired of all the remarks about the size of his head. He is a gentleman with a lot of heart! Why are so many pinheads, consumed with appearances instead of what is in the heart? I wrote O'Reilly and Hannity each, two letters, begging for help and never got a response. What angered me at Bill, was a while back, he made a statement, that basically, "False accusations are out of control." Yes Bill, but you don't have a clue with this one. Are you going to simply leave it at that?

I love Fox News, but rapidly growing weary, with all the attention and their fixation with nude models and Hollywood entertainment. I have satellite, for Fox News, PAX, sports, Christianity and educational programs, many of which are tainted or shall I say, too "Politically Correct" for me. **Love those remotes**! I refuse to watch any reality shows. <u>I have to live reality</u>.

I gave up Network TV programs, years ago, with their slanted News, pushing their personal and political agendas down my throat, as well as their sitcoms. I am amazed at the bad taste in shows on other Fox channels. I detest programs with all their token actors, attempting to force me to believe all is normal! Homosexuality is not normal! That is not a hateful remark. I lost a gay friend years ago to aids. I loved him dearly, (not his lifestyle) and he loved me in return.

Hollywood idiots couldn't care less what you think. I've stopped going to the movies, unless it's G rated and some PG. 13. Even many of them

189

aren't viewable. The only series we watch faithfully is Doc, the Gaither's Homecoming, and It's A Miracle on PAX TV. Plus episodes of Seventh Heaven.

I have drawn a line with all my former favorites, like Sarandon, Robbins, Clooney, Babbs, and her hubby, Penn, Baldwin and Martin Sheen, to name a few. I have done the same with music. Freedom of speech or freedom to incite? Some movies look good, but if one of the "Motor- mouths," are in it, or I hear G-d, I will walk out of the theater. If at home, I just grab my remote! There are exceptions, but too few. I can't believe some family networks. I will wait to see a movie, cleaned up, but still leave in the G-d and Christ, omitting other words I can deal with. I wish Michael Moore and Al Franken would get lost. We need a **RIOT**! That's Christian talk for a, **"Righteous Invasion Of Truth**!**"** As Jack would say, **"You can't handle the truth!"**

I gave up Pepsi over Madonna's commercial. It was difficult, but worth it. If more people drew lines, we would bring about changes! I will not water-down or compromise any longer! Money talks. The only way we stand a chance of being heard is, **hit them in the wallet**, that will get their attention! And look for "Made in America." Reminds me of an old joke, a lady went shopping and found something made in America, so she bought it! Funny? Yes, but sadly, so true.

I respect and admire Ann Coulter, Cal Thomas, Max Lucado, Sean Hannity, DR. Lora, Billy Graham, his daughter Ann Lotz and son Franklin. Bill O'Reilly, Rush Limbaugh, Jesse DuPlantis, Joel Osteen and like our President Bush, the most important person in my life is Jesus. I love Pat Robertson and the 700 Club. He knows the truth about Muslim faith and speaks up about it, and is then crucified for telling the truth. Generally, his words are taken out of context! I know, I watch it daily and have supported it for years. What you have to realize is, Pat Robertson is not running for office or attempting to get votes! Cynical? Yes I am, with no apology. Yes, most Christians are. We have to be. Experience is a fine professor! Knowledge is even better.

I adore and respect Mel Gibson for his boldness in doing the Passion. There is a story behind this, but not my place to tell it. Anti-Semitism? Oh please, give me a break! The Romans killed Jesus, aided by a couple of Political Jews, but all of this was preordained by God, with blame being on all of us, not the Jews! Read the Book, don't wait for the movie! Why crucify Gibson? Didn't Jesus ask "Father forgive them, for they knew not what they do?" No matter who killed Jesus, they are forgiven, yet we still want to debate the event.

I think you all have gotten the point and know where I stand. I didn't even jump on PETA and those criminal environmentalists, or how sick I am of being at the mercy of foreign oil! No, I shall not go there. Not in this book. I think I have made my feelings clear. For those that find this awful or perhaps wanting change, then I strongly suggest that you get to the Polls and let your voices be heard. Otherwise, you might as well be prepared to lose many more of your rights!

While on the dark side, this country is full of attorneys and Politicians writing bad checks, abusing Government credit cards, getting traffic tickets, (let's see you try that) without being punished and the taxpayers pay the bills. Tax dollars for a lap dance, in a topless bar? Eighty million dollars a year to tap phones.

Look at the IL mess, with six men in prison, but never proving Wright guilty of anything. A truck driving school with one hundred fifty four men, not able to read or speak English, getting their license, with the same address. Which happened to be a Motel 6. The truck driving school donated greatly to the election of said man! I still remember the parents watching all their children burn alive in the van, because of this. It took this travesty in IL. to expose the corruption.

Can you imagine working for a company with just over five hundred employees with the following statistics;

29 have been accused of spousal abuse

07 have been arrested for fraud

19 have been accused of writing bad checks

17 have directly or indirectly bankrupted at least two businesses, 3 having done time for assault

71 cannot get a credit card due to bad credit

08 have been arrested for shoplifting

21 are currently defendants in lawsuits

14 arrested on drug related charges

84 arrested for drunk driving in the last year. Can you guess who this company is? The 535 members of the United States Congress. The group of fools cranking out new laws each year, to keep us in line! Since 1991,

seventy-eight politicians have been sent to prison. It should be more but, it's a good start.

A perfect example of why I cannot get any attention regarding Rick's rights. Just look at who I am forced to deal with. Are you kidding? I must resort to liars for honesty? To right a wrong, in this great country called America? Where are, **"WE, THE PEOPLE?"** I'm just spinning my wheels in my effort for assistance. Can you grasp the purpose of this book by now?

What we must learn, is that for every wrong done, by anyone, no matter how trivial it might seem, I assure you someone will pay the price. I guarantee you, the one that pays will be an innocent victim! Nothing is done without a price. Everything we do touches another life. I've had enough and I assure you, something will be done in God's perfect timing. Call it a crutch, call it whatever pacifies you, I don't care nor, am I finished yet. How have we managed to take Ten Commandments and turn them into a minimum of tens of thousands? That's organized religion.

I will say, there are some Muslims that are not at a dangerous degree, yet! To them, Jesus was a good Prophet, at best. However, Jesus is the only one that teaches us to love your enemies, opposed to killing them. If you're not a Muslim, you are an infidel and you will be forced into submission. Islamic faith, I will acknowledge, but I will ever accept it as a peaceful religion. I love them and pray for them, but there is a huge difference between faith and religion. You ridicule and mock any bold enough to take this stand. Why don't you investigate? I love and admire our President, but refuse to join him in being politically correct, in that Muslim faith is peaceful. I am convinced he doesn't have the facts! We truly are fighting evil.

Allah, Muhammad nor Budda, ever died for anyone and all have graves. If Bin Laden is such a devout Muslim, why doesn't he set an example and blow himself up? Jesus set quite an example in giving His life for our sins, His final words were asking for our forgiveness. Love your neighbor as you love yourself. Jesus says to love your enemies. Now this is a peaceful faith!

Muslims have five levels of faith, with no level coming with a guarantee of heaven. The fifth level is shedding your blood, called Jihad, which should get you there! But, Allah can change the rules at any time. It appears that the men decide what woman achieve, while the men joke about hell being full of women.

Can it be that Jesus simply makes it too easy? He is the way, the truth and the life. We simply accept His gift at the cross, His life for our sins. I can't imagine, daily working to earn nothing more than a hope of making it to their heaven.

I have learned that being saved does not make me a Savior! The message is more important than the messenger! I am not trying to convert anyone, but I pray I give you something to think about! Animals have more rights and protection than people have. Are Christians are so depraved in believing we are to be gentle, honest, trustworthy and accountable? Are we going to continue to allow the heathen to slowly misguide and desensitize us, like sheep off to the slaughter? What will it take to open our eyes to the state of this nation? Downhill runs much quicker than up. Islam is not a peaceful faith! Christians are not weak and I am sure this year's election will prove this fact. We do not hate the homosexuals, but will not condone their lifestyle. We have been silent too long, but it is not too late to speak up.

I dare any reader to read **"The Lambda Conspiracy."** A novel by Spenser Hughes. I read it years ago. I am not surprised regarding gay and lesbian rights and their place in politics. I thought it was a novel, but I have witnessed it come to pass! It was very prophetic. I strongly urge all to read it!

As for the Muslims, they are marrying ten thousand American women yearly? Plus, the men can marry four wives. If they cannot force us to convert, they'll infiltrate America in this way. Know this, their religion instructs, "Kill the infidel, or force them to accept the faith." Once a woman is married to a Muslim, she loses her name and must be totally submissive to her husband. Once she has a boy, a heir, she can be beaten repeatedly. Should she not wear enough gold, she opens the door to abuse. Her children can be taken and the wife has no way of having them returned. She gave up her rights to this, unknowingly. A Muslim marriage contract is only good for twenty years. This goes on in our own backyard. What are we doing about it? Over two hundred women with acid burns and no attorney will assist them. They are forced to go underground. They need prayer and lots of it. This is our job, as Jesus loves them all, enemies or not. Jesus says to love them as yourself. Where is peace and love in this? Don't take my word for it, read "I Married Muhammad," by Cati. What an eye opener!

I suggest the next time you run into a female Muslim, instead of turning away, talk to her! Ask her how she is and tell her God loves her. Because under that veil, will most likely be a black eye, or bruised bones and the last thing they need is to be spurned by anyone! Muslims are permitted to beat their wives I am well aware of being terribly, politically incorrect. Need I tell you again, I do not care! If we are to be truly "Politically Correct," then I challenge you. **Why does no one use Budda, Allah or Muhammad before damn, like we do our God?** I shudder to think of the results, but I dare the Hollywood idiots to attempt it! Why do we only use the God of this land to blaspheme? If you wish to be truly "Politically Correct," then go all the way or bring this farcical, secular scam to a halt!

Now, let's look at Israel and our stance with or against them. First, forget the Road Map. It will never work. Like it or not, the Bible plainly states, "I will curse those that curse Israel and I will bless those that bless Israel." Why has this nation been so blessed for so long? Go back and check the weather patterns, disasters etc. I will relate what I have seen this year alone. Last May, we had a record five hundred tornadoes! How many fires have we had, in how many states? I do cast some blame on that EPA crap. We do need controlled burns. In less than ten days we have seen some unbelievable earthquakes! Over 30,000 lives lost, just in the Iran earthquake.

We've lost many brave men in two countries. I couldn't be more proud of our Military, with what defense the last two term President left us with. The many closed bases and defense cut- backs. Our soldiers are forced to learn to fight without real bullets! I marvel at the many fine, brave Americans willing to place their lives on the line for us! But, let us be real. Yes, we have lost lives in Iraq, but not as many as in two cities, in one year, with over seven hundred murders. We haven't been in Iraq that long! Are you getting the picture? There is so much we are ignorant of. Remember, ignorance is not the same as being stupid. If we don't wake up and face some facts, then it will become stupidity!

How many are aware of HR-35? This is a law that L.B.J. got passed in the fifties. I don't believe he had a clue as to the depth it would go to, in order to get votes. This law means that Preachers and any Church is not allowed to talk about politics or verse their opinion on who to vote for. The IRS has a problem with enforcing this law, as they are dependent on someone turning them in. If caught, they will forfeit their tax exemption. Now, if this doesn't sound like Communism, tell me what it is? Turning one an another in.

Or how about HR3717, "the Decency Law. C-SPAN has been broadcasting the hearings all week, due to the Super Bowl's notorious half-time, under the guise of entertainment, porno show.

Will we ever get our fill of such brazen, repulsive and vulgar behavior? When will enough be enough? Or does that shenanigan fall under the First Amendment also, in freedom of speech? The music I heard was bad enough to hit the mute button for the audio. But, we had no options for the video portion in seeing Janet Jackson's breast. Justin is in denial or simply a liar, as Janet did at least confess her guilt. I'm so weary of "I'm sorry." Try to feed your children I'm sorry and they will die of starvation.

Such mixed signals here. Let a child in the first grade, kiss a girl or look up her dress and you will have a law suit. Better yet, should a student, at any age, turn in a school report about Jesus and it will be rejected, with the student being chastised! If it would be on Charlie Manson, Bin Laden or Ted Bundy or anyone of that caliber, and it's fine.

Is anything sacred anymore? Certainly not marriage. Too many are of the attitude of, "Do you want to get married? If it doesn't work, we can always get a divorce." Many prefer to shack-up opposed to making a commitment. However, vows and commitments are not taken seriously anymore either, so why bother? Our former President taught our children all about oral sex and how to commit perjury. I wonder why the Courts even bother to swear anyone in, under oath. The latest definition for truth, is <u>anything that you perceive it to be, is the truth</u>. No wonder so many students cheat. Noah Webster must be rolling in his grave, I'm sure. Webster could quote the entire Bible, chapter and verse, from Genesis to Revelation. Dr. Dobson of Focus on the Family did an entire show on the dictionary and how many times the word truth has changed over the last several decades. I was dumbfounded. By the time his program was over, I did my own research. It is amazing how far we have fallen.

We are living in a nation of "anything goes," as long as you can justify your words or actions, it is totally acceptable. I expect the word LOVE to become a noun, opposed to a verb. Daily, as I go online, I am appalled at what I see in my e-mail. Thank God, at least I stopped hearing from Ms Cleo's desire to give me all the answers to my life.

Most talk shows should be renamed "Shock shows." As for myself, I am tired of dancing with the enemy. My dance card is filled, but not with television. Reality shows have hit an all time low.

Are we all so miserable with our own lives that we are dependent on such rubbish? Once again, I am so proud of Mel Gibson for the boldness he is exhibiting with the Passion of Christ. An actor investing his own money and years on a movie about Christ. So, what happens? He's crucified too for doing so. He stirred the water, renewed anti-Semitism and open hatred against the Jews and angered all the journalists and Networks because he won't suck up or back down. David Meese did a song on his latest CD. A favorite line of mine is, "The black hates the white, the white hates the Jew, if you're any different, everybody hates you." Everyone on the defense about this movie, when the very subject, Jesus, is politically incorrect.

Have you any idea that the crucification of Christ was predicted numerous time in the Old Testament and it is plainly states <u>that all are guilty</u>? Not the Jews! Or is this just another fact that most do not want know? Is it, **<u>Don't confuse us with the facts.</u>** Do we just wish to pick and choose who we want to hate? Why would anyone want to hate anybody? It's so easy to love those that loves us, but more arduous to love those that do not love us. We are so busy being politically correct that we are failing to notice the terror camps in our own backyards. Does any know what is transpiring in Mosques right here in our nation and the hatred being taught? Not all of them but enough that you should be horrified! Again, "United we stand, divided we fall." We are living dangerously in the hands of God.

CHAPTER 56
THE DANGEROUS SUPREME COURT!

This nation was blessed for so long because it was established and founded on God and the Ten Commandments, not ten suggestions! Why have they now become the Ten Offenses? Why have we abandoned the God we prayed to, for the country's freedom, foundation, blessings and the right to worship. We have thrown Him out of school, Courtrooms and too many Churches! Porno floods our streets. Worse yet, porno on computers have devoured and often killed or ruined our children, under the guise of Freedom of Speech, thanks to Clinton taking care of his buddies!

This is an election year and all are duty bound to vote! Voting is a gift and should be seen as one. Get your facts, know the issues, do your American duty. Vote! I know in my heart that few are truly conscious of the great importance of our direction. So, for you that don't care enough to vote and prefer playing the "Blame Game," look in the mirror for the enemy, and blame them!

When did, **"We the People,"** become **"We the Judges?"** What are they doing handing down cultural laws? What happened to a once proud, successful, blessed country, where freedom used to ring? People from all over the world, would leave their homeland, for the promise of this once great, land of the Free and home of the Brave? Seeking the freedom to worship and to escape tyranny!

George Washington once said; " It is impossible to rightly govern the world without God and the Bible."

Thomas Jefferson once warned, if the Supreme Court became the sole arbiter of the land, America will come under tyranny. What do you know? These old time, backwoods boys really knew what they were talking about.

As for The Declaration of Independence, fifty-two of the fifty-five signatures on it, were not just practicing Christians but, active members of their Church. It kind of coincides with Genesis, does it not? All are created and equal in God's eyes, but apparently not with the Supreme Court, nor with some others like the Ninth Circuit Court in CA. What a joke. I would laugh, but it is too scary.

The United States Supreme Court is the nation's highest Federal court, consisting of nine judges. It's decisions are final, taking precedence over all other judicial bodies throughout the country. The President nominates them. These lifelong appointments are made with the advice and consent of the Senate. These judges are to be guardians and interpreters of the Constitution and it's amendments and not to be confused with Dictators!

With the current, dangerous combination of these Judges, it only takes five of them to lead our country down a hazardous spiral, leading to an ethical and moral form of anarchy. Let us take a good look at our Supreme Court. See if you do not see a frightening trend, explaining why the Dems are so upset with our President's selections, possibly taking a seat on the Supreme Court. We still have a bit of hope, but not enough. It's very possible a couple of these Judges will step down or retire. I have chosen to reveal their voting record, law school and by whom they were appointed. Please take notice of those voting on the laws and those that break the ties, generally by Sandra Day O'Connor, and she tends to go with the majority, but not always. Much like the wind, I find very little comfort here. Let's see what you think about my concerns. Remember, it is their job to abide by law that is legislated. Notice how they tend to write their own laws!

Now, I shall elaborate on our miserable, dangerous Supreme Court. Why are the Dems really so fearful of the Bush nominees? Glad you asked, because I am going to enlighten you. I'm not alone on this, (Pat Robertson beat me to a lot of facts) so you self proclaiming Patriots, Christians and true Americans better learn the facts and then speak up, loudly! Another reason and a warning of grave concern, but we are not hopeless nor helpless. The clock is running though. We have very little time in which to accomplish this mission. I and many others are acutely aware that God is angry! I am so grateful He is giving us another chance. We do not deserve it, but He is a God of love and mercy. He promises us, if we lift Him up from the earth, He will draw all men unto Him, hear us and heal our land. If we lift up our voices, repent and change our ways. Albert Einstein once said, the more he saw and learned, the more he knew there had to be a Creator, and he was going to seek Him. I pray he found him.

Now, please study these Supreme Court Judges and their rulings. See if you can separate Legislated laws from Cultural Laws. Remember, it only takes five Judges for a ruling. I hope you can do a better job than I did, I am underwhelmed and frightened.

THE SUPREME COURT, OUR NATION'S HIGHEST COURT. UN-ELECTED JUDGES, REQUIRED BY LAW TO UPHOLD THE LAW, NOT TO REWRITE IT!

William H. Rehnquist, Stanford U. Nominated, Nixon, 1972. Nominated for **Chief Justice** by Ronald Reagan, 1986. One of my two favorites!

AGAINST a ruling that sodomy laws are unconstitutional in Lawrence v. Texas. **6-3 decision!**

FOR Boy Scouts of America in Dale v Boy Scouts. **In a 5-4 decision.** Affirmed the organization can bar homosexuals from leadership ranks.

FOR upholding the Child Pornography Prevention Act in Ashcroft v. Free Speech Coalition. On April 16, 2002. A majority decision struck down this act, which is aimed at the prevention of production or distribution of pornographic material pandered as child porno, stating it violates the First Amendment guarantee of freedom of speech! Clinton's buddies (My own thoughts) and I think every parent in this country should still be screaming! Total confusing, **6 & 1/2-2 & 1/2***

FOR requiring parental consent of minors requesting an abortion in Lambert v. Wicklund. Decision of court was **7-2** to uphold the right of state legislatures to adopt laws requiring parental consent.

FOR allowing Bible clubs in public schools, in Good News Club v. Milford public schools. **5-4**

***Sandra Day O'Connor**, assoc. justice. Stanford U. Nominated by Ronald Reagan, 1981.

This woman frightens me when I attempt to recognize her ways of thinking.

FOR the sodomy law being unconstitutional.

FOR the Boy Scouts' rights.

FOR and AGAINST (concurring in part and dissenting in part) with the Child Pornography Act. You figure that one out!

FOR requiring parental consent for abortion.

FOR allowing Bible clubs in school.

John Paul Stevens, assoc. justice. Northwestern U. Nominated by Gerald Ford, took seat 1975.

Easy, saving me a lot of time and space! Two words, NEGATIVE and CONSISTENT! Yet, this is the type of what the Dems want more of!

FOR the sodomy law as unconstitutional.

AGAINST Boy Scouts' rights

AGAINST the Child Prevention Pornography Act.

AGAINST parental consent.

AGAINST allowing Bible clubs in school!

Antonin Scalia. assoc. justice. Harvard Law, nominated by Ronald Reagan, took seat in 1986.

Another easy, but enjoyable man.

AGAINST sodomy being Constitutional.

FOR Boy Scouts' rights.

FOR upholding Child Prevention Pornography Act.

FOR requiring parental consent for abortion of minors.

FOR allowing Bible clubs in public schools.

Anthony M. Kennedy, assoc. justice. Harvard Law. Nominated by Ronald Reagan, seat in 1988.

This one is a puzzle.

FOR sodomy law being unconstitutional

FOR Boy Scouts' rights.

AGAINST Child Prevention Pornography Act.

FOR requiring parental consent.

FOR allowing Bible clubs in schools.

David Hackett Souter, Harvard Law. Nominated by George H. Bush, took seat in 1990.

Bush Sr. dropped the ball here. Yet note the middle name, **Hackett**, which he does.

FOR sodomy laws being unconstitutional.

AGAINST Boy Scouts' rights.

FOR requiring parental consent.

AGAINST allowing Bible clubs in public schools.

AGAINST Child Porno Prevention Act

Clarence Thomas, assoc. justice. Yale Law. Nominated by George H. Bush, took seat 1991.

AGAINST sodomy law.

FOR Boy Scouts' rights.

AGAINST the Child Porno Prevention Act.

FOR <u>requiring parental consent.</u>

FOR <u>allowing Bible clubs in school.</u>

Ruth Bader Ginsberg, assoc. Harvard and Columbia Law. Nominated by Bill Clinton, seat 1993.

Just about the scariest one. I feel she would vote AGAINST my right to exist! Intellectual idiot?

FOR <u>sodomy laws being unconstitutional.</u>

AGAINST <u>Boy Scouts' rights.</u>

AGAINST <u>the Child Porno Prevention Act.</u>

AGAINST <u>requiring parental consent.</u>

AGAINST <u>allowing Bible clubs in schools.</u>

Last but not least, **Stephen G. Breyer**, Harvard Law. Nominated by Bill Clinton, took seat 1994.

Almost a male clone of Ruth, yet another Clintonista.

FOR <u>sodomy laws being unconstitutional</u>

AGAINST <u>Boy Scouts' rights.</u>

AGAINST <u>the Child Porno Prevention Act.</u>

AGAINST <u>parental consent.</u>

FOR <u>allowing Bible clubs in schools</u>. Hmm, must have dozed off on this one.

Now you have the facts and the reason for the Filibuster. Could it be more obvious to any? I rest my case. Numbers don't lie and I pray you will do the math. I think the Dems are keenly aware they cannot continue their stonewalling of our President's, more than qualified nominees, for another term. Expect all hell to break loose. I mean that in the literal sense. This will be the ugliest, most vile and nasty election we have ever seen. Remember who the Politicians are working for and who pays their salaries! "We the People," need to remind them of this fact at every opportunity we can find!

So, I am expected to deal with our problem of corruption, trusting in courts like this, seeking justice in the midst of such riffraff?

CHAPTER 57
MY TURN AT FREE SPEECH

The Iowa Caucus is over and Edwards came through great. I find him to be the only Democrat I can relate with. I am impressed at his determination to keep his campaign clean, but question his faith and allowing states to make laws. I thought the states came together and formed the United States of America! I find Kerry's survivor in Vietnam surfacing, to be bad timing. I do applaud Kerry for fighting in Vietnam, but I seek a leader with values, morals and ethics. I have neighbors I see as heroes, but that alone doesn't qualify them to run for the highest office in our country. I see arrogance and a rich kid in Kerry. And, I think I can still hear Howard Dean screaming, as though he won.

I noticed a banner in Iowa that I questioned; "Give America Back It's Future and It's Soul" I'm not exactly sure of it's meaning. I know what I want it to encompass, but nothing I have seen yet, would indicate my desire. We have lost our focus. We have sold out, compromised and kept quiet far too long. We do need change, but we must first go back before we can move ahead. Back to the basics of life. Again, why was America the Promised Land for so long? Why were we so blessed, prosperous and able to achieve such results? Have we ever lost a war?

I saw the tasteless spot on Moveon.org with our President as Hitler. What a disgrace! I ask you to research factual history. (that will eliminate our current school books) President Bush is a man of faith. Hitler? For those that know the Bible, you know that the Jews are God's chosen people.

Hitler's desire, following the total annihilation of the Jews, was to eradicate the blacks. This man was consumed with purity. I know that many do not accept the Holocaust occurred. But, it did! Hitler was worse than any megalomaniac. A real war monger, extremely close to Saddam's own goals. The weak, the unfit and those amounting to nothing, had to be exterminated.

Most Jews considered themselves German first, then Jews. Very few were cognizant of the reality and madness of Hitler until, in most cases, it was too late. In 1941 the Olympics were held in Germany. When America's

Owens and Lewis won all those Medals, Hitler remarked, "The way is clear for America." Why did he say this? What could he have envisioned? I shudder to think of what he had in his warped, demented mind.

Germany actually saw Hitler as their savior! It happens so easily when you wear blinders and become dependent on government. Look at his legacy, the devastation and destruction Hitler left behind. I find Al Gore's book, "Earth in the Balance," more closely related to Hitler, than Bush on his worst day!

Who is pure? White supremacy frightens me. Not one of us are a pure, white American! We all migrated here for a better life. A life of freedom to worship, freedom of tyranny, with the promise of hopes and dreams. If any are truly an American, then it is the Indians, not us! Why do so many whites think they are better or more pure? Let's look at the Indians. What would we have done without them in W.W.II? They were in short, instrumental in our victory! As well as the blacks!

In 1995 HBO, (I have no movie channels) produced an excellent movie, "The Tuskegee Airmen." I watched it on the History channel. In 1941 in Alabama, Roosevelt setup a trial base for black pilots. The movie was extremely factual, with few exceptions. Lt. Col.'s' James Warren and Lee Archer of the 332nd, having been two of the pilots, were there. The First Lady did go up, in a plane with one of them, prior to them becoming Cadets. She was instrumental in the project. Of course our Politicians at Capitol Hill got involved with crap like their blood vessels were smaller etc., and wasting the taxpayer dollars, yada, yada, yada. Just the usual tainted opinions.

They traveled by train to Alabama. At one point the train was stopped and all the colored men were taken off and sent to the front car. The front car was the coldest and caught most of the smoke. Why were they moved? To give their seats over to German prisoners!

These brave men fought every obstacle imaginable to make the grade. In all, one thousand made it. They were sent to North Africa in the beginning, far from the war. Finally, being sent to Italy where they were able to prove themselves worthy, but not greatly appreciated. Commander Davis was tough, very tough, but he had to be. He wouldn't accept defeat, knowing well the grave importance of their success. These brave men were sent to escort our bombers. In one mission alone, we lost sixty-five bombers, one third of the total. That was prior to the Tuskegee Airmen. Eventually, a massive strike on Berlin resulted with the whites requesting of the 332nd to escort them. In this strike the first three German jets were shot down by those brave men! Result, successful mission.

Commander Benjamin O. Davis, a combat pilot with the Royal Canadian Air Force, led this trial force. Against facing incredible odds Davis was immeasurably responsible for their great success. The 332nd never lost a bomber to the enemy! Unlike the movie "Top Gun," they weren't allowed to leave the bombers to go after the enemy and shoot them down. From May1943 to June 1945, four-hundred and fifty men received eight-hundred and fifty medals! Why has this been such a secret for so many decades?

Upon returning from the war, these black heroes walked down the gangplank to find signs with arrows, --> **"Colored Troops this way" "White Troops this way."** This was how we welcomed our heroes home! Men willingly placing their lives on the line for God, country, family and we, the people. Many did not return. How do you think their families felt? Civil Rights actually began in 1948, when Truman chose to integrate our armed forces. It was said that the whites would walk out. They didn't, though I am not claiming it was problem free. God willing, we will learn to unite. They have fought every war since WW I. Having to sit in the back of the bus. Having their own restroom, drinking fountains and not allowed to eat with the whites. Not allowed to attend a white school and ineligible to vote until Johnson signed the Civil Rights in the sixties! I truly hope all whites are as ashamed as I am.

The same goes for the unsung Indian heroes, who went to such great lengths to fight for the country we took from them. I am sure many are now aware of the movie "The Wind Talkers." Again, how many decades passed with us unaware of their value to our nation and our victory in the war? What disease are we suffering with? I find this inexcusable. If anything makes my blood boil, it's the "N" word and the attitude of one thinking they are better than another. When anyone or any race is deprived of an education we tend to look down upon them. This does tend to make them appear inferior. How dare we be so judgmental. It's like comparing Jesus to His followers.

One was a thief, liar and betrayer. A few were weak, but the other eleven finally got with the program.

I will not go into the details of the undeclared war in Vietnam or how we called our soldiers baby killers. How can anyone fight the enemy when you don't know who the enemy is? The awful way we welcomed them home, should be a criminal offense. For what it's worth, gentleman and women, I bow to you! For everyone, in every war that has fought to defend me, I thank God for you. With all my heart, I humbly thank you. I must also apologize for all the empty-headed, prejudiced or simply ignorant people. You truly are heroes! We are truly in your debt. Please forgive our stupidity!

Speaking of heroes, aside from our Forefathers, mine are Robert Kennedy, Martin Luther King, and Gracia Burnham. I love Ronald Reagan, but not happy with him supplying Saddam with weapons, (for Mustard and Serin gas) to take on Iran. We should have gone after them and not depended on a sadist to do the job. In truth, we helped create that monster! My heroes are any that see a wrong and stand up to right it.

Martin Luther King was one of the finest men ever to grace this country. I don't have to be black to adore, love, admire and respect this man! I admire boldness and anyone courageous enough to address critical issues in the name of peace! I was too young to join his peace march but, oh, how I wanted to. What an honor it would have been. Martin Luther King was a man that truly walked the walk and talked the talk. I'm sure he would have preferred to have stayed home to raise his children and preach, but he was called, and he answered that call with magnificence.

I am filled with disgust at most of the five-hundred cities with Avenues and Boulevards named for King. Most all are in terrible areas. St. Louis is one of the longest and worst. I am impressed with Miami and their desire to do it properly, As it should be. But hats off to Muncie IN. Wow, you folks showed them! Atlanta GA. has one several blocks from Martin Luther King's Museum. This peaceful man of God, should be revered and his message remembered by all, every time we see his name.

Bobby Kennedy was my answered prayer. I actually blamed myself for his death. I had spent months on my knees praying he would run for President. I saw no hope otherwise. Losing King and Kennedy in such a short time was so difficult for me. I left the Church and Politics for two decades. Bobby cared so much about people. Years later, I ran across a book of events of 1963.

I was shocked. I was aware of less than one third of what I read. Bobby learned that NY City had more rats than people. He found high school graduates couldn't read above a sixth grade level. Another reason to not favor the NEA. Bobby had many enemies and I can see why. He didn't tell us what we wanted to hear. Bobby was against the war in Vietnam, a great patriot and truly loved his country. Of course we know how he took on Jimmy Hoffa, as our United States Attorney General and won!

Of course I loved John Kennedy, but I know less about him. We have never had a perfect President, but I feel he would have been one of our greatest, as well as Bobby. All the more reason to have no patience with Teddy! I would never call John or Bobby <u>liberal</u>!

For those thinking I might be a Bible-thumper, I will now convince you of that. In the Book of Acts, chapter 6, verse 9-15. Peter was constantly being cast into prison for preaching. The Lord and His angels would release him, often. Stephen had just been chosen to join the Apostles, to care for the widows, poor and preach. There was a synagogue of the <u>Libertines</u> who didn't like this and stirred up the people. Stephen was falsely accused and the Libertines didn't stop until Stephen was stoned to death. Does any of this sound or look familiar to you? Is this where Liberals came from? Just a thought....................

Gracia Burnham is a survivor of a kidnapping with her husband, Martin, in the Philippines. What a lady. What a Christian! Her husband Martin, was killed. She has a picture of one of their captors on her refrigerator and still prays for him. Gracia does not play the victim or the blame game. What an example.

Faith is not organized religion. Faith has no "signs and wonders" drive through window. There are no fast faith food places, accepting orders for "<u>miracles to go</u>." There are no short cuts. You take it all or you take none of it. Faith is a relationship with the Creator.

My Pastor Jerry, my husband, daughter and Lori keep me grounded. They can't keep me silent, but they are my support and inspiration, always encouraging me. I am blessed. Pastor Jerry is a true man of God, who refuses to compromise the Word. Jerry is filled with a holy boldness. He has been through so much with me and has never deviated from what he believes the Word says. He can sure make you squirm in your seat and I wish we had thousands many more just like him!

I have just returned from dad's funeral. I am very grateful for being allowed to talk with Rick and give him the bad news. Of course he took it hard, but you cannot show weakness in prison! Dad had a beautiful Veteran's service. I was in awe of the respect he was given and I am blessed to have received the American flag on behalf of President Bush. I shall keep it for Rick.

When I left town, I thought this book was done, but too much has occurred this week. I listened to President Bush's speech tonight. I was most pleased. I paid a price for it though, in not turning the channel immediately. There were the Dems! I heard Nancy Pelosi's speech and how she misquoted President Kennedy, miserably. I am still attempting to comprehend her "A light not a missile," remark. Did I miss something? Naturally Tom Daschle had to spew his rubbish.

I will say, the Democrats are never boring. They get my attention every time most any one of them spout off. (not all) They cannot hold my attention, but they do manage to get it. I wish the Democrats had an overwhelming responsibility to allow our views to flow, with civility.

Apparently, I am really old fashioned. I believe the more things change, the more they remain the same, actually, the continue to worsen. We just cannot seem to learn from the past. It is obvious we are doomed to repeat history. God have mercy on us.

I sit in amazement, wondering what one Democrat has to offer this nation. Kerry, Kennedy and the their respective state! Dean in Vermont, not much difference. All are in favor of abortion, gay marriages, (or wanting the states to legislate it) makes me ill. I find my prayer and hope for our nation depends on the Christians going to the Polls. Let's clean up there, then go after all of the un-elected Judges! Oklahoma really threw me with Clark. What's with the Bible belt? I know the pickings are slim, but geez.............
....

CHAPTER 58
IN GOD'S HANDS, FORGET THE STATE BAR!

In closing, I have forgiven the people involved, but I detest <u>that city</u> to this day. I feel the devil himself resides there. A Deputy killed himself, (so they say) and a policeman was killed. No one ever runs against the Criminal Judge. And the Assistant DA lied at the hearing! Do you realize that they too, are under oath. I still do not have all the files, but they have finally confessed to having no transcript of either of the two court appearances, in the same month, in the same year! What angers me so, is their lack of abiding by the law. Have you any idea what would happen to you if you forged a document? If you kept records like they do?

Regarding the final decision of the Texas Star Bar, I feel broken, but do not forget, God is still on the throne! I have said from day one, He has the plan! For the last month I have been telling myself, "Wow, Lord. You must have one fantastic plan here." I truly believe this. Does anyone think we can place any faith in our system, to right this wrong? You have to be kidding.

It is not over yet, no matter what the worthless State Bar says. I detest injustice and sadly, many of you do too, if not, your turn is coming. I will be there for you, God willing and I pray your journey will be far less painful than ours has been. Every day I venture out, I run into another horror story. Everyone I meet is fighting the system in one way or another. Just one wrong after another. Perhaps if the Dems would cease leaving the state over redistricting, maybe, just maybe, something worthy could be accomplished. Whether you agree with me or not, if you have an opinion, then stand up and be heard, at the Polls or keep your silence and settle for what you get, then cast the blame at the one in the mirror!

I am not attempting to be the Prophet of Doom. Only, "We the people," can change this. We have to go to the Polls and send a message, with much prayer and repentance, only then will He hear us and heal our land!

I pray for the day I can come forth and introduce myself, as that will mean Rick will be free and I will take all the crap you wish to throw at me. We would prefer he be cleared in the Courts, but will accept His plan. I wouldn't wish this on anyone else, not even the accuser or the crooked attorney! May God be with you and may you have a happy, stable marriage or have wealth.

For any lacking in faith, or completely void of it, I suggest you find a substitute, fast! If not I strongly encourage you to find the best attorney money can buy! I do wish the worst for the State Bar. I hope they all lose their jobs. I pray they will be haunted every time their head hits the pillows. Small chance of that. Remember, what goes around comes around, and my saying, "You shall surely get your come-uppance!" I hope God smites you all!

I have just learned of another Texas injustice. I am livid! I shall call him Joe. Joe was sentenced eight years ago, to two nine year sentences, to run concurrent. Since then, the Texas prison system has changed the sentences to run consecutive. Meaning, Joe has to serve the first nine years before the next nine begins. This was not the original plea that Joe agreed to. Joe has the Court documents to prove it. Upon Joe writing the Judge in this case, he was informed that the Judge did not wish to be involved! And, much like Max, Joe's attorney has been barred from practicing law too. I told you the money the prisons receive per year, per inmate. Joe has already spent eight years in prison. He will end up spending fifteen to seventeen years before being offset by the Parole Board on a nine year sentence. But, few prisoners have any funds or connections, so that's just tough! This is criminal! Another shinning example of the Texas system gone amuck!

I want to share two e-mails I have just received. The first one is Chairman Michael Powell of the FCC has changed his mind about the use of the F-- word on radio and TV. **PRAISE GOD!**

I do not know who to credit for the second one. A "masterpiece." My Country is simply too good to leave out. The more I read it the more I would like to include all Politicians and Judges! The subject is,

"My Country."

Will we still be the Country of choice and still be America, if we continue to make the changes forced on us by the people from other countries, that came to live in America, because it is the Country of Choice? All I have to say is, when will they do something about My Rights? I celebrate Christmas, but because it isn't celebrated by everyone, we can no longer say Merry Christmas. Now, it has to be Season's Greetings. It is not Christmas vacation, it's Winter Break. Isn't it amazing how the winter break always occurs over the Christmas holiday? We've gone so far the other way, bent over backwards to not offend anyone, that I am now being offended! But, it seems that no one has a problem with that! The following is an editorial written by an American citizen, published in a Tampa newspaper.

IMMIGRANTS, NOT AMERICANS, MUST ADAPT!

I am tired of this nation worrying about whether we are offending some individual or their culture. Since the terrorist attacks on *September 11*, we have experienced a surge in patriotism by the majority of Americans. However, the dust from the attacks had barely settled when the "politically correct" crowd began complaining about the possibility that our patriotism was offending others.

I am not against immigration, nor hold a grudge against anyone who is seeking a better life by coming to America. Our population is almost entirely made up of descendants of immigrants. However, there are a few things that those, who have recently come to our country, and apparently, some born here, need to understand. This idea of America being a multicultural community has served only to dilute our sovereignty and our national identity. As Americans, we have our own culture, our own society, our own language and our own lifestyle. This culture has been developed over centuries of struggles, trials, and victories by millions of men and women who have sought freedom.

We speak ENGLISH, not Spanish, Portuguese, Arabic, Chinese, Japanese, Russian or any other language. Therefore, if you wish to become part of our society, learn the language!

"In God We Trust" is our national motto. This is not some Christian, right wing, political slogan. We adopted this motto because Christian men and women, on Christian principles, founded this nation and this is clearly documented. It is certainly appropriate to display it on the walls of our schools. If God offends you, then I suggest you find another part of the world as your new home, because God is part of our culture! If Stars and Stripes offend you, or you don't like Uncle Sam, then you should seriously consider a move to another planet. We are happy with our culture and have no desire to change and, we really don't care how you did things where you came from.

This is **OUR COUNTRY**, our land, our lifestyle. Our First Amendment gives every citizen the right to express his opinion and we will allow you every opportunity to do so. But, once you are done complaining, whining and griping about our flag, our pledge, our national motto, or your way of life, I highly encourage you to take advantage of one other great American freedom, the right to leave.

I am convinced I could not have said it better. I wish I had written it. I certainly hope it will strike a nerve in the true Americans and Patriots! Dare I dream the Politicians will open their eyes? I don't think so. However, they may be so furious it could serve as a diversion, giving President Bush a break. Now, I am really dreaming!

I have just been notified that our mother is near death, given hours, perhaps days to live. This has been a very difficult month. Part of me wants to keep her here. Another part wants her to have peace and be pain free. Again, I will have to trust the Lord. With His help, I will, get through whatever tomorrow holds.

This book is finished, for now! However, the fight will continue, as long as I am breathing and until Rick receives the justice due him! Rick is just the beginning. It has become a mission now, and we will continue forward, helping others. Trust me, there are many others! One day, Washington will have to deal with us and that's a promise!

EPILOGUE

It is my pleasure to announce that an Innocent Project has contacted us. We might have some legal assistance in this case. I am trying not to be over hopeful, after all, the Project is in Texas.

Upon my reviewing and filling out the endless questionnaire, (over 100) even more information has been uncovered.

I had informed you earlier, that Rick had signed a "Judicial Confession," well concealed in the "Stipulation of Evidence." The new attorney described it as a "mousetrap." I had to once again read the Revocation Hearing transcript and found some dazzling information. With that so-called expert, Sam, on the stand? I found some most interesting testimony by Sam, under oath, on the stand. Max asked Sam the following questions;

Max Q. "You do know that Rick plead "no contest" at his hearing?"

Sam A. "That is correct."

Max Q. " You do know that Rick did not even testify?"

Sam A. "Yes."

Max Q. "The file will clearly show Rick did not even sign a judicial confession. He just entered a "no contest" plea?

Sam A. "That is correct."

Even more interesting is the DA's cross examination of Sam. It was most brief and the DA never asked a question or made one remark regarding the "no signed judicial confession." I simply had to insert these amazing facts! No judicial confession! Once again, it does not stop there.

In the dedication, I said mother would never see this book. We lost our mother. We lost both mom and dad in six weeks. I will not ask for your empathy. I do ask for your anger towards our inept, corrupt system. I asked that Rick be allowed to attend the Funeral. The family had been told by a Marshal to call the prison and the Bureau of Classifications telling them to "begin the paperwork." All data had to come from the Funeral Home, with date, time and name etc. They would know before we would. We held back on the ceremony as long as we could, in order to accomplish this feat. The results were typical of all we have known from the great state of Texas. Nothing functions as it should!

I drove to the prison the next day to inform Rick personally. I vowed Rick would not hear this dreaded news via the telephone. No, I had to be there with him. Rick's worst fear had come to pass. He would not be able to hold his mother once again. I spent the weekend there and it did help Rick, knowing that I would return the next day. I found the Warden and the Chaplain to be very kind. I truly feel they went beyond the call in granting my requests regarding this matter. I am very grateful to both of them. I don't know if I could do it again, but it is finished.

Suffice it to say, Rick was denied a leave. Geanie, (my daughter) tried to take the task off my shoulders and handle it for me. She spoke to a very kind man at the Bureau who closed their conversation with, "We'll know in forty-five minutes, don't you worry about it." Unfortunately, I have had this experience on numerous occasions, but not Geanie. Geanie actually got her hopes up and truly believed that Rick would be there. Like many of us, she was convinced that one day we would wake up to find the nightmare over. After all, this is America! When she learned Rick had been denied, she became so angry she began calling all the numbers again, convinced there had been a mistake. Denial! Oh yes, I am quite familiar with that pain.

Upon my departure, Geanie was still on the phone, ash white, weeping and breaking my heart. I knew she would hear the same message I had heard. A cold employee of the state describing an Uncle and a brother no one knew, with atrocious terms Rick's life is reduced to a single piece of inaccurate paper, depicting what a terrible man he is! Through tears Geanie asked, "Mother, who are they talking about?"

Remember McElyea, in Austin, finally admitted to me, "There was no weapon." As for Rick's repeated criminal, brutal crimes? The DWI back in 1985. Rick fully served two years probation on that, so why is it on his record? I couldn't find it on his record prior to his sentencing! Rick could not have been hired at his Company had that DWI been on his record. How in God's name could the state go back and add it on, legally? Because this is Texas!

Geanie knows her Uncle for the person he truly is. Geanie has been a different person since that day. She too, is now filled with a righteous anger. I have another in my corner, but how it came about is most aggravating. After all the years I have been the one to receive the bad news of our on-going injustice in Texas. Geanie merely got her tongue wet and yet, daily, she is more angry, asking me, "Mother, how could you survive this more than once? I couldn't go through it again." We felt the state owed Rick and the family some closure in the death of our mother.

By now I assume you are aware of my faith. The laborious trip would have it's rewards. In short, I am so glad I went alone. I needed the time alone after days of being at mother's bedside, surrounded by family, Nurses and Doctors, until she passed. I was not truly alone, but welcomed the Lord's love and strength to keep me and prepare me for the awful news I had to share with Rick. I so desired to tell Rick that he would be there for the Funeral.

As it turned out, Rick was upset that we thought he would be able to attend the Funeral. He told me there was no chance of him being there. He said no matter what charges he was there for, no one got such a leave and hadn't for years. Rick said the state brought that to a halt years back. Remember, the Texas prisons are a huge corporation and they don't spend money on inmates!

My trip was truly rewarding and I am still learning more. I seemed to have stumbled onto a "smoking gun." I ran across an article in a Houston newspaper about an inmate that had filed an "Extraordinary Writ," against the state of Texas and the prison system, involving time credited. Time consists of good time, work time and sentencing time as an incentive for inmates. By law, inmates are allowed to accumulate time while serving their sentence. However, Texas denies inmates of such. From what I have been able to glean, upon parole, each inmate has to return all work time credit before they are allowed to leave the prison. (I asked if any had refused to do this) Yes, one guy, still incarcerated.

Inmate, Mr. Gross, filed the "Writ," based on good time and work time. I was very impressed at what I read. Via a phone interview, Gross responded, "We are not looking for a free ride, nor are we asking for the prison doors to be opened and let everyone out. All we are looking for is the Courts to look into these claims. To decide if legislative intent is being followed. If the procedure the parole board is employing may be violating Constitutional instructions. I fully understand I may have blown my chances for parole due to raising this type of claim. I have placed my trust and the future of thousands of inmates into the hands of this Court. I can only pray that something positive will occur, benefiting taxpayers, prisoners and prisoner's families alike. We understand peoples concern about radical changes. However, the elected officials created good time statues for a purpose. It is less expensive to house inmates that do not require maximum or super segregation. The inmates that conduct themselves properly deserve those credits. Inmates work in metal fabs, furniture, clothing and school bus repair industries which saves taxpayers millions of dollars. Those inmates who work deserve work time credits. These credits were designed by legislation to lessen our sentence or time for release to parole. My claim is the Board of Pardons and Paroles is unconstitutionally denying and applying those credits to inmates, thereby violating statues created by the elected officials."

Also in the article, the Texas Attorney General's office had filed an Injunction concerning an appeal. It was denied. Rehnquist and Justices' O'Connor, Thomas and Scalia appear to have a problem with Texas also. Thank You Lord, bring on the investigation!

I researched a Texas state prison web site to learn, "good time is a privilege not a right," and even worse, the Board of Pardons nor the Parole Division are involved in the awarding of good time. So who does? What is the purpose of forcing an inmate to return all work credit? When the inmate returns to prison, (the state generally sees to this, by design) the inmate must then begin anew. The inmate is forced to do this, violating Federal law! Each time I visit Rick, I see inmates working on the roads, buildings and all over town. This is free labor? It's not enough that one is sentenced to prison without any evidence, but to force them to work for free while they lose medical care, education and such? Quite an enterprise they have going on in Texas.

Since the US States Supreme Court denied the office of the TX Attorney General their appeal and God willing, Texas will be investigated! Federal Law states if a man works, he must be paid. The state matches each day served by an inmate. For instance, Rick's prison record is perfect, therefore, every day he serves the state gives him a day. Since Rick works, he earns an additional one half day for each day served. For every thirty days Rick serves he gets sixty days credit, add work time of one half day and Rick earns a total of seventy-five days per each thirty days. Few inmates see any money, only credit for time worked and served. Thus, Rick has done an equivalent of nearly sixteen years so far!

There are exceptions to the rule in that most inmates do not earn money. The exception is an inmate I know of that made badges for the state of Texas, for years. (13 I think) In this case the state did pay, for some time. The money was deposited in his account, but suddenly the funds ceased, without warning or explanation. The inmate repeatedly asked for a reason or explanation., to no avail. He then filed a complaint, an attempt I should say but, the letter was seen in the mailroom, having never arrived at it's destination, because the complaint would make the Unit look bad! Immediately this inmate was demoted and sent back to the worst populated dorm, after 13 years with an excellent record. This is a crime.

While on my computer I found another disturbing web site in Texas, about getting rid of "Chief Justice Rehnquist and the 5." Where do you think this comes from? The best hope we have are the five they want out. Dear God, does this not bring fear bumps all over you? The problem here is that the Supreme Court is considering one being appointed from within the Bureau to investigate the matter. Are you kidding? This is Texas. For God's sake, do not place a chicken snake in the hen house! The Supreme Court will soon receive my letter. (already mailed) I want to see "Due Process and that equal justice," I hear about but, fail to see it. However, I would also like to know who the other four Justices are. For the life of me, I cannot imagine more than three being conservative, let alone too conservative.

I stand amazed at the stance the U S Supreme Court has taken and I applaud their efforts, but I beg them not to trust Texas to investigate or police themselves. The entire system is so volatile and not capable of such an arduous task!

I also have the documents for Joe. (the one with the paperwork wrong and corrected) Yes, the Judge did make the corrections on his paperwork. I have the corrections as well as the letters to the Bureau and the Board of Pardons and Paroles. Their reply was eleven months later, "It stays 3G." They would not acknowledge the inmate or the corrections made by the judge! This is Texas, where prison rules. Joe's attorney has since been disbarred and the judge will go no further. The system seems to especially take advantage of those with bad attorneys and with those having no family or friends willing to take the state on.

Another was arrested and probation revoked for buying gas on the wrong side of the street! He lived in Texarkana, which is a border town. Again, this was in 1998. Had to fill the empty prisons!

I feel in my heart, even though Rick is in minimum security and a model prisoner, once they figure out where all this is coming from, all will change, for the worse. I did share some personal feelings at the prison and am quite aware I can be exposed. I can live with this if they come after me, but leave Rick alone!

My last visit with Rick was so painful, after an hour Rick asked if we could not talk anymore about mother. Of course I agreed. I felt he needed time and with my returning the next day, I knew he would suffer a very, very long night. That gave us a lot of time to go over facts and the lingering questions we had in respect to Rick's ordeal. As for the IRS. Yes, Rick said Sue did do all the filing. He doesn't recall signing his name and confesses that for a fact, Sue did mention she had a problem with the IRS. Recall all of those checks Sue wrote for parts, cars and such, on her mother's account? The remark to Rick, "I'm sorry, but I've done something and either you or mother will have to take the fall?" We are reasonably sure the IRS was involved.

Rick is fully aware of this book. With mother and dad being gone, he suggested I should use the real names. I cannot at this time and reminded Rick of the children. We agree, we have no desire to hurt them unnecessarily. I know Rick is hurting and grieving in his own way with losing five family members since he has been gone. Rick is fed up with all the errors, forgeries and such. He sees many come and go on technicalities, absorbing the many that readily confess of their guilt. It has been a nightmare for all involved, but imagine being sentenced to prison for twenty years for a crime you never committed! Wait, let's back up. First, consider living with the accusation for over two years. Followed by the "Plea," Rick was coerced into, then spending the next seven years of his life, full of the "State of Texas employees and governmental department, criminal idiots!" Add an inadequate, inept, criminal attorney, a questionable Judge and the miserable failure of the Department of Human Services and CPS and you have the perfect recipe for disaster.

Rick reminded me of his verbal threat to the CPS workers not long before it all came down. You cannot sue the Departments, but you can sue an individual and Rick vowed to do just that, with both of them. Rick also told me something he had never shared with me previously. Rick said he had heard a voice telling him, in the first year of his involvement with Sue, "You need to get away from this woman." Rick added, "but I didn't sis and that's my fault." I know that had to be difficult for Rick to share with me. The more I think about it, the more I can appreciate it.

I will share some unbelievable statistics. (off the computer) Most people know little about how the system functions. Most are dependent on the media. (scary but true) The media will always expose violent crimes among the minorities. They will stress violent crimes by Afro-Americans and Hispanic-Americans to evoke fear and emphasize "Tough-on-crime" polices for sale to those who benefit from them, politically and or economically. This is done under our noses as they attempt to assure us that "due process" is at work. I will give you some startling facts now;

Texas has a higher incarceration rate than any country. Yes, this includes China and Russia. On the other hand, Louisiana barely tops Texas. I will focus on Texas, not Louisiana, for now.

The Texas prison population has tripled since 1990, rising 61.5% in the last five years. Recall my statement, "Word came down in 1998 to arrest anyone on probation or parole to fill the empty prisons the voters were forced to build?" In 1998 the Department of Criminal Justice reported that 54.8% of the prison population were held by "NON-Violent crimes."

1998 was indeed, a very good year for the prison system, whereas 37,000 inmates entered into the system, with more than two out of every three of that 37,000 were due to probation or parole violations. It is estimated that half were charged not for breaking the law by committing new crimes, but for committing "technical violations," such as missing a meeting with a probation officer! Let's not forget the criminal buying gas on the wrong side of the street, meaning, he left the state when he crossed the street!

All prisoner responsibilities are shared (to be viewed) between the Governor, Senators, the Courts and the Representatives. It's painfully obvious that with one Governor, 31 Senators and 150 Representatives, their influences over, and responsibilities for, criminal justice decisions are not equal!

Remember, follow the money! It's much cheaper to "put them in prison," than to spend money fighting it out in the courts. Fact is, most legal penalties are largely determined by the accused accepting the least afflictive guilty plea offered by the DA. The state collects money per inmate which enables them to make a profit, while spending the minimum in the courts.

Between 1995 and 1998 crime substantially fell 23% in California, 21% in New York, 10% nationally, but in Texas it was a mere 5.1% decline. What happened to the Texas "get tough policy?" Texas inmates are generally imprisoned in remote locations from friends and family. In their confinement, they receive very little education or training, drug and alcohol treatment and counseling. Often experience works as a crime school. Wow, that was one of the first things Rick told me on my first visit at a transfer facility. He said, " prison is the place to go to learn how to be a criminal." No, he has no tattoos and very few friends there. He does say there are some fine people and that he is not the only innocent man there. I received a letter from Rick the day after I returned home from the funeral. Enclosed was a beautiful sympathy card to Rick. It had been signed by about ten fellow inmates. I was so taken by the messages they shared with Rick. I saw real love, compassion, hope and faith.

Rick said upon his return to his cell following our last visit on Sunday, the card was on his bed. He wanted to send it to me to keep, but also, that I might see the goodness in several of his friends there. Their penmanship and spelling was incredible. The messages were riddled with faith, hope, encouragement and love for God. Should any see it, they would never associate it with a prison or inmates. I find this heartening, as I know the state works endlessly to not emanate any reason to hope.

When the Texas prison system finally considers an inmate appropriate for parole, opposed to what the judge says, prisoners return to a society with increased handicaps. With a tarnished record, no employment credentials and weakened family ties, the inmate is faced with a difficult task in finding employment. The inmate has had more criminal education than self-help, exposed to sources of income, through crime and this knowledge undoubtedly continues to feed the prison system. I think the state depends on this, as the inmates future crime and return to prison is very likely. With their prior criminal record, a new prison sentence will be even more severe. This is what Rick has told me often. Rick has witnessed the coming and going of so many. He said, "In here, you pretty much know those that will return, as they seem to be the only ones that achieve a parole." This infuriates me! Quote, "over all, this is a system that works to destroy people." I will add families too.

Rick is very blessed in that he will have a job, a place to live and transportation. I am thinking of all those that do not have these gifts or family support. The guilty should be punished, but more importantly they should receive help, health and education. Texas offers a vicious cycle of replay.

Parole and probation, too often, are nothing more than set-ups to ensure failure. Inmates are doomed to return before they are released. The "grand plan" to keep the money coming in, mixed with power and greed and I thought slavery had been abolished. Texas is the Poster Child for slavery and tyranny.

While one out of every 20 Texas adults are in some form of criminal justice control daily, (in prison, jail, probation or parole) is horrifying, a more shocking statistic is that one of every 3 black men between 21 and 29 are involved! This is truly discrimination! Rick is white, but these facts still infuriate me and hopefully you too. This is called, "Due process?" I don't think so. Federal and state constitutions call for "due process" in the enforcement laws. Due process requires effective defenses for all accused of crimes. If only our system would function according to law. I am so beyond expecting anyone to stand accountable for such atrocities. What will it take to wake this once great country up? Just remember this, if nothing else, you could be next! Unless we awaken to the fact that we are witnessing the worst extinction yet, our constitutional rights, nothing and I mean nothing will change.

I have learned that according to the "Code of Criminal Procedure," our Governor could give Rick a full pardon, just like he did with the falsely accused in Tulia, Texas. I have contacted the Governor's office more than once. Governor Perry, I assume, gave the information to DeDe Keith. I received two letters from him with the appearance of assistance. The more I learn the facts in Texas and the refusal to obey the law, the more angry I get. I do not ask to be stroked!

I seek justice, equality and truth.

Now, I must make a retraction. In chapter 22, I said Sue went to Rick's shop and took all of his tools. This may be fact, but I cannot prove it. I was staying with Randy and doing therapy daily. While Rick was in jail, Sue did call Rick's landlord constantly in an effort to get the keys to the shop. Rick says he cannot prove Sue got his tools. He got so far behind on rent and with the lack of business Rick chose to simply walk a way.

This is a new day and we must continue onward and upwards. I do not know what tomorrow holds, but I know who holds it. I am still convinced that God has "A plan" and one day this will be behind us. We are ever hopeful as we carry on, considering not, but fully persuaded that JUSTICE is just around the corner. Our prayer is to be able to help another and we will not relent until someone stands up accepting accountability and responsibility for such a judicial tragedy! Washington might as well begin making room for us. We shall lobby until there is change! As I stated earlier, this will not be over when Rick comes home. Rick's prison departure will be the arrival of a new era within our judicial process. That is a promise!

Why did I name this book, "A Judicial Terror in Texas?" Because the state has literally terrorized our family and many more I can assure you!

Now, may God show His power however He chooses! Dare I hope? Oh, you better believe it!

Faith is the substance of things hoped for, the evidence of things not seen!

D. LAINE

ABOUT THE AUTHOR

This is not a novel, but a fifteen year nightmare forced upon her family. D. Laine does not claim to be an Author, but a voice for the many *"falsely accused."* Compliments of the state of Texas. She is consumed with a burning desire for TRUTH and EQUAL JUSTICE, for one and all! Her quest became a mission upon learning the issue has become an epidemic, crossing the nation, like a wildfire, leaving a trail of victims. A once proud American. Very passionate about her faith and greatly concerned with the country's downward spiral. She brings a warning to every reader. "The same can happen to you, anytime, anywhere, without warning, life will never be the same."